David Bevan

Financial Policy Workshops:

The Case of Kenya

IMF Institute
Financial Policy Workshops:

The Case of Kenya

International Monetary Fund
Washington, D.C. 1981

Library of Congress Catalog Card Number: 81-4123
AACR2

International Standard Book Number: 0-939934-00-0

Price: US$12.50

International Monetary Fund
Washington, D.C. 20431

FOREWORD

The workshops presented here comprise an actual case study. The book is intended primarily as a text for the IMF Institute's training course in Financial Analysis and Policy, but it may also be of interest to policymakers at the national level.

Established in 1964 to conduct training courses for officials from financial agencies of the Fund's member countries, the IMF Institute aims to assist principally, but not exclusively, representatives from the developing countries. In recent years, its activities have expanded rapidly to meet the growing needs of these countries for financial and technical assistance with their economic problems. Conducted in English, French, and Spanish, the courses have helped to disseminate knowledge about the statistical framework and techniques of analysis developed by the Fund, as well as to make the Fund's activities and procedures better known; nearly 3,000 officials from 134 countries have participated in over a hundred courses.

The Financial Analysis and Policy course draws heavily on the Fund's techniques of analysis and reflects the Fund's experience with programs of balance of payments adjustment. A policy-oriented course, it focuses on effective demand management policies while stressing the importance of measures to improve supply and to increase saving and investment. It also reviews the statistical framework and the tools of quantitative macroeconomic analysis by presenting studies of the effectiveness of the instruments of monetary, fiscal, and balance of payments policies as related to economic objectives. These workshops represent an effort to illustrate in a practical manner the kind of techniques studied in the course.

I am confident that this publication will prove useful to interested institutions and individuals in Fund member countries, particularly developing countries, by enhancing the understanding of the working of the major financial policy instruments. I hope that this improved understanding will contribute to better management of national economies. It should at the same time promote international monetary cooperation, which is the main purpose of the Fund's existence and which is essential for the orderly development of a world economy that has become increasingly interdependent.

J. DE LAROSIÈRE
Managing Director
International Monetary Fund

PREFACE

This book offers a series of workshops on Kenya that are used as a case study in the IMF Institute's course on Financial Analysis and Policy for officials of the Fund's member countries. They represent a practical application of economic concepts and theories.

Since its inception, the IMF Institute has steadily endeavored to make its courses relevant to the needs of the participants, who are officials of financial agencies of Fund member countries. One way to reach this general objective has been to develop teaching material based on recent country experiences. A major step in this direction was the introduction in the early 1970s of a series of workshops on a specific country used as a case study in the Financial Analysis and Policy courses. This has served to achieve a more appropriate balance between the theoretical and the applied parts of these courses.

The workshops are designed to involve the participants in all phases of work leading to the formulation of a consistent financial program so as to enable them to apply what they have learned to their own countries. Each workshop deals with a particular sector of the economy, provides relevant background information, and contains exercises and questions relating to the statistical data. Some workshops also require the participants to make sectoral forecasts based on assumptions about the "state of the world" and about policies; these forecasts are brought together in a consistent whole in the final workshop. Participants must adjust policies and objectives in order to formulate their own financial programs.

The decision by the Fund to publish the workshops has been taken in response to the increasing number of requests for copies of these workshops, which could not be met because of the confidential nature of some of the material contained in the original version of the workshops. In order to ensure that the published version contains only nonconfidential material, discussions on the content of the workshops have been held with the Kenyan authorities, who have agreed to their publication and have also made valuable suggestions that have been incorporated in the published version.

The workshops presented by the IMF Institute have been changing over the years in the light of the Fund's experience with economic problems of member countries. They will certainly continue to evolve in the future. Therefore, from this point of view, the published version is not a final product.

I wish to stress that these workshops must not be construed as representing necessarily the techniques used by the Fund staff in dealing with member countries. They reflect, however, the general approach utilized by the Fund's economists in their analysis of the economy of a country.

While the workshops included in this publication incorporate the comments received from other departments of the Fund, the responsibility for any errors or inconsistencies rests with the IMF Institute.

GÉRARD M. TEYSSIER
Director
IMF Institute

Acknowledgments

The workshop publication project has been carried out by the IMF Institute under the overall direction of Mr. U Tun Wai, Deputy Director, with the assistance of Mr. Ciro Tognetti, Senior Advisor, and has been coordinated by Mr. M. Haris Jafri, Advisor. Many present and former staff members of the IMF Institute have contributed to the drafting of the chapters included in this publication: in particular, Mr. Herbert K. Zassenhaus, Deputy Director (retired); Mr. Andrew Gantt, Chief, English Division; Mr. Chorng-huey Wong, Assistant Chief, English Division; Mr. Øystein Pettersen, Senior Economist; Mr. Jeffrey M. Davis, Senior Economist; Mr. Sotirios Kollias, formerly Senior Economist, at present with the Bank of Greece; and Mr. Ivan A. Bello, Economist.

Valuable comments on the workshops have been received from other departments of the Fund, including the African Department, the Exchange and Trade Relations Department, the Fiscal Affairs Department, the Research Department, and the Bureau of Statistics. Particular mention should be made of the following staff members for their comments: *Exchange and Trade Relations Department*—Mr. Subimal Mookerjee, Deputy Director, and Mr. Manuel Guitián, Advisor; *Fiscal Affairs Department*—Mr. Sheetal K. Chand and Mr. Charles Y. Mansfield, Senior Economists, Fiscal Analysis Division; *Research Department*—Mr. Carl P. Blackwell, Assistant Director, and Mr. Michael C. Deppler, Assistant Chief, Current Studies Division; Mr. George von Furstenberg, Chief, and Mr. Mohsin S. Khan, Assistant Chief, Financial Studies Division; *Bureau of Statistics*—Mr. Akira P. Nose, Assistant Director; Mr. Arie C. Bouter, Assistant Director, and Mr. Mahinder S. Gill, Assistant Chief, Balance of Payments Division; Mr. Jonathan V. Levin, Assistant Director, Government Finance Statistics Division; and Mr. Jai B. Gupta,

Chief, and Mr. Samir I. Fawzi, Assistant Chief, Financial Statistics Division-A. The volume has been edited by Mrs. Ella H. Wright, in consultation with Mr. Norman K. Humphreys, Chief Editor.

CONTENTS

4 Workshop 2: Government Finance Statistics *(concluded)*

6 Workshop 4: Flow of Funds *(concluded)*

9 Workshop 7: Revenue Forecasting *(concluded)*

Chapter 1

Introduction to Workshops

In its courses on Financial Analysis and Policy, the IMF Institute for many years has utilized a set of integrated workshops designed to enable the participants to apply the analytical tools discussed in these courses to an actual situation in a member country of the International Monetary Fund. These workshops, which have been elaborated upon and refined over the years in the light of teaching experience, assist the participants in preparing a financial program for a given country. Such a program consists of a set of policies in the monetary, fiscal, and balance of payments fields to achieve a balance between financial resources and their use. Therefore, these workshops deal with the organization of statistical data in a relevant framework, the economic analysis of the data, and the formulation of policies to achieve desired objectives.

The nine workshops presented in this publication use Kenya as the case study country. After a brief chapter entitled "Kenya: The General Setting" (Chapter 2), giving some background on the Kenyan economy, the workshops follow in separate chapters. The basic plan of the series of workshops is to familiarize the reader with the statistical framework and institutional setting relevant for the formulation of financial policy, to analyze the data, to forecast sectorally significant macrovariables on the basis of assumed policies and assumed values of other independent variables, and finally, to bring together the sectoral forecasts in a consistent whole in the workshop entitled "Financial Programming."

It is assumed that the reader of this publication already has some familiarity with the elements of general macroeconomic theory, as well as an understanding of the rudiments of public finance, monetary theory, and international economics. Some knowledge of the principles of statistics and of simple econometric techniques, such as regression and solution of simultaneous equation models, is also assumed.

The methodology of the workshops follows a consistent pedagogical approach. Each workshop provides data (including the institutional setting, where needed) on some aspect of the economic and financial performance of Kenya. On the basis of the data, readers are asked to do exercises involving some calculation. Finally, each workshop contains a number of issues for discussion, which aim at exposing readers to the kind of problems faced by economic analysts and policy advisors.

The data for the workshops have been taken from published sources, and care has been taken to ensure that no confidential information has been included. In the case of the statistical or accounting workshops, the data are generally provided for a period of five years. For the forecasting workshops, the data cover a longer period, usually ten years. For the accounting workshops, the exercises relate to calendar year 1976 or fiscal year 1977, whichever is appropriate, and answers are provided. In the case of the forecasting workshops, the forecasts are to be made for calendar year 1977 or fiscal year 1978, whichever is appropriate. No answers are given for the exercises in the forecasting workshops, except for the purely numerical or algebraic questions, because no unique forecast is possible and answers will vary according to the assumptions made with respect to policy measures and the values of other exogenous variables.

ACCOUNTING WORKSHOPS

The first four workshops in the series are statistical or accounting workshops. Their objective is to acquaint readers with the structure, coverage, and limitations of the Kenyan data in the monetary, fiscal, and external sectors, as well as to provide an economic interpretation of statistical relationships as a prelude to policymaking. These workshops are divided into two parts. The first part deals with concepts and principles for the compilation of the respective data. The second part illustrates how these concepts and principles are applied to the Kenyan data.

The workshop entitled "Monetary and Financial Survey" (Workshop 1) discusses the organization and consolidation of data for the financial institutions of Kenya, in accordance with the format used in *International Financial Statistics (IFS),* a monthly publication of the International Monetary Fund. Particular attention is focused on the accounts of the monetary system of Kenya and on the information that these accounts provide in regard to general monetary developments.

The workshop "Government Finance Statistics" (Workshop 2) analyzes the conceptual framework for the organization of the government finance statistics of Kenya, using the format in the *Government Finance Statistics Yearbook,* an annual publication of the International Monetary Fund. The workshop examines some statistical problems of Kenyan data on government finance, the consistency of budgetary accounts with monetary and other accounts, and the information provided by the government finance statistics of Kenya on overall budgetary developments.

The workshop "Balance of Payments Statistics" (Workshop 3) explains the principles for the compilation of the balance of payments statistics of Kenya, as set forth in the fourth edition of the *Balance of Payments Manual,* published by the International Monetary Fund. It then deals with the organization of the balance of payments data of Kenya into both a standard presentation and an analytic presentation, according to the format used in the *Balance of Payments Year-*

book, an annual publication of the International Monetary Fund. The workshop emphasizes the significance of different indicators of balance of payments performance and examines the relationship of balance of payments data and monetary accounts.

The workshop "Flow of Funds" (Workshop 4) demonstrates how the income and financial transactions in the economy of Kenya can be summarized in a set of interrelated sectoral accounts. It then explains the relationship of flow-of-funds accounts with the monetary survey, government finance statistics, and balance of payments statistics. The significance of flow-of-funds accounts for policymaking is emphasized.

FORECASTING WORKSHOPS

Following the four accounting workshops, there are the workshop on the Polak model, three sectoral forecasting workshops, and the final workshop on financial programming.

The workshop entitled "The Polak Model: An Application" (Workshop 5) applies to Kenyan data the Polak model, a simple macroeconomic model incorporating the monetary approach to the balance of payments. While the Polak model is not used for forecasting purposes in subsequent workshops, this workshop illustrates the uses of the Polak model for the forecasting of imports and for the formulation of monetary policy to achieve balance of payments equilibrium.

The aim of the three sectoral forecasting workshops is to teach a particular methodology of sectoral forecasting, based on past trends as well as on certain assumptions about economic outlook and policy stance. In each of these workshops, information is given on the institutional background, the legal framework, and recent developments (including policy actions) in the field covered by the workshop, in order to facilitate the making of assumptions needed for forecasting. It must be emphasized that these workshops do not envisage that the forecasts will be made solely on the basis of past trends, and hence they are not designed to yield forecasts which can then simply be "fed" into the final workshop. In fact, the methodology shown in these forecasting workshops can yield any number of alternative forecasts, depending on the assumptions made as to future economic developments or policy actions. Furthermore, different, and equally acceptable, forecasting techniques may be used to produce different forecasts. All the forecasting workshops stress that forecasting is not a mechanical process and that it is essential to make the forecasts on the basis of economic evaluation of actual and expected developments.

In the workshop "Projection of Monetary Aggregates" (Workshop 6), an approach is shown for projecting monetary aggregates—the major components of the balance sheets of the banking system. These forecasts are to be made partly on the basis of given information about economic developments, as well as policy actions and intentions, and partly on the basis of functional relationships, with the values of the parameters, such as the money multiplier, being computed on the basis of regression analysis. The workshop makes projections for money and quasi-money on the basis of both supply factors and demand factors, and it also examines the policy implications of the forecasts.

The workshop "Revenue Forecasting" (Workshop 7) describes an approach to the forecasting of the revenues of the Central Government of Kenya, based on functional relationships adjusted for the effect of discretionary changes in the tax system and using the proportional data adjustment method. Among the issues discussed are the significance of proper classification of government revenues, the choice of proxy bases, and the effect of price changes.

The workshop "Balance of Payments Forecasting" (Workshop 8) contains methods and guidelines for the forecasting of different components of the balance of payments of Kenya through the use of regression equations as well as judgmental factors. Emphasis is placed on the need to take into account economic developments in Kenya and in the rest of the world.

The final workshop, entitled "Financial Programming" (Workshop 9), is devoted to the formulation of a comprehensive and consistent financial program—that is, an appropriate mix of fiscal, monetary, and balance of payments policies, designed to achieve stated macroeconomic targets within specified constraints. Forecasts made in previous workshops may be used, but it often happens that these sectoral forecasts may not be consistent, in a macroeconomic setting, with each other or with the assumptions and policies in other parts of the financial program. New forecasts may have to be made (using the methodology expounded in the earlier workshops) repeatedly, following an iterative process, until the desired consistency among the different parts of the financial program is achieved. Considerable stress is laid on the need to analyze the significance of constraints, the existence of different policy trade-offs within these constraints, the need to assess the impact of recommended policies on other parts of the financial program, and the importance of specified consistency tests.

The forecasting workshops adopt an analytical approach based on sectoral econometric models. Many problems of a statistical nature arise in the process of estimating these sectoral models. The econometric forecasting methods utilized in these workshops are not very sophisticated but are tailored to the availability of data in a developing country such as Kenya. The forecasts obtained through the application of these methods are, in general, useful for purposes of analysis and as a guide to policymaking. Because of the data limitations and the importance of isolated events in the underlying series, econometric forecasts may not be sufficiently accurate for the formulation of concrete policy measures and must therefore be supplemented by experience and judgment to arrive at realistic values.

The problems discussed below are presented to caution the potential user against relying on purely mechanical application of statistical tools to obtain accurate forecasts. These problems are related to limitations of the data base, simultaneous equation bias, misspecification, multicollinearity, and evaluation of residuals.

1. *Limitations of the data base.* The data available in a developing country such as Kenya have four major deficiencies. First, as most of the data series for the majority of macroeconomic variables cover ten years or less and are available on an annual basis only, they are too short for the use of statistical techniques requiring numerous

independent variables or involving similar losses in degrees of freedom. Second, for a variety of reasons, the existing data tend to contain errors of measurement and therefore tend to be unreliable. Third, major data series are revised frequently, with little or no information available to enable the researcher to reconcile differences between these revisions. Finally, when the timing of the recording of statistical data differs between series, such as between fiscal statistics and other national accounting statistics, estimation based on two sets of statistics requires adjustment of the data and information may not be available to adjust them.

2. *Simultaneous equation bias.* As mentioned above, partial equilibrium or sectoral models have been used. In the workshop "Balance of Payments Forecasting" (Workshop 8), for example, aggregate import-forecasting equations relate the quantity of imports demanded (a) to the ratio of import prices to domestic prices, and (b) to domestic real income. It is assumed in these equations that the forecast values for domestic real income and domestic prices are independent of the resulting forecast for imports. This assumption may not be realistic in specific cases and may thus yield only an approximate forecast. The bias introduced by the forecast values for gross national product and prices, which may not be compatible with estimates for other important variables, is referred to as the simultaneous equation bias.

3. *Misspecification.* This problem arises from misspecification of the "true" model underlying a given economic relationship, such as the demand for imports. Misspecification can take several forms. For example, a misspecification bias is introduced if some of the relevant explanatory variables are not included in the equation because of the unavailability of data. Another kind of misspecification of relationship arises if a linear relation is assumed when in fact a nonlinear relation exists.

4. *Multicollinearity.* In an economy characterized by average rates of inflation at the double-digit level, any two macroeconomic variables in current prices are bound to be highly correlated. Collinearity among explanatory variables could lead to implausible

results. Thus, in the presence of multicollinear data, the sample data contain little information to enable the researcher to estimate individual parameters with a reasonable degree of precision.

It is, however, worth noting that the tolerance level of the bias due to multicollinearity and specification bias depends on the *end use* of the model or equation. If the model is to be used for forecasting, specification errors or multicollinearity might not be very serious. However, if the estimated parameters, such as propensities and income elasticities, are used to formulate precise policy prescriptions, more attention to such bias would be necessary.

5. *Evaluation of residuals.* In a forecasting exercise, the evaluation of residuals for the most recent observations is important in assessing the adequacy of a point estimate for a coming period. In a typical less developed country, the errors in data base, the splicing of series, and the lumpiness of events, as well as actual serial correlation, may all generate residuals which appear significantly different in the most recent period from those in earlier years. A graphical depiction of regression results is an essential tool in identifying large residuals and their patterns. For example, a recent export boom may lead to a significant positive residual in the demand for money equation. It is extremely important that the pattern of this residual be evaluated, as it will affect the values utilized for policy variables. Although statistical techniques reducing serial correlation are well known and are widely used in correcting equations used for forecasting, these techniques are generally inadequate for satisfactory forecasting and the policymaker must also use prudent judgment.

Chapter 2

Kenya: The General Setting

Kenya, which gained independence from the United Kingdom in December 1963, covers a land area of 582,647 sq. km. (225,000 square miles), which extends about 280 miles north and south of the equator and which is almost 560 miles wide along the equator. Kenya shares boundaries with Ethiopia, Somalia, Sudan, Tanzania, and Uganda. Its coastline along the Indian Ocean on the southeast is about 250 miles long. The Rift Valley, which runs the entire length of the country in the west, contains a series of lakes, and a small part of huge Lake Victoria lies within Kenya's territory. While a narrow fertile belt of tropical vegetation borders the Indian Ocean, more than half of the country is an arid lowland, stretching north and west from the coast and having a natural vegetation of poor grass and scrub. The rest of the country consists mainly of a plateau, with an altitude varying from 2,000 to 9,000 feet. The highest point is Mount Kenya, which rises about 17,000 feet and is centrally located to the northeast of the capital, Nairobi.

The country has a wide range in climate, mainly because of variations in altitude. The climate is tropical in the narrow coastal belt along the Indian Ocean. As the land rises, the climate becomes subtropical and even temperate, with heavier rainfall, improving the vegetation and the prospects for intensive cultivation. The mean temperature at 9,000 feet is about 55 degrees F., in contrast to over 80 degrees F. on the coast. The annual rainfall is about 100 inches around Mount Kenya, decreasing to about 10 inches near the northern frontiers. Over most of the country, rainfall comes in distinct seasons, but it varies greatly from place to place and from year to year in the same area.

In the middle altitudes, the grasslands provide good grazing for game and domestic cattle, while the southwestern quarter of the country, ranging from 5,000 to 9,000 feet, includes some of the best farming land in Africa. Although forests cover only about 3 per cent of the land area, they are valuable for land cover and water retention. Land suitable for intensive farming without irrigation is mainly confined to the coastal belt and to the higher elevations, which commonly receive 35 inches or more of rain a year. Expansion of the cultivated area through irrigation is limited by the availability of water. A number of rivers drain into Lake Victoria; only two rivers, the Tana and the Galana (Sabaki), have sufficient water to reach the ocean throughout the year, while other streams dry up for several months of the year. The greater part of the country can, therefore, support only extensive, rather than intensive, grazing.

Kenya's population, estimated at 14.34 million in mid-1977, is believed to be increasing at about 3.5 per cent a year. The population density in 1977 was 24 per square kilometer for the overall land area and 139 per square kilometer for the arable land area. Africans constitute over 97 per cent of the population, with the remainder being, in numerical order, Indians, Pakistanis, Europeans, Arabs, and persons of other ethnic origin. Kenya's African population consists of many ethnic groups, of which the most numerous are Kikuyus, Luo, and Luhya. Although these groups speak many dialects, Swahili is commonly understood. English is used primarily in government and business.

Eight cities in Kenya had over 20,000 residents in 1977. Urban population accounts for about 11.3 per cent of the total population.

Nairobi, the capital, is the largest city, with over 700,000 inhabitants; next is Mombasa, the principal port, with a population of over 400,000.

ECONOMIC STRUCTURE

The economy of Kenya is predominantly agricultural, although the relative importance of agriculture has been steadily declining in recent years as a result of the more rapid growth of the industrial sector. In 1977, agriculture, forestry, and fishing accounted for about 29 per cent of the gross domestic product (GDP), compared with over 40 per cent at the time of Kenya's independence in 1963. The share of manufacturing, mining, and construction in GDP was some 21 per cent in 1977, while government services and commerce accounted for about 18 per cent and 10 per cent, respectively.

Agriculture

The important role of agriculture in the Kenyan economy is highlighted by the fact that almost 85 per cent of the population depends on agriculture for a livelihood, mainly in a self-employment status. Slightly less than half of the value added in agriculture is in the monetary sector, the remainder being in production for home consumption. Since Kenya became independent, the rate of growth in the agricultural sector engaged in production for the market (hereinafter called the market sector of agriculture) has been almost twice that of the agricultural sector producing for home consumption (hereinafter called the subsistence sector of agriculture).

Kenya has a diversified agriculture, producing a variety of both food and cash crops, unlike many developing countries in Africa which cultivate only one or two cash crops. As a result, agricultural exports are rather diversified, reducing the vulnerability of the Kenyan economy to fluctuations in world prices. However, as the area under irrigation is limited, agricultural production is greatly affected by changes in the weather. For example, agricultural output was reduced in 1965 and 1973 as a result of droughts and in 1975 as a result of a drought in one part of the country and excessive rainfall in another part.

The principal food crops are maize, pulses, root crops, fruits and vegetables, wheat, sorghum, millet, and nuts, while the major cash crops are coffee, tea, sugarcane, sisal, pyrethrum extract, cotton, and wattle (for sale as bark). Four of these crops—coffee, tea, maize, and wheat—account for three fourths of the gross value of sales of farm products. Livestock and dairy production are also important agricultural enterprises for both domestic consumption and exports.

Of the principal food crops, maize and wheat are largely consumed domestically. Maize, the most important food crop, is cultivated mainly on small farms, and most of the output is consumed by the subsistence sector. Wheat is grown chiefly on large farms, which have to some extent shifted from maize to wheat production. While the output of maize has steadily increased over the years, wheat production rose strongly until 1970 and then declined sharply until 1973, followed by a recovery. However, the output of wheat in 1977 was still 13 per cent below the peak of 1970. Kenya has recently had small exportable surpluses of maize almost every year, and production of rice, mainly on small farms, has expanded rapidly. The production of other food crops, mainly on small farms, has followed a generally rising trend.

The livestock and dairy industry has slowly recovered during the 1970s after several years of stagnation and even decline. In recent years, the value of the output of livestock and dairy products has represented some 22 per cent of total gross farm revenue, and exports of these products, though relatively minor, have increased steadily during the 1970s.

Exports of agricultural products have accounted for 50–60 per cent of total exports in recent years. Coffee, the leading export crop, has traditionally accounted for some 20 per cent of total export earnings. Owing mainly to the sharp increase in coffee prices, this share rose to 27 per cent in 1976 and to some 40 per cent in 1977. Coffee production, after increasing strongly in the early 1960s, remained relatively stagnant until 1976–77 when the sharp rise in prices stimulated a strong recovery in output. Tea has been a rapidly expanding export crop, displacing sisal in 1964 as the second largest foreign exchange earner. Both tea production and tea exports have increased steadily in recent years and, as a result of higher prices, tea exports represented about 14 per cent of total exports in 1977. Production and exports of sisal and wattle bark have been declining as a result of falling prices in the face of excess world supply and competition from synthetic substitutes. Kenya produces about 70 per cent of the world's pyrethrum, and both production and exports have been well maintained. Cotton, which was one of Kenya's major exports before World War II, lost its importance mainly because of the persistence of pests. However, cotton production and exports showed a recovery in the late 1960s, and cotton's position as a relatively minor export has been maintained during the 1970s. Output of sugarcane, which is largely consumed domestically and is grown mainly on large farms, has expanded steadily.

Manufacturing, Mining, and Construction

As a result of the high rate of growth of manufacturing compared with agriculture (an annual average of 8–9 per cent, compared with 5 per cent) since Kenya became independent, the share of manufacturing rose from about 9 per cent of GDP in 1963 to more than 15 per cent in 1977. Early industrial development was spearheaded by the food, beverage, and tobacco industry, followed by the establishment of other industries based on domestically produced raw materials—such as textiles and clothing, leather and footwear, paper and paper products, cement, and clay and glass products. A more recent evolution has been the establishment of capital-intensive and often import-intensive industries, such as petroleum and chemicals, plastics, rubber, metallurgy, motor assemblies, paper mills, electrical goods, and machine tools.

The food, beverage, and tobacco industry continues to be the leading manufacturing sector in size, even though its rate of growth has not been as rapid as some of the newer, more dynamic industries. Together with textiles and leather, this industry accounts for a large part of the exports of manufactures, which have recently amounted to 40–50 per cent of total exports. The establishment in 1967 of the East African Community (EAC), comprising Kenya, Tanzania, and Uganda, was an important factor in stimulating Kenya's industrial development by offering expanded export opportunities. It is significant that, even with the early *de facto* breakup of the EAC, Kenyan industry has been able to maintain its share of total exports.

Although Kenya's industrial development has been accomplished largely through the initiative of the private sector, it has also been assisted by the Government through tariff protection, regional integration (the short-lived EAC), tax incentives, and the provision of development finance.

Mining and construction together accounted for close to 6 per cent of GDP in 1977. While Kenya is believed to have exploitable mineral deposits (copper, gold, silver, iron, and limestone), the development of mining has been hampered by a shortage of capital for exploration and exploitation. The most important mining products have been soda ash, raw materials for cement, salt, limestone products, and copper. Construction activity has maintained a steady growth, based on industrial construction, roadbuilding and other public works projects, and residential construction related to increasing urbanization.

Other Sectors

Kenya's transport and communications sectors, which serve Tanzania and Uganda as well, constitute about 5 per cent of Kenya's GDP. Mombasa, which has a fine deep-water harbor, is the chief port of East Africa and handles almost all of the overseas traffic of Kenya and Uganda and part of that from Burundi, Rwanda, eastern Zaïre, and southern Sudan. Boat services on Lake Victoria form an important link between Kenya and the other East African countries and provide useful feeder routes to the railways. Kenya's main railway, reaching about 1,200 miles from Mombasa via Nairobi into Uganda, is the principal means of transportation to and from the coast and carries the overseas traffic of both Kenya and Uganda. Branches extend through the rich farming area of Kenya's Central Province into Tanzania. Kenya has an extensive road network of about 30,000 miles, but only a small proportion of the road surface is bituminized.

The installed capacity of Kenya's electric power plants increased at the moderate pace of some 3 per cent a year in the early 1960s, but since 1965 annual growth in the domestic generation of electric power has averaged some 15 per cent, which has been in line with the growth of demand, so that the volume of imported electric power has increased only slightly.[1] The domestic generation of electric power amounted to some 1 million kilowatt hours in 1977.

ECONOMIC AND FINANCIAL PERFORMANCE

This section focuses on Kenya's economic and financial performance prior to 1974. Developments since then are reviewed in detail in the workshops on Projection of Monetary Aggregates (Workshop 6), Revenue Forecasting (Workshop 7), Balance of Payments Forecasting (Workshop 8), and Financial Programming (Workshop 9).

The Period 1964–72

During the first decade of its independence, Kenya was remarkably successful in achieving an economic growth well above average for a country at its stage of development. During the eight-year period 1964–72, GDP at factor cost (constant prices) grew at an average annual rate of about 6.5 per cent, leading to a significant increase in real per capita income, despite one of the highest rates of population growth in the world. This favorable outcome may be attributed to the Government's success in mobilizing resources for growth, to the creation of conditions conducive to a high level of private investment, and to a consistent and generally sound management of the economy.

Other indicators of performance are equally impressive for this period. The mobilization of domestic savings was remarkably high for a country at such an early stage of development. As the Kenyan

[1] Kenya, *Development Plan, 1974–1978,* p. 315.

authorities generally followed a cautious financial policy, inflation and external debt were kept well within manageable proportions and serious balance of payments problems were avoided. The Central Government was able to turn the deficit in the recurrent budget into a sizable surplus, increase its development expenditures sevenfold, and reduce its relative dependence on foreign aid. At the same time, the Government greatly expanded its provision of basic social services.

Some aspects of this performance, however, were less satisfactory and created problems for economic management in the period after 1972. First, the benefits of development were not distributed as widely as the Government had intended, leading to the twin problems of growing unemployment and continuing poverty of the "working poor," [2] particularly in the rural areas. Thus, there persisted the core of the distribution problem—the low productivity and with it the poverty of the mass of the Kenyan people.[3] Second, the Government's policy of encouraging import substitution through protection and other incentives resulted in the establishment of a number of capital-intensive and import-intensive industries, contributing to some of the balance of payments problems.

Growth of GDP during the period 1964–72 was distributed unevenly among the economic sectors. While the average annual rate of growth of manufacturing, mining, and construction was over 8 per cent and that of government services almost 10 per cent in real terms, the agricultural sector as a whole grew at an average annual rate of 5 per cent. It is significant that the market sector of agriculture showed an average real growth of 6.5 per cent, which is very satisfactory in comparison with most countries. However, the subsistence sector of agriculture, whose production is for home consumption and where the bulk of the population is employed, grew at an average

[2] International Labor Office, *Employment, Incomes and Equality: A Strategy for Increasing Productive Employment in Kenya,* ILO/UNDP Report (Geneva, 1972), pp. 9 and 60–61.

[3] International Bank for Reconstruction and Development (World Bank), *Kenya: Into the Second Decade* (Baltimore: Johns Hopkins University Press, 1975), p. 5.

rate of only 3.7 per cent in real terms, roughly equal to the rate of population increase.

Although a high degree of price stability prevailed during the period 1964–72, with the increases in the consumer price index being less than 2 per cent in most years, rather large price increases took place in 1965 (6 per cent) and 1971 (7.5 per cent) as a result of the drought and of food shortages.

Relative price stability, coupled with sustained efforts by the Government in the fiscal and development fields, contributed to an impressive savings performance in aggregate terms during the period 1964–72. Gross domestic savings as a proportion of GDP were about 19–20 per cent in most of these years—an achievement matched by few developing countries. Household savings (including unincorporated business savings) amounted to about 10 per cent of personal disposable incomes, representing the major item of domestic savings, although their relative share fell as corporate savings accounted for an increasing part of total savings in the expanding economy. Depreciation allowances alone contributed about 30 per cent of total savings during this period.[4]

The Central Government's efforts in generating public savings, and thus indirectly influencing the growth of household and business savings, were a striking aspect of Kenya's development after its independence. In fiscal year 1964 (year ending June 30), the Government had a sizable recurrent budget deficit and had to rely on foreign aid and borrowing to fill this gap as well as to meet all of its slender development budget. Over the next eight years (1964–72), the situation changed dramatically. As a result of a creditable tax effort by the Government, recurrent revenue showed an average annual increase of over 14 per cent during this period. By the end of this period, government revenues accounted for 23 per cent of GDP, an exceptionally high ratio for a developing country, and government savings amounted to more than 20 per cent of total domestic savings. While recurrent expenditures increased by 11 per cent a year, the good revenue performance enabled the Government not only to meet its expand-

[4] *Ibid.*, p. 7.

ing recurrent budget expenditures but to make a substantial contribution—an average of 28 per cent over this period—to development expenditures, which increased nearly sevenfold during this time. The Government was able to finance its overall deficit largely by noninflationary borrowing on the domestic market and by borrowing on concessional terms from abroad. Over the entire eight-year period, the Government financed 80 per cent of its total (recurrent and development) budget out of recurrent revenue, 10 per cent from net domestic borrowing, and the remaining 10 per cent from net foreign borrowing. Prior to fiscal year 1971, the Government did not have recourse to borrowing from the central bank but rather had a positive outstanding balance with the central bank. However, in the last two fiscal years of this period (1972 and 1973), the momentum of increases in revenues slackened significantly and the Government resorted to some net borrowing from the central bank, while maintaining the rate of growth of government investment.

During the period 1964–72, Kenya had overall balance of payments surpluses in every year except 1964, 1967, and 1971. Until quite late in this period, Kenyan authorities were not particularly worried by a foreign exchange constraint. The growing domestic resource gap was certainly reflected in a widening current account deficit. But, although Kenya was increasingly dependent on a free flow of imported goods and services, the country did not experience any great difficulty in obtaining the foreign exchange necessary to finance these imports through exports and a large inflow of foreign capital. Kenya traditionally has had a deficit in the merchandise trade account, which gradually widened as domestic resources came under pressure. The trade deficit grew quite slowly during the 1960s, when imports increased a little faster than GDP and exports a little more slowly. Most of the trade deficit was covered by Kenya's net receipts from "invisibles," particularly the sale of services to Uganda and Tanzania and expanded earnings from the tourist industry. Thus, until the end of the 1960s, the current account was either in surplus or showed a moderate deficit that could easily be met by private and official capital inflows.

The situation changed dramatically in 1971, when a large overall deficit was registered. The value of imports increased by 62 per cent, largely due to higher world prices, while exports increased by only 34 per cent. At the same time, as the trade deficit widened, the net earnings from invisibles also leveled off because of a disruption in Kenya's service trade with Tanzania and Uganda, some slackening in tourist inflow, and increasing repatriation of dividends. The overall payments position reverted in 1972 to a surplus, although a small one, largely as a result of reduction in imports in response to corrective measures, while export earnings improved slightly.

The Years 1973 and 1974

Some deterioration in fiscal performance and in the balance of payments position had begun to be noticeable in the last two years of the period 1964–72. The economic environment was adversely affected by a number of factors. Worldwide inflation became pronounced from 1972 on, and a sharp increase in petroleum prices occurred at the end of 1973. Domestically, the situation was further exacerbated by the effects of a severe drought in 1973.

Given these adverse developments, Kenya's overall economic performance in 1973 could be considered rather satisfactory, but there was a strong upsurge in prices. While economic growth continued at a high rate, with a rise of 6.5 per cent in GDP in real terms, similar to that of 1972, the rate of inflation accelerated to 15 per cent, compared with 3 per cent in 1972. The overall economic growth rate was maintained despite the drought, which reduced the rate of growth of the market sector of agriculture from 7.6 per cent in 1972 to 5 per cent in 1973, mainly as a result of an increase of 11 per cent in the output of the manufacturing sector. Real gross fixed investment rose by 4.7 per cent in 1973, compared with a decline of 4 per cent in 1972. This increase in fixed investment occurred entirely in the public sector. About 95 per cent of total investment was financed by domestic savings, which reached a record high of 27 per cent of the GDP in 1973. In addition, in fiscal year 1974, the Government was able to reverse the unfavorable budgetary trend of 1972 and 1973, reducing the overall deficit by half and practically eliminating government borrowing from the banking system. The main factor in this fiscal improvement was a 25 per cent increase in recurrent revenues, largely due to new tax measures. Only a small overall balance of payments surplus was registered in 1973 (even smaller than in 1972), in spite of a 30 per cent increase in the value of exports, because of a rise in imports of 6 per cent over the low level of 1972 as restrictive credit measures were relaxed and because of a reduction in net income from services and transfers.

Economic developments in 1974 were not favorable, reflecting the impact of the adverse factors mentioned earlier, particularly the rise in petroleum prices. There was a slowdown in economic growth, with real GDP increasing by only 3.6 per cent, about half the average rate of the previous ten years, and barely matching the rate of population increase. The main factors were a minimal increase (1 per cent) in the output of the market sector of agriculture, largely due to continued dry weather and a smaller rise (7.5 per cent) in manufacturing output than in 1973. There were declines in real fixed investment and in the ratio of domestic savings to GDP. Inflation continued at the high rate of 1973, with an increase of 16 per cent in the consumer price index. The budgetary position deteriorated sharply in fiscal year 1975, with an increase over fiscal year 1974 of 86 per cent in the overall deficit which, for the first time in recent years, reached a level of 6 per cent of GDP. About half the deficit was financed from the banking system. While recurrent revenues increased by 20 per cent as a result of additional tax measures, both recurrent and development expenditures recorded much larger increases, substantially exceeding budget estimates. The balance of payments registered a large overall deficit in 1974 because of a dramatic deterioration in the terms of trade, led by the rise in petroleum prices.

By 1974, it was clear that an adverse trend in the external terms of trade, together with the effects of long-standing policies that contributed to increases in both capital-intensive and import-intensive production, had led to mounting pressures on Kenya's balance of payments. These developments were viewed by the Kenyan authorities as threatening a reduction in Kenya's future economic growth to considerably below the average annual rate (6.5 per cent) achieved in the decade prior to 1975. The unfavorable developments in 1974 lent urgency to the need for corrective action. Accordingly, in July 1975, the Government of Kenya undertook a three-year program, supported by the resources of the International Monetary Fund under an extended facility arrangement, seeking the attainment of (1) an annual rate of growth in real GDP of 5 per cent, (2) a rate of increase in domestic prices substantially less than that of import prices, and (3) the elimination of balance of payments assistance after five years. To achieve these objectives, the program included policies relating to demand management and structural policies, such as a shift of public and private investment toward agriculture (for example, through increased development outlays on agriculture, water, and rural development; maintenance of remunerative producer prices; and the provision of adequate agricultural credit facilities); reform of the tariff structure which, in the past, favored imports of capital goods and raw materials; the gradual elimination of fiscal incentives for certain types of investment; and the possible modification of Kenya's interest rate structure.

Details of the three-year economic and financial program and of developments during the period 1975–77 are presented in the workshop on Financial Programming (Workshop 9). In this workshop, these details serve as background material for the preparation of a financial program for 1978 within the framework of the medium-term objectives incorporated in the program adopted by the Kenyan authorities under the extended facility arrangement concluded with the International Monetary Fund. The workshops on Projection of Monetary Aggregates (Workshop 6), Revenue Forecasting (Workshop 7), and Balance of Payments Forecasting (Workshop 8) provide additional information about fiscal, monetary, and balance of payments developments during the period 1975–77.

REFERENCES

Kenya, Ministry of Finance and Planning, Central Bureau of Statistics, *Economic Survey* (annual).

———, Ministry of Finance and Planning, Central Bureau of Statistics, *Statistical Abstract* (annual).

———, Ministry of Finance and Planning, Central Bureau of Statistics, *Statistical Digest* (quarterly).

———, Central Bank of Kenya, *Annual Reports.*

———, *Development Plan, 1970–1974.*

———, *Development Plan, 1974–1978.*

International Monetary Fund, *Surveys of African Economies,* Vol. 2 (Washington, 1969), pp. 137–209.

———, *International Financial Statistics* (monthly), 1978 Supplement, May 1978.

———, *Balance of Payments Yearbook* (annual).

———, *Government Finance Statistics Yearbook* (annual).

———, *Direction of Trade* (monthly).

———, African, Exchange and Trade Relations, and Fiscal Affairs Departments, "Kenya: Industry and Tourism Lead Other Sectors in Sustained Growth," *IMF Survey* (September 21, 1973), pp. 284–86.

International Bank for Reconstruction and Development (World Bank), *Kenya: Into the Second Decade* (Baltimore: Johns Hopkins University Press, 1975).

International Labor Office, *Employment, Incomes and Equality: A Strategy for Increasing Productive Employment in Kenya,* ILO/UNDP Report (Geneva, 1972).

APPENDIX I

Map of Kenya

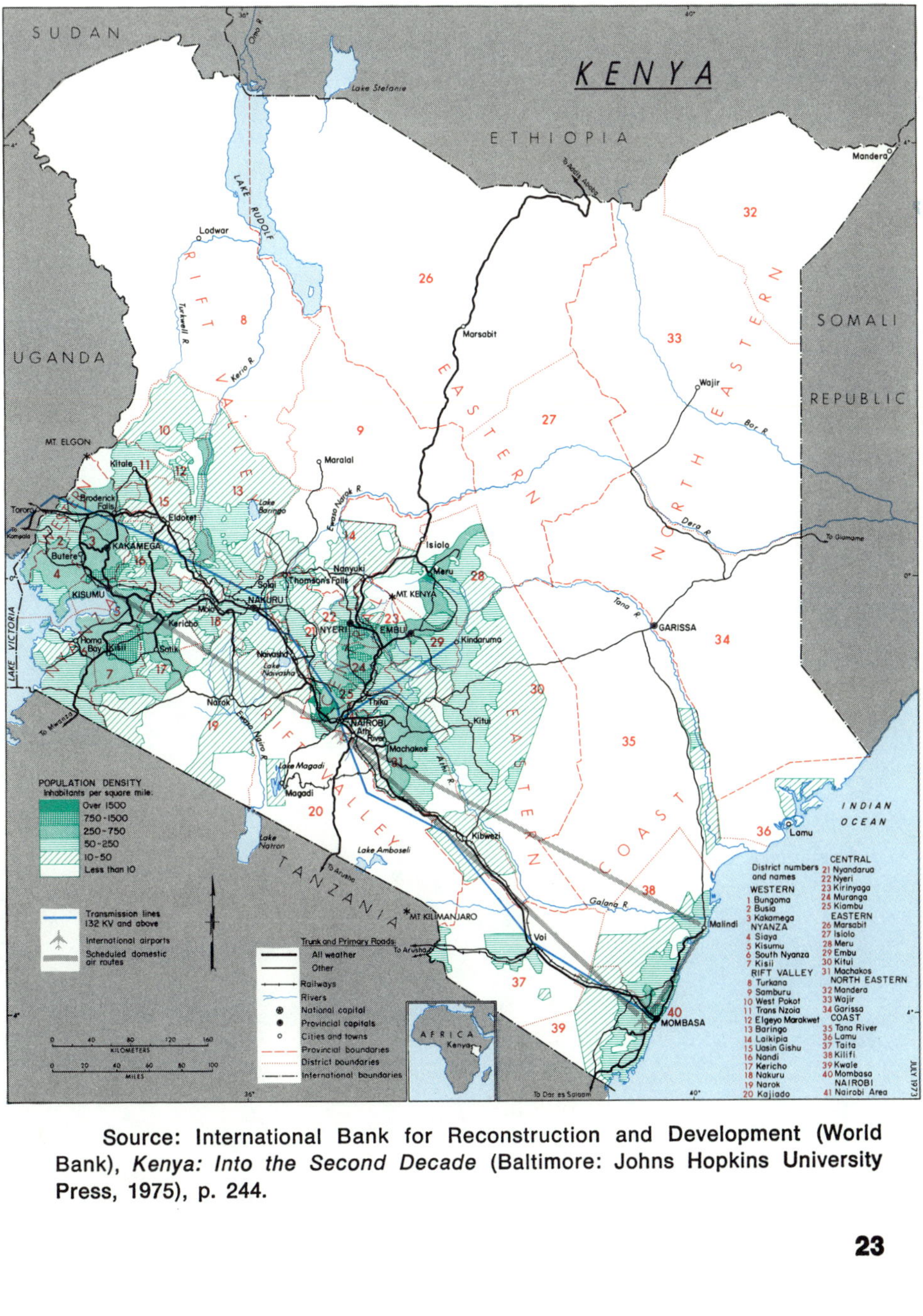

Source: International Bank for Reconstruction and Development (World Bank), *Kenya: Into the Second Decade* (Baltimore: Johns Hopkins University Press, 1975), p. 244.

APPENDIX II

Kenya: Selected Economic Data, 1963–74

(In millions of Kenya shillings, unless otherwise indicated)

	1963	1966	1970	1972	1973	1974
Output and prices						
GDP (at market prices)	6,440	8,224	11,453	14,447	16,761	20,343
Consumer prices (Index: 1975 = 100)	52.4	57.0	59.3	65.0	71.2	83.9
Government finance [1]						
Total revenue and grants	*773*	*1,040*	*1,621*	*2,712*	*2,828*	*3,696*
Total expenditure and lending minus repayments	*983*	*1,444*	*1,978*	*3,278*	*3,730*	*4,283*
Overall deficit (—) or surplus	—210	—404	—357	—566	—902	—587
Money and credit						
Net foreign assets	. . .	775	1,617	1,358	1,558	969
Claims on government (net)	. . .	—79	31	346	479	930
Claims on official entities	. . .	30	108	191	237	223
Claims on private sector	872	1,049	1,732	2,481	3,143	3,813
Money	. . .	1,333	2,410	3,029	3,862	4,016
Quasi-money	294	552	1,095	1,265	1,494	1,803
Balance of payments			*(In millions of SDRs)*			
Exports, f.o.b.	190.4	243.6	285.5	310.8	394.2	483.1
Imports, f.o.b.	198.5	276.8	371.8	418.4	457.0	746.6
Current account balance, excluding officials transfers (deficit —)	—10.4	—27.2	—76.4	—89.6	—127.6	—283.7
Overall balance (deficit —)	8.7	20.1	50.7	27.0	18.2	—73.4

Sources: All items: International Monetary Fund, *International Financial Statistics,* 1978 Supplement, May 1978. Additional sources for gross domestic product: Kenya, *Statistical Abstract,* 1976 and Kenya, *Economic Survey,* 1976, 1977, and 1978; consumer prices: Kenya, *Statistical Digest,* various issues; government finance: International Monetary Fund, *Government Finance Statistics Yearbook,* Vol. 1, 1977 and Vol. 2, 1978; and balance of payments: International Monetary Fund, *Balance of Payments Yearbook,* 1977.

[1] Year ending June 30.

Chapter 3

WORKSHOP 1

Monetary and Financial Survey

This workshop discusses the sectorization and consolidation of data on financial assets and liabilities of the financial institutions of a country. The format described here is the one used in the International Monetary Fund's monthly publication, *International Financial Statistics (IFS).* In presenting the data on financial institutions, *IFS* aims to provide a measure of the volume of liquidity and to cover the accounts of the banking sector whose activities are of the greatest importance in finance and liquidity creation. Such accounts also permit the derivation of a large part of the data on intersector finance and of much useful information on the origin of changes in liquidity.[1]

PRESENTATION OF THE STATISTICS

In the *IFS* scheme, the monetary and financial data are presented on three levels. The first level contains a consolidation of financial data into three functional groups: the monetary authorities (MAs),

[1] Earl Hicks, Graeme S. Dorrance, and Gerald R. Aubanel, "Recent Developments in Monetary Analysis: Monetary Analyses," *Staff Papers,* Vol. 5 (February 1957), pp. 342–433.

deposit money banks (DMBs), and other financial institutions (OFIs). *IFS* attaches special importance to the accounts of the monetary authorities; these accounts form a core data base for timely evaluation of monetary developments, including foreign reserve movements, and for formulating monetary policy. The second level consolidates the data for the monetary authorities and deposit money banks into the "monetary survey"; it provides a statistical measure of money and credit. The third, or most consolidated level, combines the other financial institutions and monetary survey into the "financial survey," [2] in order to measure overall private sector liquidity, contribute to an explanation of its origin, and provide information useful in a description of the relationship between the financial system and other sectors of the economy. The purpose of each of these levels of consolidation is to present financial data for an economy in a way that will best facilitate economic analysis, i.e., the behavior of these financial aggregates and their interactions with the economic activity of the country concerned. *IFS* concentrates its attention on financial data because they serve to explain the financing of sectoral and aggregate expenditure; in addition, these data have the advantage of being readily available even in the developing countries.

The First Level: Monetary Authorities

The monetary authorities data, which are reported in lines 11 through 17r on the country pages of *IFS* (as shown in Table 1), consolidate and present the accounts of the central bank and other institutions that create reserve money; issue currency; hold the national reserves of gold, foreign exchange, and special drawing rights (SDRs); control the monetary system; and act as the bank for the government. Generally, most of these functions are carried out by the central bank, but there are many countries where the treasury issues coin and some countries where the treasury or a treasury-controlled exchange stabilization fund holds the official reserves of gold and foreign exchange. These monetary functions of the govern-

[2] Presented in *IFS* for only a limited number of countries, because of the lack of adequate data.

ment should be consolidated with the accounts of the central bank in order to present all of the functions of the monetary authorities together in one section.

Data from the balance sheets of the institutions in this category need to be classified so as to furnish as much information as possible on their functions. Thus, it is important to know how countries' transactions with the rest of the world affect the monetary authorities' holdings of foreign assets, how these institutions operate to control the credit expansion of the deposit money banks, and how credit to the government and other sectors has been allocated.

TABLE 1. Line Items on Country Pages of *International Financial Statistics*

Exchange Rates	
SDR Rate	aa
Market Rate (end of period)	ae/ag
Market Rate (period average)	af/ah
Par or Central Rate (end of period)	de/dg
Par Rate/Market Rate (period average) & Trade Conversion	rf/rh
International Liquidity	
Total Reserves Minus Gold	1l.d
SDRs	1b.d
Reserve Position in the Fund	1c.d
Foreign Exchange	1d.d
Gold (million fine troy ounces)	1ad
Gold (national valuation)	1and
Fund Position	
Use of Fund Credit	2e.d
of which: by Facility	2e*d
Quota	2f.d
Trust Fund Loans Outstanding	2etd
Monetary Authorities: Other (Foreign) Liabilities	4..d
Deposit Money Banks: (Foreign) Assets	7a.d
Deposit Money Banks: (Foreign) Liabilities	7b.d
Other Financial Institutions: (Foreign) Assets	7e.d
Other Financial Institutions: (Foreign) Liabilities	7f.d
International License Banks: (Foreign) Assets	7k.d
International License Banks: (Foreign) Liabilities	7m.d
Monetary Authorities	
Foreign Assets	11
Claims on Government	12a
Claims on Official Entities	12b
Claims on Businesses and Individuals	12d
Claims on Deposit Money Banks	12e
Claims on Other Financial Institutions	12f

TABLE 1. Line Items on Country Pages of *International Financial Statistics*
(continued)

Monetary Authorities *(continued)*	
Reserve Money	14
Currency held by Private Sector	14a
Demand Deposits	14d
of which: Other Government Entities	14dx
of which: Other Financial Institutions	14dy
Quasi-Monetary Liabilities	15
of which: Foreign Currency Deposits	15x
Bonds	16a
Import Deposits	16b
Foreign Liabilities	16c
Long-Term Foreign Liabilities	16cl
Government Deposits	16d
Counterpart Funds	16e
Capital Accounts	17a
Other Items (net)	17r
Deposit Money Banks	
Reserves	20
Foreign Assets	21
Claims on Government	22a
Claims on Official Entities	22b
Claims on Businesses and Individuals	22d
Claims on Other Financial Institutions	22f
Demand Deposits	24
of which: Other Government Entities	24x
of which: Other Financial Institutions	24y
Quasi-Monetary Liabilities	25
of which: Foreign Currency Deposits	25x
Bonds	26a
Import Deposits	26b
Foreign Liabilities	26c
Long-Term Foreign Liabilities	26cl
Government Deposits	26d
Counterpart Funds	26e
Credit from Monetary Authorities	26g
Capital Accounts	27a
Other Items (net)	27r
Monetary Survey	
Foreign Assets (net)	31n
Domestic Credit	32
Claims on Government (net)	32an
Claims on Official Entities	32b
Claims on Businesses and Individuals	32d
Claims on Other Financial Institutions	32f

TABLE 1. Line Items on Country Pages of *International Financial Statistics* (continued)

Monetary Survey *(continued)*	
Money	34
Quasi-Money	35
Bonds	36a
Private Sector Import Deposits	36b
Long-Term Foreign Liabilities	36cl
Counterpart Funds	36e
Other Items (net)	37r
Money, Seasonally Adjusted	34..b
Bank Clearings	39c
Bank Debits	39d
Other Financial Institutions	
Reserves	40
Foreign Assets	41
Claims on Government	42a
Claims on Official Entities	42b
Claims on Businesses and Individuals	42d
Claims on Deposit Money Banks	42e
Demand Deposits	44
Quasi-Monetary Liabilities	45
Bonds	46a
Import Deposits	46b
Foreign Liabilities	46c
Long-Term Foreign Liabilities	46cl
Government Deposits	46d
Counterpart Funds	46e
Credit from Government	46f
Credit from Monetary Authorities	46g
Credit from Deposit Money Banks	46h
Capital Accounts	47a
Other Items (net)	47r
Financial Survey	
Foreign Assets (net)	51n
Domestic Credit	52
Claims on Government (net)	52an
Claims on Official Entities	52b
Claims on Businesses and Individuals	52d
Liquid Liabilities	54
Bonds	56a
Import Deposits	56b
Long-Term Foreign Liabilities	56cl
Counterpart Funds	56e
Other Items (net)	57r

TABLE 1. Line items on Country Pages of *International Financial Statistics*
(concluded)

Interest, Prices, Production	
Discount Rate (end of period)	60
Treasury Bill Rate	60c
Government Bond Yield: Mid-Term	61a
Long-Term	61
National Accounts	
Exports	90c
Government Consumption	91f
Gross Fixed Capital Formation	93e
Increase in Stocks	93i
Private Consumption	96f
Less: Imports	98c
Gross Domestic Product	99b
Less: Net Factor Payments Abroad	98e
Gross National Expenditure = GNP	99a
National Income, Market Prices	99e
Gross Domestic Product: 1975 Prices	99b.p

Source: International Monetary Fund, *International Financial Statistics* (monthly).

On the *IFS* country pages, foreign assets (11)[3] include gold, foreign bank notes, deposits in foreign exchange held abroad, investments in the debt instruments of other countries, SDRs, and the member's reserve position in the International Monetary Fund. The last is the outstanding amount a member country may draw unconditionally under the Fund's regular tranche policies plus the equivalent of its outstanding lendings to the Fund under borrowing arrangements.

Defining the government sector of a country often poses difficult problems. In *IFS,* an attempt is made to separate banking system claims on, and liabilities to, public institutions into two categories: government per se and official entities. The term "government" formerly included state and local, as well as central government, but now an attempt is made to limit it to the central government, government enterprises directly under its control, and social security funds. For those countries where data are available, this category is based on the same definition of government as that used for "government

[3] Numbers in parentheses refer to line items on the country pages of *IFS* (see Table 1).

finance," which comprises lines 80–89 of *IFS*.[4] The treatment of government enterprises is based on the same general criteria as those used for government finance statistics: namely, the existence of government ownership and/or control, the extent to which the decision-making process is based on commercial considerations, and whether the market for the output of these enterprises is largely in the government or private sector. Official entities include the financial accounts in the banking system of government entities other than those presented as "government," such as state and local governments and autonomous nonfinancial public enterprises. The autonomous financial public enterprises (e.g., official development banks, postal and other official savings banks, official mortgage banks, etc.), together with similar private institutions, are included in a separate category, called "other financial institutions" (OFIs), discussed below in the section on The First Level: Deposit Money Banks. The title used in *IFS* for this category varies from country to country, depending on the nature of the institutions.

Table 2 presents a typical balance sheet of the monetary authorities of a country, with the regrouping necessary for presenting the above information and for constructing the monetary survey.

In the accounts of the country's monetary authorities, following the above distinction, claims on the public sector are subdivided into claims on government (12a) and claims on official entities (12b), while claims on official development and savings banks are included in claims on other financial institutions (12f). In general, claims on the private sector (12d) are likely to be insignificant. Rediscounts are treated as claims on deposit money banks (DMBs) since they are viewed as a transaction between the central bank and the DMB to replenish the liquidity of the latter. At the DMB level, they are reported as a claim on nonresidents, government, or private sector (according to the case) with a contra-entry on the liability side as credit from the central bank.

---

[4] See also International Monetary Fund, *Government Finance Statistics Yearbook* (annual).

TABLE 2. Typical Balance Sheet of Monetary Authorities

Assets		Liabilities	
Gold	Foreign assets (11)	Reserve money	(14)
Foreign exchange		Currency in circulation	
Reserve position in IMF		outside banks	(14a)
Holdings of SDRs		in bank vaults	(14b)
Foreign correspondents		banks' deposits	(14c)
Foreign investments		private sector deposits	(14d)
Loans to the government	Claims on government (12a)	official entities' deposits	(14dx)
Treasury bonds		Time deposits	(15)
Discounts and guaranteed government obligations		Deposits in foreign exchange	(15b)
Claims on official entities	(12b)	Import deposits	(16b)
Claims on the private sector	(12d)	Foreign liabilities	(16c)
Claims on other financial institutions	(12f)	Government deposits	(16d)
Discounts	Claims on deposit money banks (12e)	Counterpart funds	(16e)
Advances		Lending funds of government	(16f)
Claims on the money market			
Fixed assets	Unclassified assets (13)	Capital	Capital accounts (17a)
Other items		Reserves	
		Counterpart of SDR allocations	Other items (17r)
		Profits	
		Other accounts	

Note: Numbers in parentheses refer to line items on country pages of *International Financial Statistics* (see Table 1).

The main item on the liability side is reserve money. This is the monetary base through which the central bank influences the liquidity of the DMBs and, hence, their ability to create deposit money. The main component of reserve money is currency in circulation outside banks, i.e., currency in the hands of the public. Private sector deposits (14d), like claims on the private sector, are generally small. The deposits of official as well as private nonbank financial intermediaries are included in private sector (demand) deposits (14d) or in time deposits (15), as appropriate. Currency in bank vaults (14b) and banks' deposits with the monetary authorities (14c) are important for economic analysis, since they serve as the base for total demand deposits of the community. Foreign liabilities (16c) include all liabilities to nonresidents in domestic and foreign currencies. Deposits of government are shown as item (16d). A member's use of Fund credit, which measures the net use by a member country of its conditional drawing rights in the Fund, is included as item (16c). However, the counterpart of SDR allocations is shown in other items (17r) rather than as a foreign liability. Thus, any allocation of SDRs will add to net as well as gross reserves of the participating member countries. As defined in *IFS,* deposits in foreign exchange (15x) include liabilities to residents only, and therefore are not included as foreign liabilities. Counterpart funds (16e) in local currency are generated from the sale to residents of commodities imported under bilateral aid agreements, particularly under U.S. Public Law 480 (PL–480). These funds usually serve as a source of financing for projects mutually agreed on by the contracting governments.[5]

In the presentation of the accounts of a country's monetary authorities, a number of problems are encountered.

1. Even at the first level, the presentation of the accounts of monetary authorities involves some consolidation. First, there is a consolidation of central bank accounts with certain accounts of the treasury or other appropriate government agency, such as treasury currency or coin; government foreign asset holdings; treasury ac-

[5] Under PL–480, commodity assistance (largely in the form of grain) is provided by the United States, generally in the form of a long-term loan repayable in local currency, to countries in balance of payments difficulties. The proceeds of sales of these imported commodities generate the counterpart funds in local currency, which are owned by the United States (i.e., a liability of the recipient country to the United States). The United States and the recipient country conclude agreements regarding the disposition of these funds, which may take diverse forms in different countries. Usually, most of the funds are transferred to the local government, as long-term loans in local currency, to provide financing for mutually agreed development projects. However, a part of these funds may be set aside for use by the U.S. Embassy to finance local currency expenditure. Another part (usually small) may be used to make local currency loans to U.S. corporations operating in the country. A relatively small part may be transferred to the local government on a grant basis.

counts (if any); and transactions with the Fund,[6] including the payment of the local currency subscription. Second, an interdepartmental consolidation for the central bank is needed where separate issue and banking departments exist, each performing the functions of monetary authorities. However, in cases where the central bank performs predominantly commercial banking functions (either through a separate banking department or otherwise), or conversely, where a deposit money bank, usually official, also performs some or all of the central banking functions, a separation must be made, with the banking department or the commercial banking component of the central bank being included in the DMB consolidation and the central banking component of the DMBs being transferred to the accounts of the monetary authorities.

2. In cases where foreign assets held by the treasury, by an exchange stabilization fund, or by a similar government institution are consolidated with the accounts of the monetary authorities, the *offsetting* entries may be recorded either by deducting from claims on government (12a) or, where this would lead to a negative figure, by adding to government deposits (16d). Foreign liabilities of government, such as those related to development loans, are not recorded in the accounts of the monetary authorities.

3. The reserve position in the Fund is entered in line 11, even in cases where a part of the Fund's accounts (such as the local currency subscription) is shown in the accounts of the treasury or another government institution and does not appear in the balance sheet of the central bank. In such cases, offsetting entries are made, following a procedure similar to that in paragraph 2 above. The same is true of use of Fund credit, because the maintenance of the Fund accounts is a monetary function of the government which must be consolidated with central bank data.

4. The term "claims" (on government, banks, etc.) is used to include not only direct credit in the form of rediscounts, loans, and

---

[6] In most countries, these are carried on the books of the central bank.

advances but also indirect credit in the form of investments in securities (including both new issues and securities purchased from existing holders).

5. As regards the classification of the public sector into its various components, a uniform presentation of *IFS* data for all countries has not been possible because of lack of data. In some cases, state and local governments may not be included at all or may be included in government (12a) rather than in official entities (12b). There may be cases of autonomous public enterprises being included in government (12a) instead of in official entities (12b). In other cases, official development and savings banks may be included in official entities (12b) or even in government (12a), instead of being shown separately as OFIs (12f). Similarly, the deposits of an official entity or an official development bank may be shown in government deposits (16d), instead of in private sector demand deposits (14d) or time deposits (15). Where possible, in such cases a note is inserted in the country pages of *IFS,* pointing out the inadequacy of data.

6. The distinction between DMBs and OFIs (see the section below on The First Level: Deposit Money Banks) may present similar problems of classification for the claims of the monetary authorities on, and their liabilities to, such institutions. As in the case of paragraph 5 above, this can also have a bearing on the totals in the monetary survey.

The First Level: Deposit Money Banks

Deposit money banks (DMBs), which comprise lines 20–29 on the country pages of *IFS,* include all commercial institutions whose demand deposit liabilities are important or form a large proportion of their total liabilities. Although the commercial banks are the principal institutions in this category, such financial institutions as savings banks may also be included when their liabilities are regarded as money. Thus, the term "deposit money banks" is, in general, synonymous with commercial banks but its coverage may be somewhat different. Currently in *IFS,* the term "commercial banks" is used in some countries as a heading for lines 20–29, while the term "deposit money banks" or a different term is used in others (such as business banks for Yugoslavia, commercial and cooperative banks for India, commercial and savings banks for Spain, deposit and savings banks for Mexico, etc.).

Table 3 presents a consolidation of the balance sheet accounts from such institutions. Most of the items in this table need no further explanation than that given for the same items under monetary authorities. The most important problem in making a table of this kind lies in the division of deposit accounts between demand deposits (24) and time and savings deposits (25 and 25x). Money comprises demand deposits held by the domestic nongovernment sector. Quasi-money includes mainly time and savings deposits (25) held by the domestic private sector with those institutions included in deposit

TABLE 3. Typical Consolidated Balance Sheet of Deposit Money Banks

Assets		Liabilities	
Cash in vault; Deposits with monetary authorities	Reserves (20)	Sight deposits; Checking accounts	(24)
Gold and foreign exchange; Deposits and securities abroad	Foreign assets (21)	Savings and other deposits requiring previous notice; Time deposits	(25a)
Loans to the government; Treasury bonds; Discounts and government obligations	Claims on government (22a)	Foreign exchange deposits	(25x)
		Import deposits	(26b)
		Deposits of foreign correspondents	(26c)
Claims on official entities	(22b)	Government deposits	(26d)
Discounted bills; Advances; Overdrafts; Medium-term and long-term loans; Stocks and bonds	Claims on the private sector (22d)	Counterpart funds	(26e)
		Government lending funds	(26f)
		Credit from monetary authorities	(26g)
Fixed assets; Other items	Other items (23)	Capital; Reserves — Capital accounts	(27a)
		Profits; Other accounts	(27r)

Note: Numbers in parentheses refer to line items on country pages of *International Financial Statistics* (see Table 1).

money banks.[7] Foreign exchange deposits of the private sector and other foreign exchange deposits (25x) are considered as quasi-money and not as a foreign liability.

Some problems in the presentation of DMB accounts are noted below:

1. In the consolidation of the accounts of deposit money banks, care must be taken to eliminate interbank float and other interbank claims and liabilities, if any.

2. The separation of DMBs from OFIs presents the problem of distinguishing between monetary and nonmonetary financial institutions in practice, as well as the problem of consistency in the treatment of the monetary system's claims on and liabilities to OFIs. The problem arises, on the one hand, because many savings institutions or development banks (OFIs) also have some demand deposits and, on the other hand, because time and savings deposits in DMBs have outgrown demand deposits in many countries. The current *IFS* practice is to classify as DMBs those institutions whose demand deposit liabilities are a significant part of their total liabilities and to treat as OFIs those institutions whose demand deposit liabilities are clearly insignificant. The borderline cases (of which there are many) are decided on a case-by-case basis with reference to the legal basis, tradition, and circumstances. As for both official and private DMB claims on and liabilities to OFIs (see the preceding section on The First Level: Monetary Authorities), separate entries are not shown in Table 3. With very few exceptions, the country pages of *IFS* do not show DMB claims on OFIs separately, because these are insignificant or are not known. However, there is no conceptual reason why there should not be a line (22f), corresponding to line (12f) of MA accounts, in cases where this is warranted; in fact, there is a line (22f) in the case of Mexico.

3. The term "claims" includes both direct and indirect credit, as explained in paragraph 4 of the preceding section on The First Level: Monetary Authorities.

---

[7] The distinction between money and quasi-money is discussed at greater length below in the section on The Second Level: The Monetary Survey.

4. The problem of classification of DMB claims and liabilities, arising out of the distinction between government and official entities, is the same as that explained in paragraph 5 of the preceding section on The First Level: Monetary Authorities. Claims on government and claims on official entities are shown separately in lines (22a) and (22b), respectively. Deposit liabilities to government in line (26d) and deposits of official entities are shown in line (24), if they are demand deposits, or in line (25), if they are time and savings deposits.

The Second Level: The Monetary Survey

A major purpose of the monetary survey is to allow analysis of the financial aggregates most influenced by the monetary authorities and most influential on other economic aggregates. To this end, the balance sheet data from all the deposit money banks and the monetary authorities are consolidated into a few categories of major interest to economists and policymakers (see Table 4).

TABLE 4. Typical Monetary Survey

Assets		Liabilities	
Net foreign assets	(31n)	Money	(34)
Domestic credit	(32)	Quasi-money	(35)
Claims on government	(32an)	Import deposits	(36b)
Claims on official entities	(32b)	Counterpart funds	(36e)
Claims on private sector	(32d)	Other items (net)	(37r)

Note: Numbers in parentheses refer to line items on country pages of *International Financial Statistics* (see Table 1).

For several reasons, only the financial institutions named earlier are included in the monetary survey. First, the monetary authorities and deposit money banks form what might be called the core of the system of financial intermediaries within any particular country, and the movements of the accounts of these institutions are of primary interest for monetary analysis. Second, the balance sheets of other financial intermediaries are often not available without substantial delay, thus limiting the usefulness of these data for the formulation of monetary policy. Finally, the instruments available to central banks for the control of monetary policy often affect deposit money bank operations directly, but they usually do not impinge quite as directly on the operations of other financial institutions.

The monetary survey must be constructed so as to eliminate float and to net out all interbank accounts. The items included in the monetary survey from the two consolidated balance sheets are derived as follows:[8]

Assets

Net foreign assets (31n)=
- Foreign assets of the monetary authorities (11)
- *Plus:* Foreign assets of the deposit money banks (21)
- *Less:* Foreign liabilities of the monetary authorities (16c) and deposit money banks (26c)

Note: If the balance is negative (liabilities greater than assets), it is entered as such under (31n).

Claims on government (net) (32an)=
- Claims on government of the monetary authorities (12a) and deposit money banks (22a)
- *Less:* Deposits of government with the monetary authorities (16d) and with deposit money banks (26d)

Claims on official entities (32b)=
- the sum of (12b) and (22b)

Claims on private sector (32d)=
- Claims on the private sector by the monetary authorities (12d)
- *Plus:* Claims on other financial institutions (12f)
- *Plus:* Claims on the private sector by deposit money banks (22d)

[8] In the case of French-speaking countries, the following modifications to the table would be needed: Private sector deposits in Postal Savings Accounts and the Treasury are to be reported in (34) with a contra-entry in (32an), postal debt is included in (31n) and (32an), and custom duty bills held by the Treasury are in (32an) and (32d) [compare *IFS* pages for France and member states of the Banque des Etats de l'Afrique Centrale (BEAC) and the Banque Centrale des Etats de l'Afrique de l'Ouest (BCEAO)].

Liabilities

Money (34) =
- Currency outside deposit money banks (14a)
- *Plus:* Private sector deposits with monetary authorities (14d)
- *Plus:* Official entities' deposits (14dx)
- *Plus:* Demand deposits in the deposit money banks (24)

Quasi-money (35) =
- Time and savings deposits with the monetary authorities (15)
- Time and savings deposits with deposit money banks (25)
- *Plus:* Foreign currency deposits held by residents with the monetary authorities (15x) and deposit money banks (25x)

Import deposits (36b) = the sum of (16b) and (26b)

Counterpart funds (36e) = the sum of (16e) and (26e)

Other items (net)[9] (37r) =
- Capital accounts (17a) and (27a)
- *Plus:* Retained profits (27b)
- *Plus:* Other liabilities of the monetary authorities, including the counterpart of SDR allocations (17b)
- *Less:* Other items, including certain memorandum accounts, of monetary authorities, and deposit money banks (13) and (23)

For the most part, the entries are self-explanatory. Foreign assets (31n) comprise all types of foreign assets and gold, minus short-term and medium-term foreign liabilities of the institutions included in the survey. The intent is to show the domestic monetary impact of a country's transactions with the rest of the world, as measured by the change in net foreign assets. Domestic credit[10] (an asset of the banking system) includes all outstanding credit granted by the banking

[9] This is a balancing entry.

[10] Domestic credit and its components (claims on government, claims on official entities, and claims on the private sector) also include investments made by the banking system in securities issued by government, official entities, and the private sector.

system to government, official entities, and the private sector (including, for example, persons, corporations, or other financial institutions). All credit that banks grant to each other, as well as credit granted by the central bank to deposit money banks, disappears in the process of consolidation.

In the monetary survey, claims on government [11] are also entered as net—that is, the figures against this item include all credit granted to government by the banking system minus all deposits of the government in the banking system. This treatment facilitates measurement of the impact of government operations on the liquidity of the economy. Also, the government is the authority responsible for economic policy and, consequently, its decisions concerning expenditure do not usually depend on the amount of deposits it has but on wider measures, since it is not bound by liquidity considerations like those which apply to other sectors. Claims on official entities [11] are shown separately because of the importance and because of the special problems in regard to these entities, especially in the less developed countries. Claims on official entities are entered as gross because the amount of deposits and cash that they possess (their liquidity) is thought to influence their expenditure. Claims on the private sector [11] register all credit to private individuals and enterprises and are entered as gross because of the considerations pointed out above with regard to claims on official entities. This item also includes claims on official and private OFIs.

The term "money" is variously defined both in theory and in practice. One of the more widely accepted definitions includes all currency in circulation outside the banking system and government—that is, currency in the hands of private sector and official entities and all deposits of the private sector and official entities that can be utilized as a means of payment. Deposits are generally that part of money which may be transferred by check. However, in certain institutional arrangements, other current deposits with a high rate of turnover, such as savings deposits, may be included. Accordingly, in the monetary survey, money includes the two categories: currency in circulation and demand-type deposits. It is shown as a liability of the

[11] See footnote 10.

monetary system because currency is a liability of the monetary authorities and demand deposits are liabilities of deposit money banks. The term "quasi-money" is another liability of banks and includes all other deposits with the monetary system that are not utilized directly as a means of payment and that usually have a lower rate of turnover. This generally means time and savings deposits with the banking system. Import deposits are advance payments made in domestic currency by residents when applying for foreign exchange, and these are not included in quasi-money. Government deposits are not included in either money or quasi-money, particularly because they do not represent liquidity in the sense that they do not constrain government expenditure policies and are thus different in character from private sector deposits.

It is necessary for the monetary survey to take into account peculiarities of the financial structure in any country. In France and in countries following French banking practices, the Treasury and Postal Savings Accounts have a very special role which must be considered in constructing the monetary survey. In other countries, a formerly private bank may serve in place of a treasury as the agency for all government accounts. Since these peculiarities or departures from the norm are frequent, *IFS* contains an explanation of such institutions or accounts in the footnotes to the country tables.

Some problems of consolidation in respect of the monetary survey are worthy of mention:

1. As in the case of the consolidation of the DMB accounts, the consolidation for the monetary survey could eliminate transactions between the MAs and the DMBs. Thus lines (12e), (14b), and (14c) in the MA accounts and lines (20) and (26g) in the DMB accounts are canceled out.

2. The term "claims" has the same meaning as that explained in paragraph 4 of the section above on The First Level: Monetary Authorities.

3. As explained in paragraph 2 of the preceding section on The First Level: Deposit Money Banks, OFIs are not included in the monetary survey and, as such, any demand deposits or time and

savings deposits held in the OFIs are not reflected in the money and quasi-money figures of the monetary survey.[12] However, the amount of demand deposits thus excluded from the monetary survey is likely to be small, since the size of demand deposits, as indicated in the preceding section, is the main criterion for classification as a DMB or as an OFI.

4. While claims on official and private development and savings institutions (OFIs) may be shown separately in MA (12f) and DMB (22f) accounts (see comments in the sections above on The First Level), they are not shown separately in the monetary survey but are included in credit to the private sector (32d). The information provided by the separate entries (12f) and (22f) is necessary, however, for the financial survey consolidation (see the next section on The Third Level), in order to net out claims and liabilities between MAs and DMBs, on the one hand, and OFIs, on the other hand; items (12f) and (22f) would disappear, and so would the corresponding liability items in the OFIs (liabilities to MAs and DMBs). Similarly, OFI cash (claims on MAs) and OFI claims on DMBs (items (40) and (42e) of Table 5) would be offset in the consolidation by the corresponding MA and DMB liabilities to OFIs.

5. On the assets side, the monetary survey consolidation classifies claims by sectors or sector components in lines (32an), (32b), and (32d). However, on the liabilities side, the classification is mainly according to the nature of liquidity (as explained earlier with reference to money, quasi-money, and government deposits). Thus, deposits of official entities are considered to have the same liquidity characteristics as private sector deposits and are included in money (34) or quasi-money (35) in the monetary survey consolidation (depending on whether they are demand or time and savings deposits), even though they may have been shown separately in the first-

[12] Other financial institutions (OFIs) are not treated as monetary institutions in the monetary survey. However, claims of the monetary system on OFIs are either reported separately, if significant, or are otherwise subsumed in claims on the private sector, and their deposits with the monetary system are included in money and quasi-money.

level consolidation, as for example, item (14dx). Deposits of official or private development and savings institutions (OFIs) are included in private sector deposits in the MA and DMB accounts as well as in the monetary survey.

6. Foreign currency deposits held by residents, shown separately as item (15x) in MA accounts (for example, Chile) and item (25x) in DMB accounts (for example, Chile and Saudi Arabia), are included in quasi-money because their characteristics are similar to those of other components of quasi-money, even though they are denominated in foreign exchange.

7. Counterpart funds (36e) are shown separately in the monetary survey, if their amount is substantial. *IFS* currently shows counterpart funds separately in the monetary survey for seven countries (Bolivia, Egypt, Pakistan, Paraguay, Sudan, Tunisia, and Zaïre).

The Third Level: The Financial Survey

While the monetary survey covers only the monetary authorities and deposit money banks, the financial survey includes other financial intermediaries that are important in the financial structure of the economy. Information on their activities is useful for monetary and financial analysis. The financial survey establishes a link between money creation and the channeling of credit, on the one hand, and the collection of savings, on the other hand. The financial survey, together with the balance of payments and the financial accounts of the government sector, would make it possible to construct a statement of the financial transactions of the private sector, thus providing a link with flow-of-funds accounts.

Other financial intermediaries may include specialized credit entities, such as savings or postal banks, mortgage banks, development banks, or banks specializing in sectoral loans for mining or agriculture. Insurance and pension institutions may also figure importantly in this group of financial intermediaries.

The balance sheet of each one of these institutions reflects its particular character. Thus, consolidation of balance sheets from the major institutions of this sector into a single statement for financial intermediaries may often pose very difficult problems of netting and categorization. Where feasible, however, this statement has a form similar to that shown in Table 5.

TABLE 5. Typical Consolidated Balance Sheet of Other Financial Intermediaries

Assets		Liabilities	
Cash	(40)	Demand deposits	(44)
Foreign assets	(41)	Time and savings deposits	(45)
Claims on government	(42a)	Bonds and certificates	(46a)
Claims on official entities	(42b)	Foreign liabilities	(46c)
Claims on the private sector	(42d)	Credit from government	(46f)
Claims on deposit money banks	(42e)	Credit from monetary authorities	(46g)
		Credit from deposit money banks	(46h)
		Capital accounts	(47a)
		Other items (net)	(47r)

Note: Numbers in parentheses refer to line items on country pages of *International Financial Statistics* (see Table 1).

To the extent that the accounting practices of these financial intermediaries are compatible with those of the banking system, and where data are available, the data are presented and then consolidated in the financial survey of *IFS*.[13] The table takes the form shown in Table 6.

TABLE 6. Typical Financial Survey

Assets	Liabilities
Net foreign assets (51) = (31n) + (41) — (46c) [1]	Liquid liabilities (54) = (34) + (35) + (44) + (45)
Net claims on government (52an) = (32an) + (42a) — (46f) [2]	Bonds and certificates (56a) = (46a)
Claims on official entities (52b) = (32b) + (42b)	Capital accounts (57a) = (17a) + (27a) + (47a)
Claims on the private sector (52d) = (32d) + (42d)	Other items (net) (57r) = (17r) + (27r) + (36r) + (36e) + (47r) — (13) — (23)

Note: Numbers in parentheses refer to line items on country pages of *International Financial Statistics* (see Table 1).

[1] If long-term, item (46c) is not netted out.

[2] If long-term, item (46f) is not netted out.

[13] Claims and liabilities of the monetary authorities or deposit money banks on other financial institutions should be excluded, as for example, lines (32f) and (34).

ISSUES FOR DISCUSSION

1. *There are three levels of aggregation of monetary statistics in* IFS. *What are the purposes behind collection of statistics at each level?*

2. *On the asset side of the banking system balance sheets, classification is by sector, i.e., foreign sector, government sector, private sector, etc. On the liability side, classification is mainly by type of liability, i.e., money, quasi-money, other items, etc. What are (a) the purpose of and (b) the advantages and disadvantages of this asymmetrical classification?*

3. *Why are deposits denominated in foreign exchange and held by residents and nonresidents treated differently? Why are such deposits, when held by residents, included in quasi-money? Why are counterpart funds not treated as foreign liabilities or as quasi-money?*

4. *What are some of the problems encountered in the application of the criteria for distinguishing between DMBs and OFIs? How does such a distinction affect the figures for domestic credit and money?*

5. *How does the distinction between government and official entities (i.e., the inclusion of a particular official entity in one or the other of the above two categories) affect the figures for net credit to government, domestic credit, and money? Why are claims on official entities treated differently, in terms of sectorization, from liabilities to these entities? Why are claims on, and liabilities to, official development and savings banks not shown separately?*

6. *In the consolidation of the net foreign assets of MAs and DMBs, comment on the special problems arising out of the treatment of foreign asset holdings of the Treasury or other government institutions and of transactions with the IMF. Should bilateral payments balances (credit or debit) be included in net foreign assets?*

Should the foreign liabilities of the Central Government or of official entities be treated as foreign liabilities of the monetary authorities?

7. *Why are government deposits not treated as money or quasi-money? Why does the monetary survey present credit to government as net of government deposits? Is there a situation where this would not be the best presentation, from the point of view of economic analysis? Why are deposits of official entities treated differently from deposits of the Government?*

8. *Why does the monetary survey show foreign assets net, i.e., after deducting foreign liabilities?*

9. *How does the financial survey provide a link with flow-of-funds accounts? How could it be better presented if the primary goal was to provide a data base for such a link?*

MONETARY SURVEY FOR KENYA

It should be remembered that the claims of the monetary authorities on, and liabilities to, the commercial banks will not appear in the banking system's consolidated statement; similarly, the claims of the commercial banks on, and liabilities to, the monetary authorities will be excluded from the consolidated statement. The figure for total claims of commercial banks on the monetary authorities, as shown in the summary account for the commercial banks, does not exactly match the liabilities to commercial banks recorded in the balance sheet of the monetary authorities. These discrepancies are unavoidable because checks and other items are in transit and because a timing difference may exist in the recording of transactions. In the monetary survey these discrepancies will be reflected in "other items (net)." This item is not, therefore, equal to the sum of the corresponding items in the balance sheets of the monetary authorities and the commercial banks.

EXERCISES AND ISSUES FOR DISCUSSION

Exercise A

Table 9 below gives a consolidated balance sheet of the banking system from 1973 through 1976 in the form of the monetary survey, which has been derived from the summary accounts of the monetary authorities (Table 7) and the commercial banks (Table 8). The column for 1977 in Table 9 has been left blank, and these figures are to be filled in, using Tables 7 and 8.

Exercise B

Table 10 below gives the changes in the items of the monetary survey from 1973 through 1976. The columns for the changes in shillings and in per cent from 1976 to 1977 have been left blank, and these figures are to be filled in, using Table 9.

Exercise C and Issues for Discussion

In 1976 and 1977, the economy of Kenya experienced a sharp upsurge in economic activity, led by increases in exports of coffee. In 1977, real GDP is estimated to have grown by 7.5 per cent. Consumer prices rose by 15 per cent. Domestic aggregate demand increased by 23 per cent in current prices.

1. *Examine the accounts of the monetary authorities for 1977. How did the export boom affect their assets?*

2. *Calculate the change in* net *foreign assets of the monetary authorities in 1977. What would be the approximate first round impact of this change on reserve money? Was the actual change in reserve money larger or smaller than this?*

3. *Examine the accounts for the Government in both the monetary authorities and commercial banks in 1977. What was the change in net credit to Government in (a) the monetary authorities and (b) the commercial banks? Does it appear from these accounts*

that Kenyan policy was to move to offset or exacerbate the liquidity impact of the export boom on the banking system?

4. *Examine the monetary survey. What was the percentage change in money plus quasi-money in 1977? How does this compare with the percentage change in (a) real GDP and (b) domestic aggregate demand?*

5. *Aside from the influences of the Government on the banking system, what other accounts could the monetary authorities influence in order to affect the expansionary effect of the banking system on the economy?*

6. *What was the percentage change in domestic credit in 1977? How does this compare to the increase in aggregate domestic demand? Below are listed data for the percentage increases in domestic aggregate demand and domestic credit in recent years. Does the increase in credit in 1977 seem excessive or deficient in magnitude? Is this a reasonable comparison? What other information is needed to assess the appropriate increase in domestic credit during the year?*

(In millions of Kenya shillings and percentage changes from previous year)

	Aggregate Demand [1]		*Domestic Credit* [2]	
	Amount	*Percentage change*	*Amount*	*Percentage change*
1974	20,179	16.7	4,966	28.7
1975	24,437	21.1	6,414	29.2
1976	28,835	18.0	7,475	16.5
1977	35,039	21.5	9,255	23.8

[1] Aggregate domestic demand is defined as the sum of consumption and gross fixed investment in any particular year. Data from Kenya's *Economic Survey*.

[2] Data from *International Financial Statistics*.

TABLE 7. Kenya: Summary Accounts of the Monetary Authorities, 1973–77

(In millions of Kenya shillings)

Assets	1973	1974	1975	1976	1977
Foreign assets (11)	**1,615.0**	**1,354.0**	**1,439.0**	**2,309.0**	**4,282.0**
Fund reserve position	102.2	—	—	—	—
Holdings of SDRs	142.4	16.3	36.3	26.8	139.0
Correspondents [1]	820.3	747.0	804.9	1,581.9	3,533.7
Holdings of foreign securities	524.2	587.4	589.1	684.4	586.3
Government foreign exchange holdings	25.4	3.6	8.3	15.8	23.1
Claims on Government (12a)	**369.0**	**526.0**	**1,111.9**	**851.0**	**1,243.0**
Advances	200.0	200.0	543.1	200.0	200.0
Treasury bills	59.9	148.8	284.3	20.0	132.6
Securities issued or guaranteed by Government	108.8	176.9	150.1	496.9	726.5
SDR allocations used by Government	—	—	134.4	134.4	134.4
Trust Fund loan	—	—	—	—	49.6
Claims on official entities (12b)	**7.0**	—	—	—	—
Claims on commercial banks (12e)	—	**236.3**	**34.3**	**8.5**	**18.0**
Fixed assets and other items (13)	**179.0**	**279.0**	**36.0**	**100.0**	**24.0**

Liabilities	1973	1974	1975	1976	1977
Reserve money (14)	**1,395.0**	**1,789.0**	**1,613.0**	**2,001.0**	**3,233.0**
Currency outside banks (14a)	982.0	1,086.0	1,234.0	1,625.0	2,182.0
Currency in bank vaults (14b)	137.0	253.0	174.0	205.0	241.0
Banks' deposits (14c)	221.0	381.0	131.0	133.0	730.0
Official entities' deposits (14d) [2]	55.0	69.0	74.0	38.0	80.0
Foreign liabilities (16c)	**6.0**	**289.0**	**750.0**	**844.0**	**570.0**
Use of Fund credit	—	280.3	662.9	820.9	460.0
Other foreign liabilities	6.0	8.7	87.1	23.1	110.0
Government deposits (16d)	**464.0**	**36.0**	**—59.0**	**73.0**	**1,278.0**
Counterpart of Fund reserve position	102.1	—	—	—	—
Other deposits of the Treasury	361.8	36.0	—59.0	73.0	1,278.0
Capital accounts (17a)	**182.0**	**186.0**	**186.0**	**186.0**	**186.0**
Other liabilities	**123.2**	**94.0**	**129.3**	**163.8**	**299.9**

Sources: Central Bank of Kenya, *Annual Report for the Financial Year Ended 30th June, 1978;* International Monetary Fund, *International Financial Statistics,* July 1978.

Note: Numbers in parentheses refer to line items on country pages of *International Financial Statistics* (see Table 1).

[1] Includes balances with Banks of Tanzania and Uganda as follows:

1973	*1974*	*1975*	*1976*	*1977*
10.0	6.9	11.5	7.4	31.8

[2] Including some float.

TABLE 8. Kenya: Summary Accounts of Commercial Banks, 1973–77
(In millions of Kenya shillings)

Assets	1973	1974	1975	1976	1977
Reserves (20)	**372.0**	**514.0**	**298.0**	**313.0**	**971.0**
Cash in vaults	137.0	253.0	174.0	205.0	241.0
Deposits in the Central Bank	234.0	261.0	124.0	108.0	730.0
Foreign assets (21)	**222.0**	**304.0**	**372.0**	**407.0**	**334.0**
Holdings of foreign currency	5.0	7.1	18.9	16.0	23.3
Deposits and securities abroad	217.0	296.9	353.1	391.0	310.7
Claims on Government (22a)	**649.6**	**510.1**	**676.9**	**1,191.9**	**1,963.4**
Treasury bills	459.7	325.6	498.3	1,015.9	1,370.9
Government securities	185.4	184.4	174.0	158.6	590.2
Loans and advances	4.5	0.1	4.2	17.4	2.3
Claims on official entities (22b)	**230.0**	**223.0**	**303.0**	**215.0**	**259.0**
Claims on private sector (22d)[1]	**3,143.0**	**3,813.0**	**4,344.0**	**5,362.0**	**7,196.0**
Fixed assets and other items (23)	**647.0**	**870.0**	**953.0**	**1,057.0**	**1,485.0**

Liabilities	1973	1974	1975	1976	1977
Government deposits (26d)	**76.0**	**70.0**	**81.0**	**72.0**	**128.0**
Demand deposits (24)	**2,825.0**	**2,881.0**	**3,249.0**	**4,079.0**	**6,189.0**
Savings deposits (25)	**979.4**	**1,143.2**	**1,277.7**	**1,513.7**	**2,083.2**
Rest of public sector	3.8	4.5	13.8	23.5	19.0
Private sector	975.6	1,138.7	1,263.9	1,490.2	2,064.2
Time deposits (25)	**515.0**	**660.0**	**996.5**	**1,266.6**	**1,902.6**
Rest of public sector	141.1	209.5	397.9	440.6	580.8
Private sector	373.9	450.5	598.6	826.0	1,321.8
Deposits of foreign correspondents (26c)	**273.0**	**400.0**	**480.0**	**413.0**	**413.0**
Credit from Central Bank (26g)	—	**254.0**	**19.0**	—	—
Capital accounts (27a)	**307.0**	**373.0**	**443.0**	**537.0**	**750.0**
Other liabilities (27b)	**287.3**	**454.6**	**411.1**	**664.3**	**743.2**

Sources: Central Bank of Kenya, *Annual Report for the Financial Year Ended 30th June, 1978;* International Monetary Fund, *International Financial Statistics*, July 1978.

Note: Numbers in parentheses refer to line items on country pages of *International Financial Statistics* (see Table 1).

[1] Claims on two financial institutions—Cereals and Sugar Finance Corporation (CSFC) and Agricultural Finance Corporation (AFC)—are included here as follows:

1973	*1974*	*1975*	*1976*	*1977*
285.2	79.5	258.0	470.5	683.5

TABLE 9. Kenya: Monetary Survey, 1973–77
(In millions of Kenya shillings)

Item	1973	1974	1975	1976	1977
Net foreign assets	**1,558.0**	**969.0**	**581.0**	**1,459.0**	
Foreign assets	1,837.0	1,658.0	1,811.0	2,716.0	
Use of Fund credit	—	280.3	662.9	820.9	
Other foreign liabilities	279.0	408.7	567.1	436.1	
Domestic credit	**3,859.0**	**4,966.0**	**6,414.0**	**7,475.0**	
Government (net)	479.0	930.0	1,767.0	1,898.0	
Official entities	237.0	223.0	303.0	215.0	
Private sector [1]	3,143.0	3,813.0	4,344.0	5,362.0	
Other items (net)	**61.0**	**116.0**	**181.0**	**480.0**	
Money plus quasi-money	**5,356.0**	**5,819.0**	**6,814.0**	**8,454.0**	
Money	3,862.0	4,016.0	4,540.0	5,674.0	
Currency	*982.0*	*1,086.0*	*1,234.0*	*1,625.0*	
Demand deposits [2]	*2,880.0*	*2,950.0*	*3,323.0*	*4,117.0*	
Uncleared effects	—	*—20.0*	*—17.0*	*—68.0*	
Quasi-money	1,494.0	1,803.0	2,274.0	2,780.0	

Source: Tables 7 and 8.

[1] Includes data for CSFC and AFC (see footnote to Table 8) as follows:

1973	*1974*	*1975*	*1976*
285.2	79.5	258.0	470.5

[2] Includes official entities' deposits with the monetary authorities.

TABLE 10. Kenya: Changes in Monetary Survey Items, 1973–77
(In millions of Kenya shillings and per cent)

Item	1973		1974		1975		1976		1977	
	Amount	Per cent	Amount	Per cent	Amount	Per cent	Amount	Per cent	Amount	Per cent
1. Net foreign assets	200	14.7	–589	–37.8	–388	–40.0	878	151.1		
2. Domestic credit	841	27.9	1,107	28.7	1,448	29.2	1,061	16.5		
3. Credit to Government (net)	133	38.4	451	94.2	837	90.0	131	7.4		
4. Credit to other general government	46	24.0	–14	–5.9	80	35.9	–88	–29.0		
5. Credit to private sector[1]	662	26.7	670	21.3	531	13.9	1,018	23.4		
6. Assets = liabilities	1,056	24.3	522	9.7	1,055	18.0	1,943	27.8		
7. Money	833	27.5	154	4.0	524	13.0	1,134	25.0		
8. Quasi-money	229	18.1	309	20.7	471	26.1	506	22.3		
9. Other items	–21	–25.6	55	90.2	65	56.0	299	165.2		

Source: Table 9.
[1] Includes CSFC and AFC (see footnote to Table 8).

Chapter 4

WORKSHOP 2

Government Finance Statistics

The government influences the national economy through a variety of its transactions: purchases and payments for goods and services, receipts from taxes and sales, transfer payments, and lending and borrowing transactions. To provide data on government activities for the purpose of economic analysis, these transactions are compiled and recorded as government finance statistics. While such statistics necessarily reflect the institutions and practices of the individual countries, a common system of definitions and classifications helps users of these statistics to identify more clearly the impacts of government operations on the national economy and also permits comparisons between countries. Toward this end, the International Monetary Fund has published annually since 1977 the *Government Finance Statistics Yearbook,* presenting standardized data on the operations of member governments.[1] The definitions and standards followed in the

[1] International Monetary Fund, *Government Finance Statistics Yearbook,* Vol. 1 (Washington, 1977); hereinafter referred to as the *GFS Yearbook.* Issued annually.

compilation of the data are based primarily on *A Manual on Government Finance Statistics,*[2] which has been discussed in draft form with government officials and which is to be published in revised form by the International Monetary Fund.

This workshop discusses the types of government activities to be measured and the means of measuring them, presents the analytical framework for the organization of these statistics, and shows the categories into which government transactions may be classified. It then demonstrates some practical applications of these principles with reference to data for Kenya.

PRINCIPLES OF GOVERNMENT FINANCE STATISTICS

No single, ideal method for organizing government financial transactions will, at the same time, serve the different purposes of accountability, financial control, and economic and financial analysis. In this section of the workshop are discussed the principles adopted in the *GFS Yearbook* for the purpose of facilitating economic and financial analysis. Three basic organizing principles have been identified: [3]

> The institutional sector in the economy called government is to be defined not by legal or structural criteria but by the function it performs —primarily the provision of nonmarket services for collective consumption and the transfer of income for purposes of public policy, with funds coming mainly from compulsory levies on other sectors.
>
> To provide data for the economic and financial analysis of government and of its effects upon the economy, one should measure—not estimate or impute—the flow of payments between this sector and the rest of the economy during a given period of time.
>
> Because the ultimate effect of each transaction on the rest of the economy may be indeterminate or unclear, transactions should be classified not by their ultimate purpose or effect but by the immediate nature or characteristic of each transaction as it occurs.

---

[2] International Monetary Fund, *A Manual on Government Finance Statistics: Draft* (Washington, June 1974).

[3] Jonathan Levin, "New Tools for Measuring Government," *Finance and Development,* Vol. 12, No. 2 (June 1975), p. 15.

The meaning and practical implications of each of these three principles are discussed below in some detail.

Definition of Government

Government is defined to cover all units performing government functions—that is, the implementation of public policy through the provision of primarily nonmarket services and the transfer of income, supported mainly by compulsory levies on other sectors.[4]

General government—the broadest definition of government—is made up of (1) central government, covering all units that are agencies or instruments of a country's central authority, whose jurisdiction extends to all parts of its territory; (2) state, provincial, or regional governments, comprising governmental units exercising a competence independently of central government in a part of a country's territory encompassing a number of smaller localities; (3) local governments, consisting of governmental units exercising an independent competence in the various urban and rural jurisdictions of a country's territory; and (4) any supranational authorities exercising functions relating to tax and governmental expenditure within the national territory.

Social security funds are within the government sector, as defined above, and are treated as part of central government or other levels of government at which they operate rather than as a separate subsector of general government.[5] This treatment reflects the basic similarity between social security and other government social programs and the growing integration of social security operations in the broad mix of government countercyclical, social, and economic policies.

Departmental enterprises are treated as part of the level of government to which they are attached. Departmental enterprises are

---

[4] See *Government Finance Statistics Yearbook,* Vol. 2 (1978), p. 2.

[5] In the United Nations' *A System of National Accounts* (New York, 1968), social security funds are treated as a separate subsector of general government.

unincorporated industrial, commercial, or financial units that are closely integrated with the rest of a government department or agency and that are engaged mainly in supplying goods and services to other units of government or selling goods and services to the public on a minor scale. Examples of nonfinancial departmental enterprises are printing and publishing services for government (ancillary units), government restaurants in public buildings, and rental dwellings for government employees.

Public enterprises are considered outside the government sector. Government-owned and/or government-controlled industrial or commercial units that are incorporated, or that sell goods and services to the rest of the economy on a large scale, are classified in the nonfinancial public enterprise sector. Examples are publicly owned railways and airlines, the postal service, and industries that are nationalized or are established by the government itself. Government-owned and/or government-controlled financial institutions that accept demand, time, or savings deposit liabilities, or both incur liabilities and acquire financial assets in the market, are classified in the public financial institutions sector.

Also excluded from government are any monetary functions performed by government, such as the issue of currency or transactions with the International Monetary Fund, and any acceptance of demand, time, or savings deposit liabilities.[6] All such transactions are assigned to the public financial institutions sector, with the net flow to or from the government appearing in the statistics as a flow between the government and the public financial institutions sector.

Measurement of Government Transactions

This section discusses some basic principles for the measurement of government transactions, as adopted in the *GFS Yearbook.*

[6] In the United Nations' *A System of National Accounts,* government performance of monetary authority transactions and acceptance of deposits are included within government so long as they are not carried out by units that both incur liabilities and acquire financial assets in the market.

Cash Principle

The International Monetary Fund's standards for compiling government finance statistics provide for entering government transactions on a cash basis; money receipts and payments should be recorded as of the time they are settled in cash.[7] This reporting basis approximates the flow of funds and resources between the government and the rest of the economy, avoids problems of evaluation, corresponds closely with other financial statistics, and is therefore eminently useful for financial policy and financial programming.

In the *GFS Yearbook,* data for the principal aggregates—revenue, grants, expenditure, lending minus repayments, and financing—are generally on a payment or cash basis, representing government payments to or receipts from the rest of the economy during the chronological time period indicated. Data for the detailed components are based on the most reliable statistics available from the government accounts as close to the payment stage as possible. Where details are on a different basis from the cash totals, adjustment items are provided.

When purchases are made or revenues received in government debt instruments, the various parts of the operation are shown as separate transactions. For example, when a government makes a purchase for which it pays in the form of a fixed-term security or contractual obligation redeemable in cash, this is shown as an expenditure and a simultaneous borrowing transaction at that time, and then it is shown as a debt redemption when it is redeemed in cash.

Gross vs. Net Treatment of Receipts and Payments

As a general principle, nonindustrial receipts and payments should be shown on a gross basis, so that the statistics will reflect the full magnitude and impact of the raising of government revenue and

[7] In contrast, the United Nations' *A System of National Accounts* is on an accrual basis, so that transactions are recorded at the time claims or liabilities arise or when they are due without penalty.

its disposition.[8] Thus, school fees are not counted as an offset to the cost of providing school services and are not subtracted as a "negative expenditure," nor are the costs of collecting taxes deducted from tax receipts as "negative revenue."

An adjustment of significant magnitude may sometimes be required when receipts and payments in the accounts are shown net of appropriations-in-aid, i.e., revenues arising in the course of operations of government departments or agencies and treated as "negative expenditures" in their accounts, with only the remaining amount shown as a cost or need for budgetary appropriation. To reflect fully the magnitude of both government revenues and expenditures, receipts and payments must be augmented by the amount of appropriations-in-aid included as "negative expenditures" in the accounts.

For industrial activities carried out by departmental enterprises, only their operating surpluses or deficits are included in government revenues or expenditures, respectively, since it is the operating surplus or deficit resulting from sales and expenditures of government industries' production that provides income for the government or requires government outlays.[9] Capital transactions of industrial activities, however, are treated on a gross basis as an integral part of the government's operations.

Consolidation

In compiling government finance statistics, it is necessary to eliminate transactions between all units within the government itself and to combine in a common set of categories the sum of their transactions with the rest of the economy. This process is referred to as consolidation.

The International Monetary Fund's standards include guidelines for assembling the transactions of the general government sector,

---

[8] In the United Nations' *A System of National Accounts,* various expenditure categories are shown on a net basis; e.g., purchase of land or intangible assets are net of sales.

[9] The United Nations' *A System of National Accounts* also treats departmental enterprise activity on a net basis, but consolidates the operating deficits with surpluses.

requiring three levels of consolidation: (1) the consolidation within each government, eliminating intragovernmental transactions; (2) the consolidation of all governments at a single level, eliminating only intergovernmental transactions between regional governments or between local governments, for example; and (3) the consolidation of the central, regional, and local governments into the general government sector as a whole, eliminating intergovernmental transactions between levels of government.

Currently, however, the *GFS Yearbook* does not present data for consolidated general government, because of the practical difficulties in obtaining data for all subsectors in sufficient detail and without long delays. Emphasis is placed on compiling the transactions of central governments, which usually become available much earlier, with more frequency, and in far greater detail than those covering other subsectors of general government. Moreover, the central government is by far the most important subsector of general government from the standpoint of fiscal policy.

Detailed data are presented in the *GFS Yearbook* for consolidated central governments, as well as separately for their extrabudgetary components or social security funds. In a number of cases, however, data for central governments do not cover all central government units (as indicated at the end of the *GFS Yearbook*'s country notes). For state and local governments, only summary data are presented.

Classification of Government Transactions

This section outlines the analytical framework for the classification of government transactions into the major categories of the statistical system—revenue, grants, expenditure, lending minus repayments, and financing. Comments are made on the classification within each major category.[10]

---

[10] For titles of lines in the *GFS Yearbook,* see the Appendix. The Summary Table of central government operations contains the principal aggregates. Its component tables, Tables A through G, show the details of revenue, grants, expenditure, lending minus repayments, financing, and debt.

Basic Distinctions

In the *GFS Yearbook,* transactions are generally classified by their characteristics at the time of payment rather than by any subsequent use. Six basic distinctions in the nature of government transactions are set forth, the cross-classification of which yields the analytical framework (see Chart 1). The first two distinctions (receipts vs. payments; repayable vs. nonrepayable) apply to all transactions. The next two distinctions (requited vs. unrequited; current vs. capital) apply only to nonrepayable transactions, and the last two distinctions (financial assets vs. liabilities; currency and deposits vs. debt and equities) apply only to repayable transactions.

The meaning of each distinction is briefly discussed below.[11]

1. *Receipts vs. payments.* The basic difference between transactions lies in whether they are receipts (source of funds into the government) or payments (use of funds).

2. *Repayable vs. nonrepayable.* Repayable transactions generate or extinguish a claim for repayment and are distinguished from nonrepayable transactions involving no claim for repayment.

3. *Requited vs. unrequited.* Requited transactions involve payment for a quid pro quo, such as goods, services, use or ownership of property, or factor services received in return, whereas an unrequited transaction brings no concurrent counterpart in exchange.

4. *Current vs. capital.* The basis for this distinction lies in the fact that use of capital goods meant to be used in the process of production, and having an economic life of more than one year, affects future income and present wealth as the capitalized present value of the future income flow.

5. *Financial assets vs. liabilities.* This distinction is necessary because of the asymmetry between the government's financial assets and liabilities. While government borrowing is directed toward meeting government financial needs, government lending is generally undertaken for policy-oriented purposes and not for the management of liquidity.

---

[11] For a more detailed discussion, see Jonathan Levin, "New Tools for Measuring Government," pp. 16–18.

CHART 1. Analytical Framework for Classification of Government Transactions

	RECEIPTS	PAYMENTS
REVENUE / EXPENDITURE	NONREPAYABLE REQUITED CURRENT Fees and charges Nonindustrial sales Property income Operating surpluses of departmental enterprises CAPITAL Sales of capital UNREQUITED CURRENT TAXES Fines, forfeits Private donations	NONREPAYABLE REQUITED CURRENT Wages and salaries Purchases of goods and services Interest Operating deficits of departmental enterprises CAPITAL Acquisitions of capital UNREQUITED CURRENT
GRANTS	Current grants CAPITAL Capital grants	Current grants CAPITAL Capital grants
NET LENDING	REPAYABLE FINANCIAL ASSETS Repayment of past government lending { Sales of equities; Debt: Foreign, Domestic }	REPAYABLE FINANCIAL ASSETS Purchase of equities; Debt: Foreign, Domestic } Gross lending by government
FINANCING	GOVERNMENT DEPOSITS Net decrease	GOVERNMENT DEPOSITS Net increase
	CURRENCY HOLDINGS	CURRENCY HOLDINGS
	LIABILITIES Borrowing { Debt: Foreign; Domestic: Nonbank, Deposit money banks, Central bank }	LIABILITIES Debt: Foreign; Domestic: Nonbank, Deposit money banks, Central bank } Amortization
CLASSIFIED OUTSIDE GOVERNMENT	DEPOSITS WITH GOVERNMENT CURRENCY ISSUE	DEPOSITS WITH GOVERNMENT CURRENCY ISSUE

Source: Jonathan Levin, "New Tools for Measuring Government," *Finance and Development*, Vol. 12, No. 2 (June 1975), p. 18.

6. *Currency and deposits vs. debt and equities.* Important differences separate currency and deposit transactions from those involving debt and equities. Government holdings of currency and deposits constitute working balances, held for liquidity purposes. Thus, they are more akin to government liabilities, which are also incurred to generate liquidity, than they are to other government financial assets. Among government liabilities, currency and deposits have a special characteristic. Any currency issues of government are considered to represent government performance of the monetary authorities function and are shown as liabilities of the monetary authorities. Similarly, any demand, time, or savings deposit liabilities accepted by the government are classified as liabilities of the financial institutions sector.

The relevance of the above distinctions becomes apparent in their delineation of the major groups of transactions.

Revenue

Revenue includes all nonrepayable receipts, requited and unrequited, other than grants from other governments and international institutions. The detailed classification of revenue and grants is presented in the Appendix (Table A). Revenues are divided between current and capital revenue, the latter including only receipts from the sale of capital assets. Current revenue, therefore, embraces all tax revenue and current nontax revenue.

Taxes are defined as compulsory, unrequited, nonrepayable contributions, enacted by government for public purposes. Tax revenue is shown net of refunds paid out during the period and net of corrective transactions; however, it is not reduced by any governmental expenditure for collection and administration. Taxes also include compulsory social security contributions, as well as the profits transferred to government from fiscal monopolies, which reflect the use of the government's taxing power to collect excise-like revenue through the monopoly sale of selected products. Tax revenue is classified into seven major categories according to the base on which the tax is levied or the kind of action that creates the liability.

Nontax revenue includes requited receipts from property income, fees and charges, nonindustrial sales, and the operating surpluses of departmental enterprises. Also included are some unrequited receipts such as fines, forfeits, and private donations.

Capital revenue covers the value of government sales of fixed capital assets, strategic stocks, and land and intangible assets.

Grants

Grants are defined as unrequited, nonrepayable, noncompulsory receipts from other governments—domestic or foreign—and international institutions. Current grants are those made for purposes of current expenditure or for general or indeterminate purposes, including both current and capital expenditure. When either donor or recipient considers the transfer to be of a capital nature, it should be treated as a capital grant.

In arriving at an overall deficit or surplus, the *GFS Yearbook* groups grants with revenue as transactions that reduce the deficit rather than finance it. This choice follows the approach in the United Nations' *A System of National Accounts (SNA).*

Expenditure

Expenditure includes all nonrepayable payments by government, whether requited or unrequited and whether for current or capital purposes. Unlike the treatment in receipts, payments of grants or transfers to other governments form a category within expenditure rather than a separate group outside it.

Several of the distinctions within expenditure are of special significance to overall measures of government and economic activity. Thus, only requited payments contribute to the measurement of consumption, capital formation, and product in the *SNA.* The distinction between current and capital payments is essential for the measurement of government savings.

The classification of expenditure follows two main lines: the economic effect of the expenditure upon the community; and the purpose or function for which the expenditure is made. The economic classification is of particular interest for macroeconomic analysis.

In the classification of expenditure and lending minus repayments by economic type in the Appendix (Table C), prime distinctions are drawn between current and capital expenditure and between requited and unrequited payments. Current expenditure encompasses expenditure on goods and services, interest payments, and subsidies and other current transfers. Expenditures on durable goods and equipment for military purposes are classified as current expenditure, except for factories and dwellings used as households of servicemen.

Capital expenditure comprises acquisition of fixed capital assets with both a normal life of more than one year and more than a significant minimum value, purchases of strategic stocks, purchases of land and intangible assets, and capital transfers. Purchase of capital assets for use outside government, e.g., by nonfinancial public enterprises, is classified as a purchase of equities and is included as part of lending minus repayments.

In the classification of expenditure by function shown in the Appendix (Table B), expenditures are classified into nine major categories, with a number of subcategories within each. This classification focuses on the purpose for which the expenditures were made, irrespective of the government agency through which they were made.

Lending Minus Repayments

Lending minus repayments comprises government transactions in claims upon others undertaken for purposes of public policy rather than for management of government liquidity or for earning a return. It covers both debts and equities. Changes in government holdings of currency and deposits, however, are classified under financing rather than under lending minus repayments. Government lending undertaken for liquidity purposes, whether by sinking funds, social security schemes, or any other units of government, is classified under financing rather than under lending minus repayments.

In arriving at the overall deficit or surplus, the *GFS Yearbook* groups lending minus repayments with expenditure rather than with financing, differing in this respect from the *SNA,* which groups under financing all transactions affecting claims. This treatment reflects the asymmetry between government lending and borrowing. Lending, as defined above, is undertaken not to influence liquidity or to acquire a profitable financial asset, but to pursue objectives of public policy.

Lending minus repayments, which itself forms an economic category in the classification of expenditure and lending minus repayments by economic type, can also be classified by the function or purpose for which it is made. This is shown in Table B.1 of the Appendix, with categories corresponding to those for expenditure in Table B of the Appendix.

Financing

Financing, by definition, is equal to the overall deficit or surplus. In the *GFS Yearbook* (see Summary Table in the Appendix), the overall deficit or surplus is equivalent to the balance of revenue, grants, expenditure, lending, and repayments:

$$\text{overall deficit/surplus} = (\text{revenue} + \text{grants}) - (\text{expenditure} + \text{lending minus repayments}).$$

These are the items above the line; the remaining items, described as financing, would be below the line. Financing, therefore, covers all transactions involving government's holdings of currency and deposits, government liabilities, and any financial assets held by the government for the purpose of liquidity rather than public policy. Government currency issues, as well as demand, time, and savings deposit liabilities accepted by the government, are considered to be financial institutions functions, so that any net flow of funds from these sources is classified as coming from the financial institutions sector.

Financing is divided into domestic financing, obtained from residents, and financing abroad, obtained from nonresidents. It is further classified by type of debt holder (see Table D in the Appendix) and by type of debt instrument (see Table E in the Appendix). For the purpose of economic and financial analysis, the classification by debt holder is probably the more useful one, since it groups together debt holders with homogeneous patterns of economic behavior. To the extent that debt instruments are held by groups with homogeneous patterns of economic behavior, this classification can be similarly useful.

Debt

Debt represents the outstanding stock of recognized, direct liabilities of the government to the rest of the economy and the world, generated in the past and scheduled to be extinguished by government operations in the future or to continue as perpetual debt. Excluded are intragovernmental or intergovernmental debt of the sector or subsector of government being measured, currency issues and other debt of the monetary authorities, dormant or repudiated debt not being serviced, and any floating debt of unpaid obligations.

Debt is classified by type of debt holder (see Table F in the Appendix) and by type of debt instrument involved (see Table G in the Appendix). Categories correspond to those for financing.

ISSUES FOR DISCUSSION

1. *How is the overall deficit/surplus defined in the* GFS Yearbook? *Explain the rationale behind this definition. How does the definition for the overall deficit/surplus in your own country's budget differ from this? What is the rationale behind the definition utilized in your country?*

2. *How does the* GFS Yearbook *treat such funds as social security funds, sinking funds, road maintenance funds, etc.? What are the major funds excluded from your own country's budgetary accounts? What is the* GFS Yearbook's *rationale for including these funds and the rationale in your own country for excluding them?*

3. *How are transactions with the International Monetary Fund treated in the* GFS Yearbook?

4. *How does the* GFS Yearbook *treat the distinction between capital and current expenditure? What is the rationale behind this treatment?*

5. *How does the* GFS Yearbook *treat various kinds of transactions by government involving financial claims on others? Is this treatment consistent with that discussed in the workshops on the monetary and financial survey (Workshop 1) and on the balance of payments (Workshop 3)?*

GOVERNMENT FINANCE STATISTICS FOR KENYA

This section of the workshop demonstrates some practical applications of the principles discussed above, with reference to Kenya.

Coverage

The general government sector in Kenya consists of the Central Government and various local governments (see Table 1).[12]

The central government units covered by the General Budget comprise the Presidency, the Legislature, the Judiciary, and 18 ministries and departments. There are a number of funds operated by the ministries (see Table 2), the net outcome of their transactions being reflected either as a change in balance with the ministry concerned or in cash held with the Paymaster General. Most of these funds receive their income from commercial transactions (for example, the Sugar Equalization Fund). However, in a few cases, the revenue of these funds is derived from taxes or fees of a governmental nature (for example, the Hides and Skins Cess Fund), and these transactions should be included in government data on a gross basis. In the data for the Central Government published in the *GFS Yearbook,* the transactions of all these funds are in fact excluded, except insofar as they receive funds from or hold balances with the ministries and

[12] Up to early 1977, the East African Community also raised taxes and made expenditures within each of the three member countries; these operations and their financing were regarded as part of the general government sector.

TABLE 1. Kenya: Units of General Government

Ref. No.	*Units*	*Accounts Utilized* (*Table 2 Ref.*)	*Data Sources* (*Table 3 Ref.*)
	Central Government Units Covered by General Budget		
1.	Presidency, Legislature, Judiciary, 18 Ministries and Departments	1-11	1,2,4,5
	Central Government Units with Own Budget		
2.	Betting Control and Licensing Board		3
3.	Canning Crops Board		3
4.	Egerton College		3
5.	Horticultural Crops Development Authority		3
6.	Kenya Bureau of Standards		3
7.	Kenya Dairy Board		3
8.	Kenya National Parks Authorities		3
9.	Kenya National Theatre		3
10.	Kenya Sisal Board		3
11.	Kenya Wheat Board		3
12.	Museum Trustees of Kenya		3
13.	Nairobi University		3
14.	National Hospital Insurance Fund		3
15.	Pig Industry Board		3
16.	Pineapple Development Authority		3
17.	Pyrethrum Board		3
18.	Tea Board of Kenya		3
19.	Transport Licensing Board		3
20.	Miscellaneous minor boards and commissions		3
	Local Government		
21.	38 county councils	11,12	6
22.	11 municipal councils	11,12	6

Fiscal Year: Ends June 30, except September 30 for units 9 and 17, and December 31 for units 3, 4, 10, 18, 21 and 22.

Liquidation or Complementary Period: None.

Basis for Recording Receipts: Cash and checks deposited.

Basis for Recording Payments: Cash paid and checks issued.

Frequency of Data: Annual.

Lag in Availability of Data: 3 months, units 9, 11, 14; 4 months, unit 1; up to 12 months, all other units.

Source: International Monetary Fund, *Government Finance Statistics Yearbook,* Vol. 2 (Washington, 1978), p. 147.

TABLE 2. Kenya: Government Accounts and Funds

Ref. No.		*Units Using Account (Table 1 Ref.)*
	Controlled by Treasury	
1.	*Appropriation Accounts.* Receipts: revenue, loan repayments, and transfers from Consolidated Fund; Payments: expenditure and lending, authorized by accounting officers of Ministries.	1
2.	*Consolidated Fund (Exchequer Account).* Receipts: revenue, intragovernmental transfers and borrowing; Payments: transfers to Paymaster General's Account and other intragovernmental transfers, authorized by Treasury.	1
3.	*Consolidated Fund Services.* Receipts: transfers from Consolidated Fund; Payments: expenditure, intragovernmental transfers and amortization, authorized by Treasury.	1
4.	*Paymaster General's Account.* Receipts: revenue, loan repayments, and transfers from Consolidated Fund; Payments: expenditure, lending, and amortization, authorized by accounting officers of Ministries.	1
5.	*Provident and Pension Funds.* Receipts: revenue; Payments: expenditure, authorized by Treasury.	1
6.	*Sinking Funds.* Receipts: investment income and transfers from Consolidated Fund; Payments: transfers to Consolidated Fund, authorized by Treasury.	1
	Controlled by Other Units of Central Government	
7.	*Education and Scholarship Fund.* Receipts: investment income; Payments: expenditure and investment, authorized by Ministry of Education accounting officers.	1
8.	*Hides and Skins Cess Fund.* Receipts: revenue; Payments: intragovernmental transfers, authorized by Ministry of Agriculture accounting officers.	1
9.	*Renewal and Maintenance Funds.* Receipts: revenue and intragovernmental transfers; Payments: expenditure and intragovernmental transfers, authorized by Agriculture and Works Ministries accounting officers.	1
10.	*Sugar Equalization Fund.* Receipts: revenues; Payments: expenditure, authorized by Ministry of Commerce and Industry accounting officers.	1
11.	*Various cash and float funds.* Receipts: transfers from Consolidated Fund; Payments: intragovernmental transfers, authorized by accounting officers of Ministries.	1,21,22

TABLE 2. Kenya: Government Accounts and Funds (concluded)

Ref. No.		*Units Using Account (Table 1 Ref.)*
	Controlled by Local Government	
12.	*Accounts of County Councils and Municipal Councils.* Receipts: revenue, loan repayments, grants, intergovernmental transfers, and borrowing; Payments: expenditure, lending, and amortization, authorized by designated officials.	21,22

Source: International Monetary Fund, *Government Finance Statistics Yearbook,* Vol. 2 (Washington, 1978), pp. 147–48.

TABLE 3. Kenya: Sources of Data

Ref. No.	
	Treasury
1.	Appropriation Accounts and Other Public Accounts (annual)
2.	Estimates of Revenue and Expenditure for Kenya (annual)
	Other Units of Central Government
3.	Annual Reports of various statutory boards and funds
4.	Economic Survey, Central Bureau of Statistics (annual)
5.	Statistical Abstract, Central Bureau of Statistics (annual)
	Local Government
6.	Accounts and Annual Reports of County and Municipal Councils

Source: International Monetary Fund, *Government Finance Statistics Yearbook,* Vol. 2, (Washington, 1978), p. 148.

departments concerned. However, the amounts involved are generally small, except where transactions are of a commercial nature and are to be netted in any case.

Also, a relatively large number of central government units have their own budgets (see Table 1), which should be consolidated with the General Budget, but at present the data for these units do not permit such a consolidation. Included here is the National Hospital Insurance Fund, which provides cash benefits for hospital treatment to employees with earnings above a certain minimum level and to their dependents. Since its revenues are also derived from nonrepayable contributions made by both employers and employees, it is to be regarded as a social security fund.

An important question on the coverage of the Central Government relates to the appropriate sectoral assignment of the National Social Security Fund (NSSF). In spite of its name, the NSSF is in fact a provident fund, fed by compulsory contributions from both employers and employees and paying lump-sum benefits in respect of age, survivors, sickness, or emigration up to the amount of the accumulated contributions made in the name of the employee, plus interest. The NSSF should not be treated as part of the social security sector, since the participants have a vested right to their accumulated individual contributions and these contributions therefore cannot be regarded as government revenue. In view of its function, the NSSF is to be regarded as a financial institution and properly belongs in the public financial institutions sector (see Table 5). Since benefit payments are low in the initial phases of operation of the pension scheme, and since the scheme has been expanded gradually to cover an increasing number of employees, the NSSF has realized large and growing annual surpluses. Most of the accumulated surpluses have been invested in government securities.

Local government includes 11 municipal councils and 38 county councils. In addition, there are 11 town councils which account for less than 5 per cent of the total amount spent by all local authorities. The municipalities, especially the two largest councils (Nairobi and Mombasa), provide the broadest range of services and exercise the greatest degree of local autonomy in decision making. Their functions include primary education, health services, water supply, and road construction and maintenance. The municipalities account for about three fourths of the total amount spent by all local authorities. Prior to its abolition in 1974, the graduated personal tax contributed about one third of the total revenues of municipal councils, but has now been largely replaced by central government grants. The functions of the county councils were drastically reduced when their responsibilities for primary education, public health, and roads were assumed by the Central Government in 1969. The Central Government then also took over the county council's graduated personal tax and abolished the general grants.

There are more than 60 nonfinancial public enterprises owned or controlled by the Government of Kenya (see Table 4). In general, these are self-sufficient in their current operations, but they receive substantial loans and grants from the Central Government for development.

TABLE 4. Kenya: Nonfinancial Public Enterprises

African Diatomite Industries
Bomas of Kenya Ltd. (tourism)
Chianga Tea Factory Co. Ltd.
Cotton Lint and Seed Marketing Board
East African Oil Refineries Ltd.
East African Power and Lighting Co. Ltd.
Fluorspar Co. Ltd.
Ikumba Tea Factory Co. Ltd.
Imenti Tea Factory Co. Ltd.
Kangaita Tea Factory Co. Ltd.
Kebirigo Tea Factory Co. Ltd.
Kenya Coffee and Marketing Board
Kenya Engineering Industries Ltd.
Kenya Film Corp.
Kenya Industrial Estates
Kenya Mazuren Tea Co. Ltd.
Kenya Meat Commission
Kenya Mining Industries Ltd.
Kenya National Properties
Kenya National Trading Corp.
Kenya National Travel Bureau
Kenya Pipeline Co.
Kenya Poultry Development Co. Ltd.
Kenya Power Co. Ltd.
Kenya Shipping Agency Ltd.
Kenya Tea Development Authority
Kenya Tourist Development Corp.
Kenya Tourist Development Corp. Management Co. (hotel)
Kenya Wine Agencies Ltd.
Kibos Ginnery Ltd.
Kitani Safari Lodge
Lands Ltd.
Liteira Tea Factory Co. Ltd.
Livestock Marketing Division
Maize and Produce Board
Mariakani Milk Scheme
Marsabit Lodge
MEA Garment Ltd.
Meru Mulika Lodge
Ministry of Power and Communications (airport)
Ministry of Water Development (water supply)
Mombasa Pipeline Board
Mumias Sugar Co.
Mutaara Tea Factory Co. Ltd.
Mwea Cotton Ginnery Ltd.
Nakuru Lending Library
Nambale Ginnery Ltd.
National Construction Corp.
National Irrigation Board
Njiru Country Club
Nyamkoba Tea Factory Co. Ltd.
Ol-Kalou Salient (agriculture)
Panafric Hotel
Pyrethrum Marketing Board
Regati Tea Factory Co. Ltd.
Sera Coatings Ltd. (plastics)
Settlement Fund Trustees
Somerset Africa Ltd. (clothing manufacture)
Tana River Development Co. Ltd.
Tegat Tea Factory Ltd.
Wananchi Saw Mills
Zimmerman Ltd. (taxidermy)

Source: International Monetary Fund, *Government Finance Statistics Yearbook*, Vol. 2, (Washington, 1978), p. 148.

TABLE 5. Kenya: Public Financial Institutions

Central Bank of Kenya	Industrial and Commercial Development Corp.
Agricultural Development Corp.	Industrial Development Bank
Agricultural Finance Corp.	Kenya Commercial Bank
Agricultural Settlement Fund	Kenya National Assurance Co.
Cereals and Sugar Finance Corp.	Kenya Post Office Savings Bank
Cooperative Bank of Kenya	National Bank of Kenya
Development Finance Co. of Kenya	National Housing Corp.
First Permanent (East Africa) Ltd.	National Social Security Fund
Housing Finance Co.	State Reinsurance Co.

Source: International Monetary Fund, *Government Finance Statistics Yearbook,* Vol. 2, (Washington, 1978), p. 148.

Central Government Budgetary Procedures

The fiscal year for the central government units covered by the General Budget runs from July 1 to June 30.[13] The annual appropriation accounts of the Central Government are in two parts—the recurrent and the development budgets. The development budget consists of the estimated annual expenditures and lending of the Government under the Development Plan; these outlays are financed mainly by external loans and grants, and domestic long-term borrowing. Supplementary appropriations may be made with the approval of Parliament during the course of the year.

Government accounts, including the Recurrent Exchequer, the Development Exchequer, and the Paymaster General's Account (see Table 2), are held with the Central Bank of Kenya. The overseas accounts of the Government consist principally of working balances held with the Crown Agents in London. Receipts of the Government, including internal and external loans, are paid into the Exchequer Accounts, and transfers from the Exchequer Accounts require the specific authority of Parliament. Treasury control over authorized expenditures is maintained through control over transfer of funds from the Exchequer Accounts to the Paymaster General's Account,

[13] For other central government units, the fiscal year is indicated in Table 1. For local governments, the fiscal year coincides with the calendar year.

which constitute the "supply issues." Actual payments are then made by ministries from the Paymaster General's Account.

Data from the Exchequer Accounts, however, cannot be used to provide a complete picture of government budgetary operations, since they exclude revenue raised and spent by the government departments (known as appropriations-in-aid). In the fiscal year ended June 30, 1977, the appropriations-in-aid amounted to about 8 per cent of total government revenue. In addition, transactions reported in the Exchequer Accounts are recorded at the time the funds are received from or credited to the Paymaster General's Account and not when they enter or leave the government sector through that account. In practice, because of the pressure to enter into commitments before the end of the fiscal year, when the "supply issues" lapse, substantial differences sometimes arise between expenditures recorded and cash payments made. Furthermore, it is not possible to make an economic or functional analysis of government expenditure according to the *GFS Yearbook* system from the data as recorded in the Exchequer Accounts, and only a limited analysis of revenue can be made.

In order to obtain government data according to *GFS Yearbook* formats, it is necessary, therefore, to turn to the Appropriation Accounts. In the data derived from the Appropriation Accounts and published in the *GFS Yearbook,* revenues are recorded at the time the funds are received by the Receivers of Revenue and payments are recorded at the time checks drawn on the Paymaster General's Account are issued.

Statistical Tables

Table 6 presents government finance statistics tables for Kenya. These comprise the Summary Table: Budgetary Central Government and Tables A through G, showing the details of budgetary central government revenue, grants, expenditure, lending minus repayments, financing, and debt. The time series presented in these tables cover the five fiscal years 1973–77. For local governments, only summary data are presented.

TABLE 6. Kenya: Government Finance Statistics Tables, Fiscal Years 1973–77
(In millions of Kenya shillings)

		1973	1974	1975	1976	1977
				(Year ending June 30)		
Summary Table: Budgetary Central Government						
1	Total revenue and grants (A.I)	2,827.6	3,696.2	4,521.4	5,324.5	6,383.3
2	Total revenue (A.II)	2,817.3	3,625.2	4,347.0	5,123.3	6,149.1
3	Current revenue (A.III)	2,816.0	3,625.2	4,346.8	5,122.9	6,148.6
3.1	Tax (A.IV)	2,318.4	3,187.1	3,943.4	4,571.1	5,296.8
3.2	Nontax (A.V)	497.6	438.1	403.4	551.8	851.8
4	Capital revenue (A.VI)	1.3	—	0.2	0.4	0.5
5	Grants (A.VII)	10.3	71.0	174.4	201.2	234.1
5.1	Current (A.17.1 + A.18.1 + A.19.1)	4.5	6.5	9.8	61.1	23.7
5.2	Capital (A.17.2 + A.18.2 + A.19.2)	5.8	64.5	164.6	140.2	210.4
6	Total expenditure and lending minus repayments (C.I)	3,729.8	4,282.8	5,673.1	7,033.7	7,710.3
7	Total expenditure (C.II)	3,428.2	3,936.5	5,179.3	6,163.6	7,240.0
8	Current expenditure (C.III)	2,618.0	3,078.9	4,079.2	4,904.4	5,579.9
9	Capital expenditure (C.IV)	810.2	857.6	1,100.1	1,259.2	1,660.1
10	Lending minus repayments (C.V)	301.6	346.3	493.8	870.1	470.3
11	Current account surplus (without grants) (3 – 8)	198.0	546.3	267.6	218.5	568.7
12	Gross fixed capital formation (C.4 – A.14)	783.7	823.4	950.4	1,059.0	1,387.5
13	Gross capital formation (C.4 + C.5 – A.14 – A.15)	783.7	823.4	950.3	1,059.0	1,387.5
14	Overall deficit/surplus (1 – 6)	–902.2	–586.6	–1,151.7	–1,709.2	–1,327.0
15	Financing (D.I or E.I) (= 14)	902.2	586.6	1,151.5	1,709.2	1,327.0
16	Abroad (D.III or E.III)	428.8	208.8	311.8	638.6	463.6
17	Domestic (D.II or E.II)	473.4	377.8	839.7	1,070.6	863.4
17.1	Nonbank (D.1 + D.4 + D.5)	...	...	...	...	...
17.2	Deposit money banks (D.3)	...	...	...	...	...
17.3	Monetary authorities (D.2)	...	...	...	...	...
	Memorandum Items:					
18	Government debt at end of period (F.I or G.I)	4,728.7	5,309.2	6,232.0	8,014.8	8,848.0
21	Amortization abroad	63.6	71.1	89.5	99.4	131.8
Table A. Revenue and Grants: Budgetary Central Government						
I	Total revenue and grants (II + VII)	2,827.6	3,696.2	4,521.4	5,324.5	6,383.3
II	Total revenue (III + VI)	2,817.3	3,625.2	4,347.0	5,123.3	6,149.1

TABLE 6. Kenya: Government Finance Statistics Tables, Fiscal Years 1973–77
(continued)
(In millions of Kenya shillings)

		1973	1974	1975	1976	1977
			(Year ending June 30)			
Table A. Revenue and Grants: Budgetary Central Government *(continued)*						
III	Current revenue (IV + V)	2,816.0	3,625.2	4,346.8	5,122.9	6,148.6
IV	Tax revenue	2,318.4	3,187.1	3,943.4	4,571.1	5,296.8
1	Tax on income, profits, and capital gains	1,069.0	1,154.6	1,531.3	1,796.7	2,149.3
1.1	Individual	65.0	29.8	...	...	...
	Graduated personal tax	65.0	29.8	...	...	...
1.2	Corporate	1,004.0	1,124.8	...	...	...
2	Social security contributions	—	—	—	—	—
3	Taxes: Payroll or manpower	—	—	—	—	—
4	Taxes on property	8.7	10.1	11.7	8.1	11.3
4.3	Estate, inheritance, and gift taxes	8.7	10.1	11.7	8.1	11.3
	Estate duty	8.7	10.1	11.7	8.1	11.3
5	Domestic taxes on goods and services	660.5	1,182.7	1,516.9	1,734.2	2,028.9
5.1	General sales, turnover, or value-added tax	54.1	639.8	937.3	1,185.5	1,308.4
	Sales tax	54.1	639.8	937.3	1,185.5	1,308.4
5.2	Excises	501.5	429.0	461.6	420.9	574.1
	Petrol tax	47.1	—	—	—	—
	Traditional liquor tax	1.8	1.0	—	—	—
	Beer tax	53.8	—	—	—	—
	Cigarette tax	13.5	—	—	—	—
	Other consumption taxes	40.5	2.9	—	—	—
	Excise duties	336.8	416.9	453.5	412.6	564.4
	Second-hand vehicle purchase tax	8.0	8.2	8.1	8.3	9.7
5.4	Taxes on specific services	30.6	35.0	40.5	41.9	48.0
	Airport pasenger tax	8.4	7.4	8.0	8.5	8.4
	Hotel accommodation tax	15.2	17.5	19.4	23.5	28.4
	Betting tax	3.1	3.8	4.0	3.8	3.7
	Entertainment tax	2.4	3.6	4.2	4.2	5.0
	Casino tax	1.5	2.7	1.6	1.6	2.4
	Other	—	—	3.3	0.3	0.1
5.5	Taxes on use of, or permission to use, goods	74.3	78.9	77.5	85.9	98.4
5.5.1	Business and professional licenses	13.7	17.9	16.4	18.2	20.6

TABLE 6. Kenya: Government Finance Statistics Tables, Fiscal Years 1973–77
(continued)
(In millions of Kenya shillings)

		1973	1974	1975	1976	1977
			(Year ending June 30)			
Table A. Revenue and Grants: Budgetary Central Government *(concluded)*						
5.5.2	Motor vehicle taxes	52.0	53.2	55.3	57.2	66.5
	Licenses under Traffic Act	50.4	51.9	. . .	. . .	. . .
	Licenses under Transport License Act	0.8	0.5	. . .	. . .	. . .
	Fees under Traffic Act	0.8	0.8	. . .	. . .	. . .
5.5.3	Other	8.6	7.8	5.8	10.5	11.3
6	Taxes: International trade, transactions	553.5	795.4	842.2	983.6	1,057.2
6.1	Import duties	539.9	795.4	842.2	983.6	1,057.2
6.2	Export duties	13.6	—	—	—	—
7	Other taxes	26.7	44.3	41.3	48.5	50.1
7.2	Stamp taxes	26.7	44.3	41.3	48.5	50.1
V	Nontax revenue	497.6	438.1	403.4	551.8	851.8
9	Property income	219.1	156.8	144.1	238.0	305.6
9.1	Nonfinancial public enterprises and public financial institutions	60.4	49.8	24.0	122.2	93.5
	Central bank surplus	60.4	49.8	24.0	122.2	93.5
9.2	Other	158.7	107.0	120.1	115.8	212.1
10	Administrative fees and charges and nonindustrial sales	207.5	201.4	160.7	194.8	382.8
11	Fines and forfeits	15.8	18.6	20.0	27.1	48.6
13	Other	55.2	61.3	78.6	91.9	114.9
	Renewals Fund revenue	—	1.6	35.9	45.8	61.2
	Transfers from households	0.3	0.2	9.5	10.6	11.9
	Other	54.9	59.5	32.8	35.5	41.8
VI	Capital revenue	1.3	—	0.2	0.4	0.5
	Sales of fixed capital assets	—	—	0.2	0.4	0.5
16	Sales of land and intangible assets	1.3	—	—	—	0.6
VII	Grants	10.3	71.0	174.4	201.2	234.1
17	From abroad other than supranational authorities	10.3	71.0	173.6	184.9	231.3
17.1	Current	4.5	6.5	9.0	44.8	23.0
17.2	Capital	5.8	64.5	164.6	140.1	208.3
18	From other levels of Government	—	—	0.8	16.3	2.8
18.1	Current	—	—	0.8	16.3	0.7
18.2	Capital	—	—	—	—	2.1

TABLE 6. Kenya: Government Finance Statistics Tables, Fiscal Years 1973–77
(continued)
(In millions of Kenya shillings)

		1973	1974	1975	1976	1977
			(Year ending June 30)			
Table B. Expenditure by Function: Budgetary Central Government						
I	Total expenditure (same as C.II)	3,428.2	3,936.5	5,179.3	6,163.6	7,240.0
1	General public services	615.4	682.4	903.3	1,111.2	1,241.5
2	Defense	238.8	285.2	382.1	412.3	858.3
3	Education	807.6	922.4	1,242.8	1,408.3	1,577.8
4	Health	255.5	288.6	414.6	485.9	591.2
5	Social Security and welfare	78.2	98.4	12.6	13.1	13.9
5.1-6	Social Security and assistance	78.2	98.4	12.6	13.1	13.9
6	Housing and community amenities	45.1	56.6	57.6	40.1	43.5
6.1	Housing	38.3	43.5	34.6	18.3	14.2
6.2	Community development	6.8	13.1	23.0	21.8	29.3
7	Other community and social services	91.2	109.2	107.0	142.1	161.8
8	Economic services	1,047.7	1,166.6	1,561.4	1,944.0	2,082.9
8.1	General administration, regulation, and research	9.4	8.7	94.9	109.5	92.3
8.2	Agriculture, forestry, fishing	211.1	325.0	392.9	640.9	723.2
8.3	Mining, manufacturing, and construction	95.4	99.3	111.1	118.4	121.1
8.4	Electricity, gas, steam, and water	76.6	79.6	112.8	215.5	254.6
8.5	Roads	508.5	532.8	525.2	525.7	586.9
8.6	Inland and coastal waterways	—	—	33.4	7.1	8.6
8.7	Other transportation and communication	27.6	36.1	172.2	232.2	201.4
8.8	Other economic services	119.1	85.1	118.9	94.7	94.8
9	Other purposes	248.7	327.1	497.9	606.6	669.1
Table B.1. Lending by Function: Budgetary Central Government						
I	Total lending minus repayments (C.V)	301.6	346.3	493.8	870.1	470.3
	Total gross lending	341.0	384.8	532.1	913.8	540.1
1	General public services	—	—	1.0	—	—
3	Education	—	—	33.3	36.5	38.7
3.3	Universities and colleges	—	—	33.3	36.5	38.7
6	Housing and community amenities	69.8	74.5	65.7	81.7	64.9
6.1	Housing	69.8	74.5	65.7	73.8	57.9
6.2	Community development	—	—	—	7.9	7.0
7	Other community and social services	—	—	—	—	0.7

TABLE 6. Kenya: Government Finance Statistics Tables, Fiscal Years 1973–77
(continued)
(In millions of Kenya shillings)

		1973	1974	1975	1976	1977
			(Year ending June 30)			
Table B.1. Lending by Function: Budgetary Central Government *(concluded)*						
8	Economic services	236.6	290.4	396.4	733.5	356.0
8.2	Agriculture, forestry, fishing	135.0	129.7	277.6	188.8	122.5
8.3	Mining, manufacturing, and construction	1.0	1.1	1.2	2.2	0.2
8.4	Electricity, gas, steam, and water	—	—	23.2	63.9	11.7
8.7	Other transportation and communication	0.1	22.7	0.8	—	91.3
8.7.1	Other transportation	0.1	22.7	...	...	...
8.8	Other economic services	100.5	136.9	93.6	478.6	130.3
9	Other purposes	34.6	19.9	35.6	62.2	79.8
	Repayments	–39.4	–38.5	–38.3	–43.7	–69.8
Table C. Expenditure and Lending Minus Repayments by Economic Type: Budgetary Central Government						
I	Total expenditure and lending minus repayments (II + V)	3,729.8	4,282.8	5,673.1	7,033.7	7,710.3
II	Total expenditure (III + IV)	3,428.2	3,936.5	5,179.3	6,163.6	7,240.0
III	Current expenditure	2,618.0	3,078.9	4,079.2	4,904.4	5,579.9
1	Expenditure on goods and services	2,038.3	2,358.9	...	...	...
1.1	Wages and salaries	1,414.6	1,604.5	...	...	...
1.2-3	Employers' contributions	—	—	13.4	17.5	22.0
1.4	Other purchases of goods and services	623.7	754.4	945.6	917.5	1,564.0
2	Interest payments	212.7	239.5	290.6	390.7	479.1
3	Subsidies and other current transfers	367.0	480.5	...	...	...
3.3	Transfers to other levels of National Government	96.1	...	...	...	...
3.6	Transfers abroad	10.6	18.2	24.5	19.6	26.3
IV	Capital expenditure	810.2	857.6	1,100.1	1,259.2	1,660.1
4	Acquisition of fixed capital assets	783.7	823.4	950.6	1,059.4	1,388.0
6	Purchases of land and intangible assets	26.5	34.2	138.2	173.8	271.9
7	Capital transfers	—	—	11.3	26.0	0.2
7.1	Domestic	—	—	11.3	26.0	0.2
7.1.1	To other levels of National Government	—	—	11.3	26.0	0.2

TABLE 6. Kenya: Government Finance Statistics Tables, Fiscal Years 1973–77 (continued)
(In millions of Kenya shillings)

		1973	1974	1975	1976	1977
			(Year ending June 30)			
Table C. Expenditure and Lending Minus Repayments by Economic Type: Budgetary Central Government *(concluded)*						
V	Total lending minus repayments	301.6	346.3	493.8	870.1	470.3
8	Domestic	301.6	346.3	493.8	870.1	470.3
8.1	To other levels of Government	. . .	. . .	144.9	433.9	160.8
Table D. Financing by Type of Debt Holder: Budgetary Central Government						
I	Total financing (II +III)	902.2	586.6	1,151.5	1,709.2	1,327.0
II	Domestic financing	473.4	377.8	839.7	1,070.6	863.4
III	Financing abroad	428.8	208.8	311.8	638.6	463.6
	From international development institutions	165.3	96.0	207.3	373.7	224.5
	From foreign governments	85.0	59.4	108.2	269.2	258.1
	Other foreign borrowing	242.1	124.5	85.8	95.1	112.8
	Redemption	–63.6	–71.1	–89.5	–99.4	–131.8
Table E. Financing by Type of Debt Instrument: Budgetary Central Government						
I	Total financing (same as D.I)	902.2	586.6	1,151.5	1,709.2	1,327.0
II	Domestic financing (same as D.II)	473.4	377.8	839.7	1,070.6	863.4
1	Long-term bonds	367.0	323.9	218.4	925.4	385.5
2	Short-term bonds and bills	136.1	–57.8	74.3	481.6	552.0
3	Long-term loans n.e.c.	—	—	–1.7	–0.5	–0.5
4	Short-term loans and advances n.e.c.	—	—	180.1	303.1	42.2
6	Changes in cash, deposits, etc.	–29.7	111.7	368.6	–639.0	–115.8
III	Financing abroad (same as D.III)	428.8	208.8	311.8	638.6	463.6
7	Long-term bonds	. . .	. . .	–3.7	–4.3	–19.0
9	Long-term loans n.e.c.	. . .	. . .	315.5	643.0	482.6
Table F. Outstanding Debt by Type of Debt Holder: Budgetary Central Government *(at end of period)*						
I	Total debt (II+III)	4,728.7	5,309.2	6,232.0	8,014.8	8,848.0
II	Domestic debt	2,193.6	2,578.0	2,878.0	3,814.3	4,266.7
1	Other levels of Government	1,242.2	1,465.2	1,793.5	2,166.0	2,517.3
2	Monetary authorities	284.7	366.2	343.1	927.0	954.6

TABLE 6. Kenya: Government Finance Statistics Tables, Fiscal Years 1973–77
(concluded)
(In millions of Kenya shillings)

		1973	1974	1975	1976	1977
				(Year ending June 30)		
Table F. Outstanding Debt by Type of Debt Holder: Budgetary Central Government *(concluded)*						
3	Deposit money banks	218.9	204.8	194.6	177.8	173.9
4	Other domestic	447.8	541.8	546.8	543.5	620.9
4.3	Nonfinancial private sector	234.0	275.5	404.0	400.4	430.5
III	Foreign debt	2,535.1	2,731.2	3,354.0	4,200.5	4,581.3
6	International development institutions	573.6	662.5	920.1	1,577.5	1,720.8
7	Foreign governments	1,537.4	1,644.6	1,813.4	1,997.7	2,312.4
8	Other foreign	424.1	424.1	620.5	625.3	548.2
8.1	Bank loans and advances	—	—	141.3	146.4	105.8
8.3	Other	424.1	424.1	479.2	478.9	442.4
Table G. Outstanding Debt by Type of Debt Instrument: Budgetary Central Government *(at end of period)*						
I	Total debt (same as F.I)	4,728.7	5,309.2	6,232.0	8,014.8	8,848.0
II	Domestic debt (same as F.II)	2,193.6	2,578.0	2,878.0	3,814.3	4,266.7
1	Long-term bonds	1,984.4	2,370.3	2,672.1	3,608.8	4,065.8
3	Long-term loans n.e.c.	209.2	207.7	206.0	205.5	201.0
III	Foreign debt (same as F.III)	2,535.1	2,731.2	3,354.0	4,200.5	4,581.3
6	Long-term bonds	...	...	424.1	424.1	392.9
8	Long-term loans n.e.c.	...	...	2,929.9	3,776.3	4,188.4
Summary Table: Other Levels of Government: Local Governments				*(Year ending December 31)*		
1	Revenue	366.1	308.8	379.4	434.3	480.9
1.1	Tax	210.4	143.7	166.9	170.4	216.2
1.2	Other	155.7	165.1	212.5	263.9	264.7
2	Grants	29.2	87.1	98.2	103.3	105.7
2.1	From other levels of Government	29.2	87.1	98.2	103.3	105.7
3	Expenditure	414.8	385.4	423.6	516.7	631.1
5	Deficit/surplus (1 + 2) – (3)	–19.5	10.5	54.0	20.9	–44.5

Source: International Monetary Fund, *Government Finance Statistics Yearbook,* Vol. 2 (Washington, 1978), pp. 146–47.
Note: n.e.c = not elsewhere classified.

EXERCISES

Exercise A

Data on the budgetary operations of the Central Government of Kenya in the fiscal year ended June 30, 1977 are provided below. On the basis of these data, derive the following principal aggregates for fiscal year 1977: (a) revenue, (b) grants, (c) expenditure, (d) lending minus repayments, and (e) financing, as shown in the Summary Table: Budgetary Central Government of Table 6.

Kenya:
Data on Budgetary Operations[1]
(In millions of Kenya shillings)

Receipts on recurrent and development accounts,[2] net of applied appropriations-in-aid	12,922.1
Payments on recurrent and development accounts,[3] net of applied appropriations-in-aid	12,802.0
Appropriations-in-aid applied on recurrent and development accounts	509.6
Interdepartmental transfers included with receipts on recurrent account	34.0
Interdepartmental transfers included with payments on recurrent account	29.7
Revenue of departmental enterprises with an operating deficit[4]	168.5
Transfers from abroad and other levels of Government	234.1
Domestic short-term and long-term borrowing	6,180.7
Repayment of government lending	69.8
Long-term borrowing abroad	595.4
Domestic debt amortization	5,201.5
Purchase of equity and loans granted	540.1
Foreign debt amortization	131.8
Increase in cash balances	115.8

[1] Derived from the *Appropriation Accounts, Other Public Accounts and the Accounts of the Funds for the Year 1976/77* and from data submitted to the International Monetary Fund's Bureau of Statistics.

[2] Include revenue, grants, borrowing, and repayment of government lending.

[3] Include expenditure, lending, and amortization.

[4] There are no departmental enterprises with an operating surplus.

Exercise B

Explain how you would classify the following items in the Appropriation Accounts, Other Public Accounts and the Accounts of the Funds for the Year 1976/77, *with reference to Table A or C or D of Table 6.*

1. Personal emoluments
2. Construction of buildings and works for Armed Forces
3. Equity participation in commerce and industry
4. Central Bank of Kenya profits
5. Purchase of locomotives and wagons for Kenya Railways
6. Loan from the International Monetary Fund
7. Capital contributions relating to government shareholding in banks
8. Rent of government buildings and houses
9. Traveling and accommodation expenses
10. Refund of import duties
11. Passages and leave expenses
12. Loan interest receipts
13. Purchase of land
14. Construction of water supplies
15. Scholarships to students
16. Pensions and gratuities
17. Subvention to Maize and Produce Board
18. Government sinking fund contribution
    (a) For external debt redemption
    (b) For internal debt redemption
19. New building for the Treasury
20. Appropriations-in-aid
    (a) Sale of machinery and equipment
    (b) Sale of farm produce
    (c) School fees

Exercise C

The following data on the domestic financing operations of Budgetary Central Government can be obtained from the Appropriation Accounts, Other Public Accounts and the Accounts of the Funds for the Year 1976/77.

From these data, derive the classification and amounts of domestic financing by type of debt instrument for the year ended June 30, 1977, as shown in Table E of Table 6. Indicate what additional information would be needed to prepare a classification of domestic financing by type of debt holder.

Kenya:
Data on Domestic Financing Operations
(In millions of Kenya shillings)

Issue of tax reserve certificates	77.5
Surrender of tax reserve certificates	25.5
Advances from Cereals and Sugar Finance Corporation	823.2
Repayment of advances from Cereals and Sugar Finance Corporation	693.0
Repayment of advances from Central Bank of Kenya	88.0
Receipts from issue of Treasury bills	4,780.0
Repayment of Treasury bills	4,280.0
Proceeds of 1982 and 1991/92 Kenya stocks	500.0
Amortization of long-term domestic debt secured by marketable instruments	114.5
Amortization of long-term domestic debt not secured by marketable instruments	0.5

ISSUES FOR DISCUSSION

1. *To what extent are the data on Central Government presented in the* GFS Yearbook *incomplete in terms of coverage and reporting basis?*
2. *What is the rationale for the different sectoral treatments of the National Social Security Fund and the National Hospital Insurance Fund?*
3. *Comment on the practical problems that would be encountered in preparing a consolidated statement for Budgetary Central Government and local governments on the basis of the data in the* GFS Yearbook.
4. *The item "Changes in Cash, Deposits, etc." in the* GFS Yearbook *(Table E of Table 6) is essentially determined as a residual from the Government's accounts. It may be compared with the actual movements in government deposits with the banking system as follows:*

	1973	*1974*	*1975*	*1976*	*1977*
	(In millions of Kenya shillings; year ending June 30)				
Changes in cash, deposits, etc.[1] (increase −)	−29.7	111.7	368.6	−639.0	−115.8
Changes in deposits[2] (increase −)					
With Central Bank	−116.0	−3.0	443.0	−670.0	−494.0
With commercial banks	8.0	−16.0	16.0	−26.0	−19.0
Total	*−108.0*	*−19.0*	*459.0*	*−696.0*	*−513.0*

[1] *Source:* International Monetary Fund, *Government Finance Statistics Yearbook,* Vol. 2 (Washington, 1978).

[2] *Source:* International Monetary Fund, *International Financial Statistics,* various issues.

Comment on the possible reasons for the discrepancies between the data derived from the Government's accounts and those obtained from the monetary accounts.

5. *On the basis of the data in the* GFS Yearbook *tables presented above, determine the changes in the net financial position of Budgetary Central Government for the fiscal years 1973–77, vis-à-vis:*
   (a) The rest of the domestic economy
   (b) The foreign sector
   Comment on the significance of these changes in the context of a flow-of-funds analysis.

6. *Discuss the problems encountered in comparing the data on financing by type of debt holder (Table D of Table 6) and by type of debt instrument (Table E of Table 6) with the changes in the corresponding stocks of debt in Tables F and G of Table 6. What factors may account for the discrepancies between the figures for domestic and external financing by long-term bonds and long-term loans not elsewhere classified in Table E of Table 6*

and the changes in the corresponding stocks in Table G of Table 6?

7. *With reference to the data presented in the Summary Table: Budgetary Central Government of Table 6, comment on overall budgetary developments over the period 1973–77. In particular, to what extent are the developments in fiscal year 1977 consistent with the objectives of reducing the pressure on domestic prices and the balance of payments and diverting more resources to economic development? Indicate what additional information, if any, would be desirable for discussing this issue.*

APPENDIX

Government Finance Statistics Tables

Data Fund Codes, Line Numbers, and Titles of Lines in the GFS Yearbook

Data Fund Code	Yearbook Line Number	Title
		Summary Table
81	1	Total Revenue and Grants (A.I)
81Y	2	Total Revenue (A.II)
81YD	3	Current Revenue (A.III)
81YA	3.1	Tax (A.IV)
81YB	3.2	Nontax (A.V)
81YC	4	Capital Revenue (A.VI)
81Z	5	Grants (A.VII)
81ZN	5.1	Current (A.17.1+A.18.1+A.19.1)
81ZP	5.2	Capital (A.17.2+A.18.2+A.19.2)
82Z	6	Total Expenditure and Lending Minus Repayments (C.I)
82	7	Total Expenditure (C.II)
82R	8	Current Expenditure (C.III)
82V	9	Capital Expenditure (C.IV)
83	10	Lending Minus Repayments (C.V)
80S	11	Current Account Surplus or Saving (Without Grants) (3 – 8)
82SA	12	Gross Fixed Capital Formation (C.4 – A.14)
82SB	13	Gross Capital Formation (C.4+C.5 – A.14 – A.15)
80	14	Overall Deficit/Surplus (1 – 6)
80H	15	Financing (D.I or E.I) (=14)
85	16	Abroad (D.III or E.III)
84	17	Domestic (D.II or E.II)
84AB	17.1	Nonbank (D.1+D.4+D.5)
84C	17.2	Deposit Money Banks (D.3)
84D	17.3	Monetary Authorities (D.2)
		Memorandum Items:
88Z	18	Government Debt Outstanding (F.I or G.i)
84Q	19	Change in Floating Debt
84P	20	Domestic Amortization
85P	21	Amortization Abroad
		Table A. Revenue and Grants
81	I	Total Revenue and Grants (II+VII)
81Y	II	Total Revenue (III+VI)
81YD	III	Current Revenue (IV+V)
81YA	IV	Tax Revenue

Data Fund Codes, Line Numbers, and Titles of Lines in the GFS Yearbook
(continued)

Data Fund Code	Yearbook Line Number	Title
		Table A. Revenue and Grants *(continued)*
81A	1	Taxes on Income, Profits, and Capital Gains
81AB	1.1	Individual
81AA	1.2	Corporate
81AZ	1.3	Other Unallocable
81B	2	Social Security Contributions
81BB	2.1	Employees
81BA	2.2	Employers
81BC	2.3	Self-Employed or Nonemployed
81C	3	Employers' Payroll or Manpower Taxes
81D	4	Taxes on Property
81DW	4.1	Recurrent Taxes on Immovable Property
81DH	4.2	Recurrent Taxes on Net Wealth
81DC	4.2.1	Individual
81DD	4.2.2	Corporate
81DK	4.3	Estate, Inheritance, and Gift Taxes
81DG	4.4	Taxes on Financial and Capital Transactions
81DX	4.5	Nonrecurrent Taxes
81DZ	4.6	Other Recurrent
81E	5	Domestic Taxes on Goods and Services
81EA	5.1	General Taxes, Turnover, or Value-Added Taxes
81EG	5.2	Excises
81EH	5.3	Profits of Fiscal Monopolies
81ER	5.4	Taxes on Specific Services
81ES	5.5	Taxes on Use of, or Permission to Use, Goods or to Perform Activities
81ET	5.5.1	Business and Professional Licenses
81EU	5.5.2	Motor Vehicle Taxes
81EV	5.5.3	Other
81EZ	5.6	Other
81F	6	Taxes on International Trade and Transactions
81FG	6.1	Import Duties
81FA	6.1.1	Customs Duties
81FB	6.1.2	Other Charges
81FC	6.2	Export Duties
81FD	6.3	Profits of Export or Import Marketing Boards
81FE	6.4	Exchange Profits
81FF	6.5	Exchange Taxes
81FZ	6.6	Other

Data Fund Codes, Line Numbers, and Titles of Lines in the GFS Yearbook
(continued)

Data Fund Code	Yearbook Line Number	Title
		Table A. Revenue and Grants *(concluded)*
81G	7	Other Taxes
81GA	7.1	Poll Taxes
81GB	7.2	Stamp Taxes
81GZ	7.3	Other
81YB	V	Nontax Revenue
81K	8	Operating Surpluses of Departmental Enterprises
81H	9	Property Income
81HA	9.1	From Nonfinancial Public Enterprises and Public Financial Institutions
81HN	9.2	Other
81JA	10	Administrative Fees and Charges and Nonindustrial Sales
81JH	11	Fines and Forfeits
81MM	12	Contributions to Government Employee Pension Funds Within Government
81X	13	Other
81YC	VI	Capital Revenue
81MA	14	Sales of Fixed Capital Assets
81MB	15	Sales of Stocks
81MC	16	Sales of Land and Intangible Assets
81Z	VII	Grants
81ZA	17	From Abroad other than from Supranational Authorities
81ZB	17.1	Current
81ZC	17.2	Capital
81ZG	18	From Other Levels of National Government
81ZH	18.1	Current
81ZJ	18.2	Capital
81ZD	19	From Supranational Authorities
81ZE	19.1	Current
81ZF	19.2	Capital
		Table B. Expenditure by Function
82	I	Total Expenditure (same as C.II)
82A	1	General Public Services
82B	2	Defense
82C	3	Education
82CB	3.2	Schools (preprimary, primary, and secondary)
82CF	3.3	Universities and Colleges
82CZ	3.6	Other
82D	4	Health
82DB	4.2	Hospitals and Clinics
82DC	4.3	Individual Health Services
82DZ	4.6	Other

Data Fund Codes, Line Numbers, and Titles of Lines in the GFS Yearbook
(continued)

Data Fund Code	Yearbook Line Number	Title
		Table B. Expenditure by Function *(concluded)*
82E	5	Social Security and Welfare
82EQ	5.1-6	Social Security and Assistance
82EN	5.7	Welfare
82F	6	Housing and Community Amenities
82FA	6.1	Housing
82FB	6.2	Community Development
82FC	6.3	Sanitary Services
82G	7	Other Community and Social Services
82H	8	Economic Services
82HA	8.1	General Administration, Regulation n.e.c., and Research
82HB	8.2	Agriculture, Forestry, Fishing, and Hunting
82HC	8.3	Mining, Manufacturing, and Construction
82HD	8.4	Electricity, Gas, Steam, and Water
82HV	8.5	Roads
82HF	8.6	Inland and Costal Waterways
82HG	8.7	Other Transportation and Communication
82HE	8.7.1	Other Transportation
82JB	8.7.2	Communication
82HH	8.8	Other Economic Services
82K	9	Other Purposes
		Table B.1. Lending Minus Repayments by Function
83	I	Total Lending Minus Repayments (same as C.V)
83A	1	General Public Services
83B	2	Defense
83C	3	Education
83CB	3.2	Schools (preprimary, primary, and secondary)
83CF	3.3	Universities and Colleges
83CZ	3.6	Other
83D	4	Health
83DB	4.2	Hospitals and Clinics
83DC	4.3	Individual Health Services
83DZ	4.6	Other
83E	5	Social Security and Welfare
83EQ	5.1-6	Social Security and Assistance
83EN	5.7	Welfare
83F	6	Housing and Community Amenities
83FA	6.1	Housing

Data Fund Codes, Line Numbers, and Titles of Lines in the GFS Yearbook
(continued)

Data Fund Code	Yearbook Line Number	Title
		Table B.1. Lending Minus Repayments by Function *(concluded)*
83FB	6.2	Community Development
83FC	6.3	Sanitary Services
83G	7	Other Community and Social Services
83H	8	Economic Services
83HA	8.1	General Administration, Regulation n.e.c., and Research
83HB	8.2	Agriculture, Forestry, Fishing, and Hunting
83HC	8.3	Mining, Manufacturing, and Construction
83HD	8.4	Electricity, Gas, Steam, and Water
83HV	8.5	Roads
83HF	8.6	Inland and Coastal Waterways
83HG	8.7	Other Transportation and Communication
83HE	8.7.1	Other Transportation
83JB	8.7.2	Communication
83HH	8.8	Other Economic Services
83K	9	Other Purposes
		Table C. Expenditure and Lending Minus Repayments by Economic Type
82Z	I	Total Expenditure and Lending Minus Repayments (II+V)
82	II	Total Expenditure (III+IV)
82R	III	Current Expenditure
82N	1	Expenditure on Goods and Services
82NA	1.1	Wages and Salaries
82NX	1.2-3	Employers' Contribution
82NP	1.4	Other Purchases of Goods and Services
82PA	2	Interest Payments
82PJ	3	Subsidies and Other Current Transfers
82PM	3.3	Transfers to Other Levels of National Government
82PP	3.6	Transfers Abroad
82V	IV	Capital Expenditure
82VA	4	Acquisition of Fixed Capital Assets
82VB	5	Purchases of Stocks
82VC	6	Purchases of Land and Intangible Assets
82U	7	Capital Transfers
82UA	7.1	Domestic
82UB	7.1.1	To Other Levels of National Government
82UM	7.2	Abroad

Data Fund Codes, Line Numbers, and Titles of Lines in the GFS Yearbook
(continued)

Data Fund Code	Yearbook Line Number	Title
		Table C. Expenditure and Lending Minus Repayments by Economic Type *(concluded)*
83	V	Total Lending Minus Repayments
83N	8	Domestic
83NG	8.1	To Other Levels of National Government
83P	9	Abroad
		Memorandum Item:
82P	10	Expenditure Abroad (Excluding Transfers, Interest, and Lending Minus Repayments)
		Table D. Financing by Type of Debt Holder
80H	I	Total Financing (II+III)
84	II	Domestic Financing
84B	1	From Other General Government
84D	2	From Monetary Authorities
84C	3	From Deposit Money Banks
84A	4	Other Domestic
84AE	4.1	From Other Financial Institutions
84AG	4.2	From Nonfinancial Public Enterprises
84AJ	4.3	From Nonfinancial Private Sector
84X	5	Adjustments
85	III	Financing Abroad
85A	6	From International Development Institutions
85B	7	From Foreign Governments
85C	8	Other Foreign Borrowing
85N	9	Changes in Cash, Deposits, Negotiable Securities
		Table E. Financing by Type of Debt Instrument
80H	I	Total Financing (same as D.I)
84	II	Domestic Financing (same as D.II)
84R	1	Long-term Bonds
84S	2	Short-term Bonds and Bills
84T	3	Long-term Loans n.e.c.
84U	4	Short-term Loans and Advances
84V	5	Other Liabilities
84W	6	Changes in Cash, Deposits, etc.
85	III	Financing Abroad (same as D.III)
85R	7	Long-term Bonds
85S	8	Short-term Bonds and Bills
85T	9	Long-term Loans n.e.c.

Data Fund Codes, Line Numbers, and Titles of Lines in the GFS Yearbook
(continued)

Data Fund Code	Yearbook Line Number	Title
		Table E. Financing by Type of Debt Instrument *(concluded)*
85U	10	Short-term Loans and Advances n.e.c.
85V	11	Other Liabilities
85W	12	Changes in Cash, Deposits, etc.
		Table F. Outstanding Debt by Type of Debt Holder
88Z	I	Total Debt (II+III)
88	II	Domestic Debt
88B	1	Other Levels of Government
88D	2	Monetary Authorities
88C	3	Deposit Money Banks
88A	4	Other Domestic
88AJ	4.3	Nonfinancial Private Sector
88X	5	Adjustment for Valuation Differences
89	III	Foreign Debt
89A	6	International Development Institutions
89B	7	Foreign Governments
89C	8	Other Foreign
89CQ	8.1	Bank Loans and Advances
89CR	8.2	Supplier Credits
89CT	8.3	Other
89X	9	Adjustment for Valuation Differences
		Memorandum Items:
88W	10	Domestic Debt Repayment in Foreign Exchange
89W	11	Foreign Debt Repayment in Domestic Currency
		Table G. Outstanding Debt by Type of Debt Instrument
88Z	I	Total Debt (same as F.I)
88	II	Domestic Debt (same as F.II)
88R	1	Long-term Bonds
88S	2	Short-term Bonds and Bills
88T	3	Long-term Loans n.e.c.
88U	4	Short-term Loans and Advances
88V	5	Other Liabilities
89	III	Foreign Debt (same as F.III)
89R	6	Long-term Bonds
89S	7	Short-term Bonds and Bills
89T	8	Long-term Loans n.e.c.
89U	9	Short-term Loans and Advances n.e.c.
89V	10	Other Liabilities

Data Fund Codes, Line Numbers, and Titles of Lines in the GFS Yearbook
(concluded)

Code Fund Data	Yearbook Line Number	Title
		Summary Table: Other Levels of Government
		State, Region, or Province Governments
81Y	1	Revenue
81YA	1.1	Tax
81YB	1.2	Other
81G	2	Grants
81ZP	2.1	From Other Levels of Government
81ZX	2.2	From Abroad
82	3	Expenditure
82P	3.1	Transfers to Other Levels of Government
83	4	Lending Minus Repayments
83P	4.1	To Other Levels of Government
80	5	Deficit/Surplus (1+2)—(3+4)
		Local Governments
81Y	1	Revenue
81YA	1.1	Tax
81YB	1.2	Other
81G	2	Grants
81ZP	2.1	From Other Levels of Government
81ZX	2.2	From Abroad
82	3	Expenditure
82P	3.1	Transfers to Other Levels of Government
83	4	Lending Minus Repayments
83P	4.1	To Other Levels of Government
80	5	Deficit/Surplus (1+2)—(3+4)

Source: International Monetary Fund, *Government Finance Statistics Yearbook*, Vol. 2 (Washington, 1978), pp. 8–13.
Note: n.e.c. = not elsewhere classified.

Chapter 5

WORKSHOP 3

Balance of Payments Statistics

Analysis of the balance of payments position of member countries represents a fundamental part of the International Monetary Fund's work. The importance of balance of payments statistics is reflected in Article VIII of the Second Amendment of the Articles of Agreement, which lists among "the minimum [information] necessary for the effective discharge of the Fund's duties, national data on . . . international balance of payments, including (1) trade in goods and services, (2) gold transactions, (3) known capital transactions, and (4) other items." [1] In order to guide member countries in reporting such data on an internationally comparable basis, the Fund has issued a series of manuals on the preparation of balance of payments statistics. These manuals contain a conceptual framework for balance of payments accounting and set forth detailed guidelines for the classification of particular items.

[1] International Monetary Fund, *Articles of Agreement* (amended effective April 1, 1978), Article VIII, Section 5(*a*) (vi).

The first section of this workshop on balance of payments statistics discusses the principles underlying the preparation of balance of payments statistics and relates them to the analytical uses of these accounts. The discussion is based on the fourth edition of the *Balance of Payments Manual.*[2] The first section also briefly deals with the possible sources of data for balance of payments statistics. The second section uses a classification exercise to illustrate the application of these concepts to Kenyan data on balance of payments. Each section concludes with practical exercises and issues for discussion by workshop participants.

PRESENTATION OF THE STATISTICS

Principles of Compilation

The principles underlying the construction of balance of payments accounts are consistent with those used in the United Nations' *A System of National Accounts (SNA).*[3] There are, however, differences between the classification scheme used in the "rest-of-the-world" segment of the *SNA* and in the balance of payments accounts. In particular, the balance of payments accounts are based on a classification scheme that is more suited to the analysis of imbalances with the rest of the world than the broad breakdown between production, consumption, and accumulation that is used in the *SNA.*

The Manual (page 7) defines the balance of payments as "a statistical statement for a given period showing (a) transactions in goods, services, and income between an economy and the rest of the world, (b) changes of ownership and other changes in that econ-

[2] International Monetary Fund, *Balance of Payments Manual,* 4th edition (Washington, 1977); hereinafter referred to as the Manual. For an explanation of the terms used in the compilation of balance of payments, reference may also be made to International Monetary Fund, Balance of Payments Division, Bureau of Statistics, *The Balance of Payments: A Glossary of Terms in Accord with the Practice of the International Monetary Fund* (Washington, 1979).

[3] United Nations, *A System of National Accounts* (New York, 1968).

omy's monetary gold, special drawing rights (SDRs), and claims on and liabilities to the rest of the world, and (c) unrequited transfers and counterpart entries that are needed to balance, in the accounting sense, any entries for the foregoing transactions and changes which are not mutually offsetting."

This definition emphasizes the scope of the balance of payments and the type of transactions covered. The reference to a given period indicates that the balance of payments deals with "flow" rather than "stock" data. Most transactions are exchanges whereby a transactor (economic entity) provides an economic value to another transactor and receives in return an equal value. The things that are considered to have economic value may be categorized broadly as real resources (goods, services, income) and financial items. In cases where items are given away, the offsetting entry to the real or financial flow is recorded in the balance of payments under the heading "unrequited transfers." In previous editions of the Manual, valuation changes were excluded from the balance of payments, but the fourth edition calls for supplementary information on changes in the value of reserves. The method used is to show the change in reserves due to transactions as the algebraic sum of the total change in holdings and the counterpart items that represent offsets to those changes that could be labeled "reserve creation/destruction."[4] The latter have become much more common with the introduction of SDRs and the advent of widespread floating exchange rates. In addition to international exchanges, transactions in financial assets between residents or between foreigners may, under certain circumstances, be recorded in the balance of payments. For example, the sale by a private resident to the monetary authorities of a claim on a nonresident should be so recorded. By convention, shifts in a country's international investment position emanating from changes in territory are excluded from

[4] Previous editions of the Manual provided for the monetization of gold to be shown as a merchandise export and for demonetization to be shown as an import. These entries provided an offset to the changes in reserves in the capital account.

the balance of payments, although transfers of real and financial assets arising from migration are included.

The Manual contains specific recommendations on the nature of the system to be employed in constructing the balance of payments statement, on the delimitation of an economy and the principles to be followed with respect to the time of recording, and on the valuation of transactions.

The balance of payments recording system takes the form of a double-entry accounting statement, in which each transaction is reflected in both a credit and a debit entry. According to the Manual (page 9), "Under the conventions of the system, the compiling economy records credit entries (a) for real resources denoting exports and (b) for financial items reflecting either a reduction in the economy's foreign assets or an increase in its foreign liabilities. Conversely, the compiling economy records debit entries (a) for real resources denoting imports and (b) for financial items reflecting either an increase in assets or a decrease in liabilities."

The balance of payments accounts are an "open system," since only the resident aspects of external transactions are recorded. In contrast, the national accounts represent a "closed system," as it records the transactions of the rest of the world as well as those of the domestic sectors.

Following the convention that credits are indicated by a positive sign and debits by a negative sign, the sum of all entries should be zero. Information on the debit and credit components of a transaction is, however, usually obtained from different statistical sources. Deficiencies in coverage, as well as variations in the time of recording and in the methods used for valuing transactions, often necessitate the insertion of a balancing item in the accounts. This is usually referred to as net errors and omissions, with the *net* emphasizing that the heading covers a balancing item between errors on both sides of the accounts.

Development of internationally consistent accounts necessitates guidelines for the scope of the domestic economy and for the definition of residency. In general, an individual or institution is considered a resident of the economy with which it has a "closer association . . . than with any other territory" (the Manual, page 2) or where its center of interest lies. Chapter 3 of the Manual provides some guidelines for decisions on residence.

1. *General government.* The residents of a country include not only its central, state, and local governments but also its embassies, consulates, and military establishments abroad.[5]

2. *Individuals.* Most of the individuals in an economy on a permanent basis would be considered residents of that country. Tourists and other visitors and workers who are in an economy for less than one year are considered residents of their home country. Diplomatic, military, and other official representatives of foreign governments (together with their dependents) are not considered part of the host country's economy. Border workers (persons who regularly work in one country but live in another) are residents of the economy where they live and not where they work.

3. *Enterprises.* An enterprise is considered a resident of the economy in which it engages in business activity even if it is a branch or subsidiary of a foreign company. Balance of payments accounts may therefore involve the notional division of a single legal entity, with consequent problems of imputing a value for transactions between the parent and its affiliates.

Internationally comparable balance of payments accounts must be based on consistent definitions of the timing and valuation of transactions. The principle is adopted that "transactions are to be recorded when the real resources or financial items involved undergo a legal change of ownership, which [by convention] is taken to be the time that the parties concerned enter the transactions in their books" (the Manual, page 3). This approach contrasts with alternative principles, such as the time of contract or customs clearance, and may also differ from the timing convention used in an exchange

[5] Official international organizations, such as the International Monetary Fund, are not considered residents of any national economy, including that in which they are located.

record in compiling statistics on the flow of real resources. As indicated in the section below on Major Sources of Data, it may be necessary to make timing adjustments to data taken from the original statistical sources.

Transactions should be valued at the market price, which is defined as the "price that a willing buyer pays to a willing seller, when the buyer and seller are independent parties whose only considerations are commercial ones" (the Manual, page 2). These conditions are not fulfilled, however, for several types of transactions. For example, transactions between affiliated enterprises are not between independent parties, and international differences in taxation or regulation may provide incentives for the use of unrealistic pricing as a means of transferring profits between countries. A further problem arises for unrequited transfers that are not commercial transactions and that by definition do not have a price. Similarly, a price needs to be imputed for barter transactions. Prices in comparable markets or costs of production may provide some guidelines when prices have to be imputed.

As balance of payments transactions are conducted in a variety of currencies, currency conversions are necessary to present accounts in terms of a single unit of account. Moreover, a universal unit of account is needed to facilitate intercountry comparisons and to permit aggregations on a regional or worldwide basis. Transactions should, in principle, be converted at the exchange rate applicable at the time a contract was made. In countries with multiple exchange rates, balance of payments transactions should theoretically be converted at the notional unitary rate that would apply if all transactions were channeled through an uncontrolled market. This would avoid including in the balance of payments the tax and subsidy transactions between residents that are implicit in multiple exchange rate schemes. The actual basis for currency conversions usually differs from these theoretical principles. For example, information as to the contract date may not be available, and some average of the exchange rates in the accounting period often has to be used. Also, the balance of payments compiler is often presented with data that for customs or other purposes has already been converted into local currency. The principles underlying this conversion may differ significantly from those required for balance of payments purposes.[6]

Classification of Items

Balance of payments transactions are broken down into the standard components shown in Table 1. The classification attempts to distinguish variables responsive to particular economic forces and items that in terms of size or variability are likely to be important in several countries. These standard components may in turn be considered as building blocks that can be further grouped to aid in analysis of the balance of payments (see the section below on Analytic Breakdown). A broad distinction is made between current and capital account transactions.

Current account transactions are divided into those for goods, services, and income and those for unrequited transfers. Usually, the major component of the former would be the *merchandise* item, which covers most balance of payments transactions in movable goods.[7] In order to ensure consistency between the valuation shown for a merchandise export by one country and the corresponding import by another country, a rule has been adopted for the treatment of distributive services. The costs of distributive services performed up to the customs frontier of the exporting country are included in merchandise, while such expenditures incurred beyond that point are treated as shipment. In balance of payments terminology this means that exports and imports are recorded on an f.o.b. (free on board) basis. For imports, this contrasts with a c.i.f. (cost, insurance, and freight) basis, which would include all international freight and insurance up to a point of valuation at the customs frontier of the importing country.

[6] "Errors and omissions" may arise due to the conversion of a transaction by customs officials at an exchange rate that differs from that used by the central bank to value the corresponding financial flow.

[7] The exceptions cover movable goods classified as other items (e.g., goods acquired for their own use by travelers, classified as "travel," and monetary gold, treated as a financial asset).

TABLE 1. Standard Components of the Balance of Payments

	Credit	Debit
I. CURRENT ACCOUNT		
A. Goods, Services, and Income		
Merchandise		
Shipment		
Other Transportation		
Passenger services		
Port services, etc.		
Travel		
Investment Income		
Direct investment income		
Reinvested earnings		
Distributed earnings		
Other		
Resident official, including interofficial		
Foreign official, excluding interofficial		
Private		
Other Goods, Services, and Income		
Official		
Interofficial		
Other, resident official		
Other, foreign official		
Private		
Labor income, n.i.e.		
Property income, n.i.e.		
Other		
B. Unrequited Transfers		
Private		
Migrants' transfers		
Workers' remittances		
Other		
Official		
Interofficial		
Other, resident official		
Other, foreign official		
II. CAPITAL ACCOUNT		
A. Capital, excluding reserves		
Direct Investment		
Abroad		
Equity capital		
Reinvestment of earnings		
Other long-term capital		
Short-term capital		

TABLE 1. Standard Components of the Balance of Payments
(continued)

II. CAPITAL ACCOUNT
(continued)

	Credit	*Debit*
A. Capital, excluding reserves *(continued)*		
Direct Investment *(concluded)*		
In reporting economy		
Equity capital		
Reinvestment of earnings		
Other long-term capital		
Short-term capital		
Portfolio Investment		
Public sector bonds		
Assets		
Liabilities constituting foreign authorities' reserves		
Other liabilities		
Other bonds		
Assets		
Liabilities constituting foreign authorities' reserves		
Other liabilities		
Corporate equities		
Assets		
Liabilities constituting foreign authorities' reserves		
Other liabilities		
Other Capital		
Long-term capital		
Resident official sector		
Drawings and repayments on loans extended		
Other assets		
Liabilities constituting foreign authorities' reserves		
Drawings and repayments on other loans received		
Other liabilities		
Deposit money banks		
Drawings and repayments on loans extended		
Other assets		
Liabilities constituting foreign authorities' reserves: denominated in national currency		
Liabilities constituting foreign authorities' reserves: denominated in foreign currency		
Drawings and repayments on loans received		
Other liabilities		

TABLE 1. Standard Components of the Balance of Payments
(continued)

II. CAPITAL ACCOUNT
(continued)

	Credit	Debit
A. Capital, excluding reserves *(concluded)*		
Other capital *(concluded)*		
Long-term capital *(concluded)*		
Other sectors		
Drawings and repayments on loans extended		
Other assets		
Liabilities constituting foreign authorities' reserves		
Drawings and repayments on other loans received		
Other liabilities		
Short-term capital		
Resident official sector		
Loans extended		
Other assets		
Liabilities constituting foreign authorities' reserves		
Other loans received		
Other liabilities		
Deposit money banks		
Assets		
Liabilities constituting foreign authorities' reserves: denominated in national currency		
Liabilities constituting foreign authorities' reserves: denominated in foreign currency		
Other liabilities		
Other sectors		
Loans extended		
Other assets		
Liabilities constituting foreign authorities' reserves		
Other loans received		
Other liabilities		
B. Reserves		
Monetary Gold		
Total change in holdings		
Counterpart to monetization/demonetization		
Counterpart to valuation changes		
Special Drawing Rights		
Total change in holdings		
Counterpart to allocation/cancellation		
Counterpart to valuation changes		

TABLE 1. Standard Components of the Balance of Payments
(concluded)

II. CAPITAL ACCOUNT (concluded)	Credit	Debit
B. Reserves *(concluded)*		
Reserve Position in the Fund		
Total change in holdings		
Counterpart to valuation changes		
Foreign Exchange Assets		
Total change in holdings		
Counterpart to valuation changes		
Other Claims		
Total change in holdings		
Counterpart to valuation changes		
Use of Fund Credit		
Total change in holdings		
Counterpart to valuation changes		

Source: International Monetary Fund, *Balance of Payments Manual,* 4th edition (Washington, 1977), pp. 66–69.
Note: n.i.e = not included elsewhere.

Shipment covers freight, insurance, and other distributive services performed on goods classified as merchandise and on other movable goods. Consistent with the treatment of merchandise on an f.o.b. basis, shipment includes distributive services performed after the goods reach the customs border of the exporting country.[8] Further, the convention is adopted that shipment of merchandise beyond the customs border of the exporting country is a service performed for a resident of the importing economy. When services up to the customs border are performed by residents of the importing country, offsetting entries are necessary under shipment. This would involve crediting the shipment account of the importing country and debiting that of the exporting country.

Other transportation is divided into passenger and port services. The former covers the international carriage of passengers in connec-

[8] Earlier editions of the Manual allowed merchandise to be treated on a c.i.f. basis when data were not available on an f.o.b. basis, with corresponding changes in the definition of shipment.

tion with travel, and the latter applies to goods and services, such as fuel and ships' stores, acquired by carriers and consumed in their operation. *Travel* covers goods and services acquired by travelers, outside their own country, for their own use or for gifts. Travelers are persons such as businessmen, students, and tourists who remain for less than one year in an economy of which they are not residents.

Investment income covers factor earnings from financial assets, with dividends and interest payments usually representing the major items under this heading. Direct investment income is divided into reinvested and distributed earnings. The category for reinvested earnings reflects the view that undistributed income increases the capital participation of the parent company. Consequently, retained earnings are, in proportion to the direct investors' participation in the equity of the enterprise, shown as direct investment income with a corresponding entry in the capital account. Investment income payments involving official institutions (including the International Monetary Fund) are shown separately from other private investment earnings.

Other goods, services, and income represent a residual category with a broad division made between official and private flows. Official flows cover such items as transactions between embassies abroad and the host country, aid services, and insofar as they can be quantified, military services.[9] Private transactions would include labor income paid to seasonal and border workers and such items as income from patents and merchandise insurance.

Unrequited transfers provide offsetting entries for real and financial flows that do not involve a quid pro quo. For example, a gift of real resources to the compiling country is shown as a debit entry under merchandise imports and as a credit item under unrequited transfers. Private unrequited transfers include migrants' transfers, workers' remittances, and other. Migrants' transfers represent the contra-entry to the shift in net worth of the migrant resulting from migration. Transfers of migrants' goods from the old to the new place of residence would be shown as a merchandise export for the

[9] Aid services, such as shipment, should be included under their own headings.

originating economy, with an offsetting debit entry under unrequited transfers. Similarly, unrequited transfers provide offsetting entries for the change in a nation's financial assets and liabilities following migration. Unrequited transfers of income between emigrants and the compiling economy are included under workers' remittances; if, however, the length of stay is less than one year, they would be classified as labor income under other goods and services. Official unrequited transfers include government grants of goods, financial resources, and technical assistance services.

The *capital account* covers transactions in financial assets and liabilities. In addition, for the reserves category it incorporates supplementary information on total changes in holdings, together with counterpart entries that offset those changes not due to transactions. Assets except monetary gold and SDRs represent claims on nonresidents, and liabilities represent indebtedness to nonresidents. Consistent with the principle that the balance of payments records transactions, assets and liabilities must represent changes in actual claims; unused lines of credit and other contingent obligations are not included. A debit entry can arise either from an increase in assets or a reduction in liabilities, while a credit entry reflects a decrease in assets or an increase in liabilities. In order to facilitate analysis, capital transactions are broken down by using several criteria: type of capital, length of maturity, and assets and liabilities. The functional breakdown represents reserves, direct investment capital, portfolio capital, and other capital. Reserves attempt to distinguish those assets that respond to movements in "autonomous" components of the balance of payments (see the section below on Analytic Breakdown). Direct investment covers assets and liabilities involving a lasting interest in an enterprise, while portfolio capital covers other long-term bonds and corporate equities. For all components, apart from direct investment, movements in assets and liabilities are shown separately. A distinction is also made between short-term and long-term capital, with the former having a maturity of one year or less and the latter a maturity of more than one year. This distinction is not, however, believed to be relevant for reserves;

portfolio capital is long-term capital by definition. In previous editions of the Manual, considerable emphasis was placed on a sectoral breakdown of capital movements. Such a breakdown in the fourth edition is, however, provided only for "other capital," with the sector to be identified as that of the domestic creditor for assets and that of the domestic debtor for liabilities. The sectoral breakdown covers the official sector, deposit money banks, and other holders, with liabilities constituting foreign authorities' reserves being shown separately in each case.

Direct investment constitutes "investment that is made to acquire a lasting interest in an enterprise operating in an economy other than that of the investor, the investor's purpose being to have an effective voice in the management of the enterprise" (the Manual, page 136). Specific criteria for distinguishing direct investment are usually linked to the degree of foreign ownership and the amount of dispersion among the owners. In practice, the number of cases where it is difficult to decide whether investment should be classified as "direct" are few, because most such enterprises are wholly owned by foreigners. Also the quantitative importance of borderline cases is limited, as the Manual provides that only the direct investors' share in the capital and income flows is to be classified as direct investment. The contra-entry to the reinvestment of earnings entered under direct investment income in the current account is reflected in the capital account as a distinct component of direct investment capital. *Portfolio investment* "covers long-term bonds and corporate equities other than those included in the categories for direct investment and reserves" (the Manual, page 142). A division is made between public sector bonds, other bonds, and corporate equities. "Other capital" represents a residual category.

Reserves are composed of "the monetary gold, special drawing rights (SDRs) in the Fund, reserve position in the Fund, use of Fund credit, and existing claims on nonresidents that are available to the central authorities either to finance payments imbalances directly or to manage the size of such imbalances by intervening to influence the exchange rate for the national currency" (the Manual, page 147).

For the most part reserves would be held by the central authorities, although funds held by the deposit money banks, but subject to the effective control of the government, should also be included. Changes in the reserve position in the Fund (asset) are shown separately from the use of Fund credit (liability). As discussed in the section above on Principles of Compilation, reserve creation (through monetization or SDR allocations) and valuation changes are included as supplementary information with an offsetting (counterpart) entry.

International reserves usually represent the major component of net foreign assets in the monetary survey. The balance of payments shows changes in reserves—a flow figure—while the monetary survey shows the stock of net foreign assets. Also, there may be differences in the coverage of net foreign assets in the monetary survey and reserves in the balance of payments. In particular, the former includes foreign assets and liabilities of the deposit money banks that may not be considered reserves for the purpose of balance of payments classification. Problems that arise in reconciling the balance of payments and monetary survey data for international reserves often reflect different exchange rate conversions in the two sources. Furthermore, valuation changes are, in principle, included in net foreign assets in the monetary survey, with an offsetting change in unclassified liabilities. Prior to the fourth edition of the Manual, such valuation changes were not recorded in the balance of payments.

Major Sources of Data

The major sources of data for merchandise transactions are trade returns and foreign exchange records. Trade returns register the physical movement of commodities across borders, while foreign exchange records indicate payments and receipts for goods. Neither necessarily corresponds to the balance of payments principle for recording transactions at the time a change of ownership is indicated in the books of the buyer and the purchaser. Thus, adjustments for differences in coverage, classification, timing, and valuation may be required.[10] Coverage adjustments to the exchange record are necessary

[10] See the Manual, Appendix B, for a more complete list of adjustments.

in order to allow for transactions that are not settled through the banking system. Barter trade, unrequited transfers in kind, and transactions settled directly by changes in financial assets and liabilities held abroad are examples of items that would not be entered in exchange records. The inclusion of marine products caught by domestic vessels in the open sea and sold directly abroad represents an example of a coverage adjustment that should be made to trade data. Classification adjustments may be necessary in order to put transactions on an f.o.b. basis, with corresponding changes in the shipment account. Timing adjustments are likely to be particularly important when there are significant changes in the size of trade flows or when large stocks are held abroad by residents or held domestically by nonresidents. Trade returns register the physical movement of goods and should be adjusted for changes in these stocks. Timing adjustments need to be made to the exchange record to allow for prepayments and trade credits, with offsetting entries for the changes in assets and liabilities included in the capital account. Valuation adjustments are necessary when data from the basic source are not recorded at market prices. An example might be the recording of a special customs valuation in the trade returns.

Information on balance of payments transactions by financial institutions and the public sector should be readily available. Trade returns and exchange records may also provide information on other components of the balance of payments accounts. For example, trade returns may provide the basic data for "shipment" and for the stores and fuel component of "other transportation." The exchange record provides information for all balance of payments components subject to exchange control, though significant classification problems may occur. Particularly for countries with limited exchange control, some private transactions may need to be estimated through the use of questionnaires and sample survey techniques. The travel component of the balance of payments is sometimes estimated by applying an average per diem expenditure to the number of days spent by residents abroad and by foreigners in the reporting country. Estimates of the per diem expenditure may be based on information obtained from travel agents, banks, hotels, or shops. A systematic record may be kept of the number of nights spent in hotels by foreign tourists. Information on tourism may in some cases be checked by an exchange of information between countries. Questionnaires may also be used to obtain information from shipping and airline companies on passenger fares and from multinational companies on investment income and direct investment. Company accounts may provide information on business transactions that should enter the balance of payments. Data on short-term capital flows are often considered to be particularly inaccurate. This reflects the problem of obtaining separate information on trade credits when exchange records are the basic data source or of obtaining a sufficient response from questionnaires in terms of coverage and reliability.

Analytic Breakdown

A major purpose of the balance of payments accounts is to provide an indication of the need for policy adjustment to rectify external imbalance. The double-entry accounting system implies, however, that the balance of payments must be in balance. A surplus or deficit in the balance of payments involves summing a subsection of total external transactions and distinguishing the transactions "above the line" from items "below the line." The decision on where to draw the line reflects a normative view as to which set of transactions best indicates the need for balance of payments adjustment. One approach suggests that transactions undertaken for their own sake should be separated from transactions undertaken solely to compensate for these autonomous components. Another approach emphasizes the volatility of transactions, with items that are considered unstable being placed "below the line" in order to obtain an indication of the underlying balance of payments position. Unfortunately, no unambiguous criteria exist for distinguishing between autonomous and compensatory items because such a division essentially reflects the classifier's view of the subjective motivation of the transactor. Nor is it easily possible to decide which types of financial assets are likely to be particularly volatile. It is therefore not surprising that a variety of concepts of balance have been developed.

The narrowest definition of payments imbalance relates to the *trade balance*—that is, the difference between exports and imports on an f.o.b. basis. A distinction between the flow of goods and the flow of services is, however, necessarily arbitrary, and the justification for this balance lies essentially in the ready availability of merchandise data from customs returns.

The *current account* represents a conceptually more interesting balance. This balance is sometimes represented by transactions on goods, services, and income, while other proponents suggest the inclusion of private, or all, unrequited transfers. Private unrequited transfers may be included on the grounds that, from the viewpoint of balance of payments adjustment, it is artificial to place labor income not included elsewhere above the line and workers' remittances below the line. Official transfers are sometimes excluded on the assumption that they largely represent capital as opposed to current flows.[11] A problem with placing unrequited transfers below the line is that a gift of real resources would appear to worsen the balance of payments of the recipient country. The balance on goods, services, income, and unrequited transfers shows the net change in financial assets arising from an economy's real transactions. Assuming that all transfers are current, this corresponds to the current surplus or deficit in the rest-of-the-world sector of the national accounts. It is questionable whether imbalances in the current account necessarily warrant policy adjustment. A developing country might, for example, wish to have a current account deficit financed by a long-term capital inflow linked to development expenditure. Alternatively, a country may wish to have a current account surplus in order to finance external investment.

The *basic balance* tries to indicate the longer-run balance of payments position by placing below the line transactions that are likely to be reversed in the short run. Long-term capital flows are included above the line, in addition to the current account items. The exclusion of short-term capital flows reflects the assumption that

[11] The Manual does not make a distinction between current and capital transfer.

these are likely to be particularly unstable. It is, however, questionable whether this assumption is valid. Also, this balance may be sensitive to whether errors and omissions are placed above or below the line.[12]

The *overall balance* places below the line only changes in reserve assets and liabilities that serve to accommodate payments imbalances. This balance focuses on the use of reserves and the short-term constraints arising from limitations on the availability of financing. The decision on the items that constitute reserves raises certain problems, some of which were discussed in the section on Classification of Items. In particular, while monetary gold, SDRs, and assets of the monetary authorities would usually be included in reserves, the treatment of similar assets in deposit money banks is judgmental and depends on the degree of control the authorities have over the use of these assets. Further problems arise in the treatment of liabilities. Use of Fund credit is classified with reserves, and in some treatments liabilities considered by the holders as reserve assets are also placed below the line. This procedure has the advantage of providing international symmetry in the definition of balances. Some approaches also place below the line special transactions that represent sources of financing other than the use of reserve assets and the incurrence of reserve-related liabilities.

A special problem arises in applying the concepts of balance to a country such as the United States that acts as a "reserve center." The liabilities of the United States are widely used for the purpose of settling international transactions and can thereby serve as reserves for other countries. It may be argued that reserve centers perform the role of financial intermediaries by lending on a long-term basis and providing short-term investments to foreign monetary authorities. To the extent that the latter transactions are classified below the line,

[12] A variant of the "basic balance" is the "liquidity balance," which places above the line short-term domestically held claims on nonresidents. The arguments that domestically held funds are necessarily immune from official control and are more stable than short-term liabilities to foreigners would seem debatable, however.

there would be a corresponding overall deficit for the reserve center. Such a situation would not, however, necessarily warrant immediate policy adjustments by the deficit country. In part reflecting these problems, the United States in mid-1976 ceased publishing official balances on the grounds that they may be positively misleading, although balances are shown as memorandum items in the U.S. accounts. This official U.S. viewpoint emphasizes that while summary balances may have their uses, a full assessment of a country's external position must be based on an analysis of the various components of the balance of payments in the context of developments in the domestic economy.

EXERCISES AND ISSUES FOR DISCUSSION

Exercises

1. *Indicate the debit and credit entries that should be made in the accounts of the compiling country to allow for the following transactions:*

   (a) *The import of manufactured goods financed by a six-month trade credit from the exporter.*

   (b) *An export of coffee paid for by foreign exchange which the exporters deposit with the commercial banks and which the commercial banks in turn deposit with their correspondent banks abroad.*

   (c) *A gift of food to the compiling country from the U.S. Government.*

   (d) *The sale of domestically mined gold to the Central Bank.*

   (e) *Direct investment by foreigners in the compiling country financed by local currency drawn from the nonresidents' holdings of deposits in the compiling country's commercial banks.*

2. *Indicate what adjustments should be made to deal with the following data problems:*

   (a) *Unrecorded border trade.*

   (b) *Goods recorded by customs data as exported that have not yet been sold to nonresidents. These goods remain in the ownership of residents and represent increased stocks held abroad.*

   (c) *The exclusion from the exchange record of an import financed by a trade credit.*

   (d) *A transaction between a parent company and a foreign subsidiary that did not appear to be recorded at market prices.*

Issues for Discussion

1. *Comment on the sources used in your own country to obtain balance of payments data. Which items in your balance of payments accounts would you consider most subject to estimation error?*

2. *What are the possible reasons for differences between the entries in the balance of payments and in the exchange record and what are the different analytical and policy uses of the two sets of data?*

3. *Comment on the analytical uses of the trade balance, the current account balance, the basic balance, and the overall balance. Evaluate their significance as indicators of balance of payments performance in your country.*

4. *Comment on the macroeconomic significance of overall surpluses and deficits. In what sense can overall deficits be said to represent a constraint on the attainment of domestic economic policy objectives, thus needing corrective action?*

5. *What information does the financing of the current account deficit provide about changes in the external debt position of the country? To what extent would the nature of such financing affect your analysis of the balance of payments performance?*

BALANCE OF PAYMENTS DATA FOR KENYA

This section presents the data on international transactions of Kenya for 1976, in order to illustrate how the principles for constructing balance of payments accounts may be applied. The recommendations of the fourth edition of the Manual were not fully reflected in the *Balance of Payments Yearbook* [13] until 1979. Differences may therefore be noted between the standard presentation for Kenya in Table 2 and the classification recommended in Table 1. These differences do not, however, affect the principles underlying balance of payments compilation or the preparation of the standard or the analytic presentation.

International Transactions of Kenya for 1976
(In millions of SDRs) [1]

A. Goods, Services, and Unrequited Transfers	
Imports, c.i.f. (including freight and insurance paid to residents and nonresidents)	844.5
Freight and insurance on imports paid to nonresidents	90.8
Freight and insurance on imports paid to residents	19.0
Freight on exports paid to local companies	29.4
Insurance on exports paid to local companies	8.5
Freight and insurance on merchandise paid to nonresidents that is not included in imports, c.i.f.	9.5
Purchases of foreign exchange from nonresident visitors	88.8
Payments by nonresidents to local carriers for transport of persons	54.9
Payments by residents to foreign companies for transport of persons	26.5
Sales of foreign exchange to residents for foreign travel, education, and other similar expenses abroad	26.9
Port disbursements by Kenyan carriers abroad	31.3
Local expenditures by foreign embassies and by technical assistance personnel	17.6
Exports, f.o.b.	644.3
Receipts for sales of fuel and ships' stores to nonresidents	53.2

See footnotes at end of table.

[13] International Monetary Fund, *Balance of Payments Yearbook* (Washington). Issued annually.

International Transactions of Kenya for 1976 *(continued)*
(In millions of SDRs)[1]

A. Goods, Services, and Unrequited Transfers *(concluded)*	
Other port disbursements by foreign carriers in Kenya	48.8
Reinvested earnings in Kenya accruing to nonresident parent companies	24.0
Payments of interest to nonresidents by commercial banks and on official and company borrowing abroad	49.7
Distributed earnings on direct investment in Kenya remitted to nonresidents	56.9
Interest on sterling and other securities largely held by Kenya's official and banking institutions	19.7
Distributed earnings received from branches of Kenyan companies operating abroad	11.8
Amounts accruing to Kenyan companies from the retained earnings of foreign subsidiaries	0.6
Technical assistance services received by Kenya and financed by foreign grants from official sources [2]	18.4
Local expenditure by Kenya's embassies and consulates abroad	5.6
Grants received by Kenya from the United Kingdom and other sources [3]	20.7
Compensation grants paid by Kenya to former civil servants and other government unrequited transfers	5.0
Kenyan companies' receipts from nonresidents for nonmerchandise insurance	5.4
Kenyan companies' receipts from nonresidents for other private services	24.0
Payments by Kenyan companies to nonresidents for nonmerchandise insurance	8.3
Payments by Kenyan companies to nonresidents for other private services	24.6
Transfers by emigrants from Kenya and other nonofficial unrequited transfers to nonresidents	33.3
Scholarships received by Kenyan students abroad [4]	6.6
Other unrequited transfers by foreigners to nonofficial domestic recipients	20.5
B. Capital (excluding reserves and related items)	
Drawings on loans, with a maturity of more than one year, by the general government	73.5
Repayments on these loans	11.4
Drawings on loans, with a maturity of more than one year, by private enterprises	12.0
Repayments on these loans	13.4
Increase in other private long-term liabilities to nonresidents	26.3

See footnotes at end of table.

International Transactions of Kenya for 1976 *(concluded)*
(In millions of SDRs)[1]

B. Capital (excluding reserves and related items) *(concluded)*	
Increase in central monetary institutions' short-term deposit liabilities to foreign banks	0.8
Increase in private liabilities to nonresidents with a maturity of less than one year	32.1
Increase in private claims on nonresidents with a maturity of less than one year	3.1
Increase in privately held long-term foreign assets	2.5
Capital remitted by foreigners for direct investment in Kenya[5]	14.7
Capital remitted by residents for direct investment abroad[5]	2.1
Decrease in holdings of long-term Kenyan Government securities by nonresidents	2.9
Increase in other long-term liabilities of the general government to nonresidents	13.5
Decrease in liabilities of deposit money banks (DMBs) to nonresidents with a maturity of less than one year	3.6
Increase in DMB holdings of short-term claims on nonresidents	6.9
Decrease in long-term foreign securities held by the Kenyan Government against sinking funds, provident funds, and trust funds	0.8
Increase in holdings by the Kenyan Government of foreign assets, with a maturity of less than one year	1.2
C. Reserves and Related Items	
Drawings from the Fund under the compensatory financing facility	24.0
Drawings from the Fund under the oil facility	3.1
Repurchases from the Fund in the credit tranche	10.6
Net use of SDRs by Kenya	1.0
Net increase in foreign exchange and other claims of the Central Bank	91.5

Source: International Monetary Fund, *Balance of Payments Yearbook,* Vol. 28 (Washington, 1977), pp. 336–41.

[1] SDRs = special drawing rights; SDR 1 = KSh 9.6595.

[2] A contra-entry should be made under unrequited transfers.

[3] This figure includes SDR 0.9 million of grants to finance general imports and SDR 0.7 million from the International Monetary Fund's Subsidy Account that should be classified in the analytic presentation as "exceptional financing."

[4] Classified as "private unrequited transfers." The fourth edition of the Manual would include these in "official transfers" if the donor was a foreign government.

[5] Account should also be taken of the amounts recorded in item A as retained earnings.

EXERCISES AND ISSUES FOR DISCUSSION

Exercises

1. *On the basis of the information provided above for 1976, prepare the 1976 column of the standard presentation for Kenya, using the format of Table 2. Then after rearranging the data, prepare the 1976 analytic presentation as in Table 3.*
2. *From Table 3 derive the trade balance and the basic balance, as well as the various possible measures of the current account balance and the overall balance.*

Issues for Discussion

1. *Comment on whether the basic balance or the overall balance is a more appropriate indicator of Kenya's balance of payments performance.*
2. *On the basis of Tables 2 and 3, comment on the strengths and weaknesses in Kenya's balance of payments position. What further information would you require to aid such an analysis?*
3. *Has the foreign sector of Kenya added to domestic savings during the period 1974–76?*
4. *What relationship would you expect to exist between the financing of the "overall deficit" in Table 3 and the change in net foreign assets in the monetary survey?*

TABLE 2. Kenya: Standard Presentation of the Balance of Payments, 1968–76
(In millions of SDRs)

	1968	1969	1970	1971	1972	1973	1974	1975	1976
A. Goods, Services, and Unrequited Transfers	**—40.2**	**—8.1**	**—49.0**	**—111.4**	**—62.7**	**—105.7**	**—256.0**	**—177.3**	
Goods and services	**—65.2**	**—30.8**	**—74.6**	**—169.5**	**—97.8**	**—130.8**	**—282.1**	**—207.4**	
Total credit	*409.5*	*455.4*	*510.0*	*530.9*	*538.3*	*597.9*	*809.6*	*817.0*	
Total debit	*—474.7*	*—486.2*	*—584.6*	*—700.4*	*—636.1*	*—728.7*	*—1,091.7*	*—1,024.4*	
1. Merchandise: exports f.o.b.	234.8	252.7	285.5	292.8	310.8	394.2	483.1	471.4	
2. Merchandise: imports f.o.b.	—294.2	—295.5	—371.6	—476.6	—417.3	—456.6	—744.5	—662.6	
3. Nonmonetary gold	0.5	0.3	—0.2	—0.6	—1.1	—0.4	—2.1	—8.0	
4. Freight and insurance on merchandise: credit	17.0	19.2	20.7	22.2	20.1	20.9	30.3	31.1	
5. Freight and insurance on merchandise: debit	—36.0	—34.9	—45.5	—60.4	—52.8	—61.8	—98.5	—87.4	
6. Other transportation: credit	42.3	47.8	52.3	57.5	54.4	58.0	156.7	156.0	
7. Other transportation: debit	—23.8	—24.4	—26.0	—23.7	—23.9	—23.7	—52.9	—58.2	
8. Travel: credit	48.5	46.7	51.7	66.7	70.4	58.2	62.9	76.5	
9. Travel: debit	—21.6	—22.5	—20.6	—24.3	—25.5	—26.4	—30.5	—26.7	
10. Undistributed income from direct investment abroad	. . .	. . .	. . .	. . .	. . .	. . .	. . .	0.7	
11. Undistributed income from direct investment in Kenya	—19.8	—15.5	—13.8	—12.4	. . .	. . .	. . .	—24.7	
12. Other direct investment income: credit	14.9	18.9	21.7	18.2	. . .	. . .	. . .	5.1	
13. Other direct investment income: debit	—26.0	—27.9	—35.6	—32.5	. . .	. . .	. . .	—46.5	
14. Other investment income: credit	8.7	15.9	25.5	16.2	33.3	22.5	31.9	29.1	
15. Other investment income: debit	—17.4	—17.9	—20.7	—14.0	—64.7	—108.1	—115.9	—57.1	

16. Other government: credit	31.4	32.2	34.8	36.9	15.0	12.2	18.2	17.3
17. Other government: debit	—27.7	—28.0	—30.2	—34.1	—29.7	—24.9	—24.9	—23.6
18. Other private: credit	11.4	21.7	17.8	20.4	34.3	31.9	26.5	29.8
19. Other private: debit	—8.2	—19.6	—20.4	—21.8	—21.1	—26.8	—22.4	—29.6
Unrequited transfers	**25.0**	**22.7**	**25.6**	**58.1**	**35.1**	**25.1**	**26.1**	**30.1**
Total credit	*53.7*	*49.8*	*53.9*	*87.9*	*62.4*	*53.9*	*66.3*	*67.6*
Total debit	*—28.7*	*—27.1*	*—28.3*	*—29.8*	*—27.3*	*—28.8*	*—40.2*	*—37.5*
20. Private: credit	17.6	19.7	20.3	20.4	28.8	26.4	32.8	32.9
21. Private: debit	—20.1	—19.8	—22.1	—23.5	—20.6	—23.2	—34.4	—32.2
22. Government: credit	36.1	30.1	33.6	67.5	33.6	27.5	33.5	34.7
23. Government: debit	—8.6	—7.3	—6.2	—6.3	—6.7	—5.6	—5.8	—5.3
B. Capital (excluding reserves and related items)	**35.4**	**60.2**	**89.3**	**51.8**	**92.0**	**118.1**	**187.0**	**143.0**
Nonmonetary sectors	**46.7**	**57.3**	**89.2**	**43.4**	**84.8**	**121.5**	**181.4**	**140.9**
24. Direct investment in Kenya	19.8	15.5	13.8	12.4	...	...	...	40.2
25. Direct investment abroad	...	...	...	...	...	...	...	—3.3
26. Other private long-term liabilities	4.1	23.0	28.0	40.1	33.5	85.8	122.5	19.3
27. Other private long-term assets	1.7	—2.0	14.6	0.6	6.4	—10.8	—7.9	—8.0
28. Other private short-term liabilities	2.0	4.2	10.0	—	6.5	14.1	32.4	29.8
29. Other private short-term assets	1.1	—0.3	—2.3	0.3	—0.7	—1.4	—6.5	—3.6
30. General government long-term liabilities	19.3	19.1	24.6	—12.6	40.9	35.8	39.9	65.6
31. General government long-term assets	—1.2	—2.4	—1.7	2.6	—1.8	—2.0	1.0	0.9
32. General government short-term liabilities	—0.3	—0.3	—0.4	—	—	—	—	—
33. General government short-term assets	0.2	0.5	2.6	—	—	—	—	—

TABLE 2. Kenya: Standard Presentation of the Balance of Payments, 1968–76
(concluded)
(In millions of SDRs)

	1968	1969	1970	1971	1972	1973	1974	1975	1976
B. Capital (excluding reserves and related items) *(concluded)*									
Monetary sectors	**—11.3**	**2.9**	**0.1**	**8.4**	**7.2**	**—3.4**	**5.6**	**2.1**	
34. Deposit money banks: long-term	—	—	—	—	—	—	—	—	
35. Deposit money banks: short-term	—11.3	2.3	—	8.6	5.6	—1.6	5.2	1.3	
36. Central institutions: long-term	—	—	—	—	—	—	—	—	
37. Central institutions: short-term	—	0.6	0.1	—0.2	1.6	—1.8	0.4	0.8	
C. Allocation of SDRs (item 38)	—	—	**5.4**	**5.1**	**5.1**	—	—	—	
D. Reserves and Related Items	**—20.4**	**—63.4**	**—50.7**	**65.2**	**—27.0**	**—18.2**	**73.4**	**39.5**	
Liabilities	—	—	—	—	—	—	**32.0**	**36.5**	
39. Use of Fund credit	—	—	—	—	—	—	32.0	36.5	
40. Other liabilities	—	—	—	—	—	—	—	—	
Assets	**—20.4**	**—63.4**	**—50.7**	**65.2**	**—27.0**	**—18.2**	**41.4**	**3.0**	
41. Monetary gold	—	—	—	—	—	—	—	—	
42. SDRs	—	—	—5.8	—6.1	—5.1	—	15.2	—1.9	
43. Reserve position in the Fund	—	—	—7.9	—	—	—0.3	12.3	—	
44. Foreign exchange and other claims	—20.4	—63.4	—37.0	71.3	—21.9	—17.9	13.9	4.9	
E. Net Errors and Omissions (item 45)	**25.2**	**11.3**	**5.0**	**—10.7**	**—7.4**	**5.8**	**—4.4**	**—5.2**	

Source: International Monetary Fund, *Balance of Payments Yearbook*, Vol. 28 (Washington, 1977), p. 336.

TABLE 3. Kenya: Analytic Presentation of the Balance of Payments, 1969–76
(In millions of SDRs)

	Code	1969	1970	1971	1972	1973	1974	1975	1976
A. Goods, Services, and Unrequited Transfers	1 . . C Z	**—8.1**	**—49.0**	**—111.4**	**—62.7**	**—105.7**	**—256.0**	**—181.6**	
Merchandise: exports f.o.b.	1 A . A Z	253.3	285.5	292.8	310.8	394.2	483.1	471.4	
To Tanzania and Uganda	1 A 1 A Y	*80.6*	*88.1*	*94.7*	*84.6*	*94.2*	*109.0*	*102.7*	
To other countries									
Coffee	1 A 1 A Q	*47.1*	*62.3*	*54.5*	*63.9*	*85.7*	*89.5*	*78.2*	
Tea	1 A 1 A P	*31.6*	*35.6*	*33.2*	*42.4*	*40.7*	*46.3*	*50.9*	
Other (including adjustments)	1 A . A Y	*94.0*	*99.5*	*110.4*	*119.9*	*173.6*	*238.3*	*239.6*	
Merchandise: imports f.o.b.	1 A . B Z	—295.8	—371.8	—477.2	—418.4	—457.0	—746.6	—670.6	
Trade balance	1 A . C Z	**—42.5**	**—86.3**	**—184.4**	**—107.6**	**—62.8**	**—263.5**	**—199.2**	
Services: credit	1 S . A Z	202.4	224.5	238.1	227.5	203.7	326.5	345.6	
Transportation and merchandise insurance	1 C . A Y	*67.0*	*73.0*	*79.7*	*74.5*	*78.9*	*187.0*	*187.1*	
Travel	1 D . A Z	*46.7*	*51.7*	*66.7*	*70.4*	*58.2*	*62.9*	*76.5*	
Government services	1 I . A Z	*32.2*	*34.8*	*36.9*	*15.0*	*12.2*	*18.2*	*17.3*	
Other services	1 M . A Y	*56.5*	*65.0*	*54.8*	*67.6*	*54.4*	*58.4*	*64.7*	
Services: debit	1 S . B Z	—190.7	—212.8	—223.2	—217.7	—271.7	—345.1	—353.8	
Transportation and merchandise insurance	1 C . B Y	*—59.3*	*—71.5*	*—84.1*	*—76.7*	*—85.5*	*—151.4*	*—145.6*	
Investment income	1 N . B Z	*—61.3*	*—70.1*	*—58.9*	*—64.7*	*—108.1*	*—115.9*	*—128.3*	
Government services	1 I . B Z	*—28.0*	*—30.2*	*—34.1*	*—29.7*	*—24.9*	*—24.9*	*—23.6*	
Other services	1 M . B Y	*—42.1*	*—41.0*	*—46.1*	*—46.6*	*—53.2*	*—52.9*	*—56.3*	
Total (goods and services)	1 . 1 C Z	**—30.8**	**—74.6**	**—169.5**	**—97.8**	**—130.8**	**—282.1**	**—207.4**	
Private unrequited transfers	1 K . C Z	—0.1	—1.8	—3.1	8.2	3.2	—1.6	0.7	
Total (excluding government unrequited transfers)	1 . 2 C Z	**—30.9**	**—76.4**	**—172.6**	**—89.6**	**—127.6**	**—283.7**	**—206.7**	

TABLE 3. Kenya: Analytic Presentation of the Balance of Payments, 1969–76
(concluded)
(In millions of SDRs)

	Code	1969	1970	1971	1972	1973	1974	1975	1976
A. Goods, Services, and Unrequited Transfers *(concluded)*									
Government unrequited transfers:									
credit	1 H 8 AW	30.1	33.6	67.5	33.6	27.5	33.5	30.4	
Grants and technical assistance from									
U.K. Government	1 H 8 A Y	*23.2*	*24.8*	*50.8*	*17.5*	*10.8*	*12.7*	*9.3*	
Others	1 H 8 A X	*6.9*	*8.8*	*16.7*	*16.1*	*16.7*	*20.8*	*21.1*	
Government unrequited transfers:									
debit	1 H . B Z	—7.3	—6.2	—6.3	—6.7	—5.6	—5.8	—5.3	
B. Long-Term Capital, excluding									
Groups D and F	1 W 1 X Z	53.2	**79.3**	**43.1**	**79.0**	**108.8**	**155.5**	**114.7**	
Direct investment	3 Z . X Z	15.5	13.8	12.4	—	—	—	36.9	
Other private	8 Z 1 X Z	21.0	42.6	40.7	39.9	75.0	114.6	11.3	
General government	7 Z 1 X Z	16.7	22.9	—10.0	39.1	33.8	40.9	66.5	
Long-term loans received	7 P . X Q	*20.6*	*24.8*	*24.1*	*41.3*	*36.7*	*28.6*	*52.5*	
Other	7 Z 1 X Y	*—3.9*	*—1.9*	*—34.1*	*—2.2*	*—2.9*	*12.3*	*14.0*	
Total, A plus B	1 . B X Z	**45.1**	**30.3**	**—68.3**	**16.3**	**3.1**	**—100.5**	**—66.9**	
C. Short-Term Capital, excluding									
Groups D and F	1 W 2 X Z	**18.3**	**15.0**	**—2.0**	**5.6**	**15.1**	**27.1**	**23.1**	
Deposit money banks	5 Z 2 X Z	2.3	—	8.6	5.6	—1.6	5.2	1.3	
Liabilities	5 Y 2 X Z	*2.1*	*3.2*	*5.4*	*0.4*	*10.9*	*14.8*	*8.9*	
Assets	5 L 2 X Z	*0.2*	*—3.2*	*3.2*	*5.2*	*—12.5*	*—9.6*	*—7.6*	
Other private	8 Z 2 X Z	3.9	7.7	0.3	5.8	12.7	25.9	26.2	

General government	7Z2XZ	0.2	2.2	—	—	—	—	—
Central monetary institutions	4Z2XZ	0.6	0.1	–0.2	1.6	–1.8	0.4	0.8
Net errors and omissions	9A.XZ	11.3	5.0	–10.7	–7.4	5.8	–4.4	–5.2
Total, A through C	1.CXZ	**63.4**	**45.3**	**–70.3**	**21.9**	**18.2**	**–73.4**	**–43.8**
D. Exceptional Financing	1WZXZ	—	—	—	—	—	—	4.3
Grants to finance general imports	1H8AQ	—	—	—	—	—	—	4.3
Grants from Subsidy Account	1H8AV	—	—	—	—	—	—	—
Total, A through D	1.DXZ	**63.4**	**45.3**	**–70.3**	**21.9**	**18.2**	**–73.4**	**–39.5**
E. Counterpart Items	9B.XZ	—	**5.4**	**5.1**	**5.1**	—	—	—
Monetization/demonetization of gold	9B3XZ	—	—	—	—	—	—	—
Allocation of SDRs	9B1XZ	—	5.4	5.1	5.1	—	—	—
Total, A through E	1.EXZ	**63.4**	**50.7**	**–65.2**	**27.0**	**18.2**	**–73.4**	**–39.5**
F. Reserves and Related Items	2Z.XZ	**–63.4**	**–50.7**	**65.2**	**–27.0**	**–18.2**	**73.4**	**39.5**
Use of Fund credit	2M.XZ	—	—	—	—	—	32.0	36.5
Other liabilities	2Q.XZ	—	—	—	—	—	—	—
Monetary gold	2A.XZ	—	—	—	—	—	—	—
SDRs	2B.XZ	—	–5.8	–6.1	–5.1	—	15.2	–1.9
Reserve position in the Fund	2C.XZ	—	–7.9	—	—	–0.3	12.3	—
Foreign exchange and other claims	2F.XZ	–63.4	–37.0	71.3	–21.9	–17.9	13.9	4.9

Source: International Monetary Fund, *Balance of Payments Yearbook,* Vol. 28 (Washington, 1977), p. 335.

Chapter 6

WORKSHOP 4

Flow of Funds

The purpose of this workshop is to show how income and financial transactions undertaken in a modern economy, divided into economic sectors according to type of activity or pattern of behavior, can be organized and summarized conveniently in a set of interrelated accounts. The usefulness of setting up a flow-of-funds system lies in the fact that it describes the financing of the various sectors of the economy and the categories of market instruments used in financial transactions. Such a system brings out explicitly the important macroeconomic accounting identities that aid in the formulation of behavioral hypotheses; and it helps in the design and control of development plans, as well as in the design and checking of consistency of short-run financial programs.

The workshop consists of two sections. In the first section, the basic structure and the analytical uses of the flow-of-funds accounts are briefly explained, and there follows a discussion of the use of data from the monetary survey, government finance statistics, and balance of payments statistics in the construction of the flow-of-funds accounts. An exercise involving the construction of current transactions accounts and balance sheets of a hypothetical economy is also part of this section. The second section deals with the construction of an elementary summary of a flow-of-funds account for Kenya on the basis of 1976 data from various official sources. This section also includes a number of issues for discussion.

FLOW-OF-FUNDS ACCOUNTS

Basic Structure and Analytical Uses

For convenient presentation of flow-of-funds accounts, the economy of a country may be divided into five sectors: households (PS_H), private business firms (PS_C), the government sector (GS), the banking sector (B), and the foreign sector (FS). Each sector is engaged in income and expenditure, as well as financial, transactions. Thus, from the viewpoint of flow of funds, the statement of the transaction account of a sector comprises two parts. The first part registers the sources of funds, which consist of the receipts from the sale of goods and services currently supplied and transfers; it also records the uses of these funds, such as the purchase of goods and services. The second part registers the receipts from the sale of financial claims, or the assumption of financial liabilities and the outlays on the acquisition of financial claims, or the repayment of financial liabilities. In presenting the accounts, the banking sector is considered to be confined to financial transactions only. As a financial intermediary, it creates financial liabilities for the other sectors to hold as their financial assets by borrowing from them, and it acquires financial assets from other sectors by lending to them; its own relatively small income-expenditure transactions are included in other sectors. Typically, the five sectoral accounts resemble those in Tables 1–5, which can be consolidated in a summary account, as shown in Table 6.[1] All flows and all

[1] In Tables 1–6, each sector is assigned a subscript number corresponding to the table in which the accounts of that sector are presented. For example, Y_1 stands for the income of the household sector (shown in Table 1), S_2 denotes the saving of the business firms sector (shown in Table 2), I_3 represents the investment expenditure of the government sector (shown in Table 3), and so on. Where two subscripts are shown for income (Y), the second sub-

stock changes in the sectoral accounts are cash transactions. The accounts do not show accrual items in respect of which cash payments are due but have not yet been effected.

TABLE 1. Transactions and Changes in Balance Sheet: Household Sector (PS_H)
(In units of account)

Item	Source [1]	Use [1]
I. Incomes and Expenditures		
1. Current receipts		
Incomes	Y_1	
Transfers	TR	
2. Current expenditures		
Consumption (domestic goods)		C_1
Taxes		T_1
Imports (direct)		M_1
Current account balance		$(Y_1+TR)-(C_1+T_1+M_1)$
3. Saving (current account balance)	S_1	
4. Investment expenditure		I_1
5. Overall sector position	$S_1 - I_1$	
II. Changes in Financial Balance Sheet		
1. Claims		
Deposits at banks by PS_H		$\Delta(PS_H/B)$
Purchase of government securities by PS_H		$\Delta(PS_H/GS)$
Purchase of private securities by PS_H		$\Delta(PS_H/PS_C)$
2. Liabilities		
Net borrowing from banks by PS_H	$\Delta(B/PS_H)$	
3. Net financing [2]		

[1] See text for explanation of abbreviations.

[2] As explained earlier in this section, net financing is the difference between items II (1) and II (2); it is also equal to item I (5).

script shows the sector which receives the income and the first subscript indicates the sector from which income is received. For example, Y_{21} means income received by the household sector (subscript 1) from the business firms sector (subscript 2). In the second part of Tables 1–6, which contains the balance sheet of each sector, the symbol preceding the slash (/) represents the sector holding the asset or claim and the symbol following the slash indicates the sector incurring the liability or obligation. For example, (PS_H/B) means the claim acquired by the household sector on the banking sector.

The overall sector position, shown in Part I of the accounts, indicates a nonfinancial deficit or a nonfinancial net saving, depending on whether it is negative or positive, respectively. The amount of such deficit or net saving in a sectoral account should be equal to the amount of net financing shown in Part II of the same account. This means that a nonfinancial deficit of a sector will result in an increase in its financial liabilities or a decrease in its holdings of financial assets—and vice versa in the case of a nonfinancial saving. The composition of the holdings of financial assets or liabilities of a sector can be changed as long as the net change is equivalent to the sectoral saving or deficit.

TABLE 2. Transactions and Changes in Balance Sheet: Business Firms Sector (PS_C)
(In units of account)

Item	Source [1]	Use [1]
I. Incomes and Expenditures		
1. Current receipts from sale of goods and services	$C_1+I_1+I_2+C_3+I_3+X$	
Cost of factors of production		Y_{21}
Cost of imports		M_2
Net sales value	Y_2	
2. Current expenditure		
Taxes		T_2
Current account balance		Y_2-T_2
3. Saving (current account balance)	S_2	
4. Investment		I_2
5. Overall sector position	S_2-I_2	
II. Changes in Financial Balance Sheet		
1. Claims		
Deposits at banks by PS_C		$\Delta(PS_C/B)$
Purchase of government securities by PS_C		$\Delta(PS_C/GS)$
2. Liabilities		
Sale of PS_C securities to PS_H	$\Delta(PS_H/PS_C)$	
Net borrowing from banks by PS_C	$\Delta(B/PS_C)$	
Net borrowing from FS	CMP	
3. Net financing		

Note: $X = C_5 + I_5$.
[1] See text for explanation of abbreviations.

Since the expenditures of one sector are the incomes of others, the sum of all sectoral nonfinancial receipts (i.e., all domestic incomes, plus imports, plus all transfers received) equals the sum of all sectoral expenditures (i.e., all consumption expenditures, plus all investment expenditures and all transfers paid by both domestic and foreign sectors). It should be noted that imports are treated as outlays of domestic sectors and receipts of the foreign sector and that exports are considered as outlays of the foreign sector and receipts of domestic sectors. It follows that, for the economy as a whole, including the foreign sector, the overall position is zero, *ex post:*

$$\sum_{i=1}^{5} (S_i - I_i) = 0.$$

TABLE 3. Transactions and Changes in Balance Sheet: Government Sector *(GS)*
(In units of account)

Item	Source[1]	Use[1]
I. Incomes and Expenditures		
1. Current receipts (taxes)	T	
2. Current expenditures		
Domestic goods		C_3
Services (wages and salaries)		Y_{31}
Transfers		TR
Direct imports		M_3
Current account balance		$T-(C_3+Y_{31}+TR+M_3)$
3. Saving (current account balance)	S_3	
4. Investment expenditure		I_3
5. Overall sector position	$S_3 - I_3$	
II. Changes in Financial Balance Sheet		
1. Claims	—	—
2. Liabilities		
Sale of *GS* securities to *PS*	$\Delta(PS_H/GS)$ $\Delta(PS_C/GS)$	
Net borrowing from banks by *GS*	$\Delta(B/GS)$	
Net borrowing from *FS*	CMG	
3. Net financing		

Note: $G = C_3 + Y_{31} + TR + M_3 + I_3$
$S_3 - I_3 = T - G.$

[1] See text for explanation of abbreviations.

TABLE 4. Changes in Balance Sheet: Banking Sector (*B*)
(In units of account)

Item	Source [1]	Use [1]
I. Incomes and Expenditures	—	—
II. Changes in Financial Balance Sheet		
1. Claims		
Loans to households by *B*		$\Delta(B/PS_H)$
Loans to business firms by *B*		$\Delta(B/PS_C)$
Loans to government (net) by *B*		$\Delta(B/GS)$
Holdings of foreign assets (net) by *B*		$\Delta(B/FS)$
2. Liabilities		
Deposits by households with *B*	$\Delta(PS_H/B)$	
Deposits by business firms with *B*	$\Delta(PS_C/B)$	

Note: Change in domestic credit $(\Delta NDC) = \Delta(B/PS) + \Delta(B/GS)$.
[1] See text for explanation of abbreviations.

Given the vertical balance between total saving and total investment and the horizontal balance between payments and receipts, "each column and each row [in Table 6] constitutes one full account of the structure, and the relationships among columns, among rows, and between columns and rows express the interlocking nature of the accounting system as a whole." [2]

Because of the interlocking nature of the system, if the incomes of a sector change during an accounting period, not only that sector's expenditures or its overall position will change, but other sectors will also show corresponding changes. Furthermore, a change in the position of a sector—surplus or deficit—is related to changes in the amount and possibly in the composition of financial assets or liabilities held by the sector. Corresponding adjustments can be found in other sectors. Similarly, a linkage within the sector or between sectors can be traced if a change originates in the holding of a certain financing instrument in a sector. For example, an increase in government

[2] Board of Governors of the U.S. Federal Reserve System, *Introduction to Flow of Funds* (Washington, February 1975), p. 4.

TABLE 5. Transactions and Changes in Balance Sheet: Foreign Sector *(FS)*
(In units of account)

Item	Source [1]	Use [1]
I. Incomes and Expenditures		
1. Current receipts (imports of the domestic economy)	$M = Y_5$	
2. Current expenditures		
Exports of consumption goods		C_5
Investment income (net)		Y_{51}
Current account balance		$M - (C_5 + Y_{51})$
3. Saving (current account balance)	S_5	
4. Net investment (exports of investment goods)		I_5
5. Overall sector position [2]		$S_5 - I_5$
II. Changes in Financial Balance Sheet		
1. Claims on banks		$\Delta(FS/B)$
2. Claims on *PS*		CMP
3. Claims on *GS*		CMG
4. Net financing		

Note: $C_5 + I_5 = X$

$S_5 - I_5 = M - (X + Y_{51})$.

[1] See text for explanation of abbreviations.

[2] As explained earlier in this section, the overall surplus of the foreign sector is treated as use while that of the domestic sectors (Tables 1 to 3) is treated as source, since the overall position for the economy as a whole (including the foreign sector) is zero.

investment I_3 may be financed by an increase in net borrowing from the banking sector $\Delta(B/GS)$, which may decrease the availability of bank loans to business firms $\Delta(B/PS_C)$, given the total amount of domestic credit of the banking sector. The decrease in $\Delta(B/PS_C)$ may then lead to a decrease in business investment I_2. The flow-of-funds system itself does not indicate the cause and effect of the above adjustments. However, behavioral hypotheses can be investigated within the framework of this accounting system, and different adjustment patterns have different implications for policies.

The equality between the nonfinancial deficit or the nonfinancial net saving, as the case may be, and net financing for each sector, as mentioned above, can be expressed by the following identities:

$$I_1 - S_1 = \Delta(B/PS_H) - \Delta(PS_H/B) - \Delta(PS_H/GS) - \Delta(PS_H/PS_C) \quad (1)$$

$$I_2 - S_2 = \Delta(PS_H/PS_C) + \Delta(B/PS_C) - \Delta(PS_C/B) - \Delta(PS_C/GS) + \Delta(FS/PS_C) \quad (2)$$

$$I_3 - S_3 = \Delta(PS_H/GS) + \Delta(PS_C/GS) + \Delta(B/GS) + \Delta(FS/GS) \quad (3)$$

$$\Delta(PS_H/B) + \Delta(PS_C/B) = \Delta(B/PS_H) + \Delta(B/PS_C) + \Delta(B/GS) + \Delta(B/FS) \quad (4)$$

$$I_5 - S_5 = \Delta(FS/B) - \Delta(FS/PS_C) - \Delta(FS/GS) \quad (5)$$

Alternatively, where PS_H and PS_C are consolidated into private sector *(PS)*, the identities can be rewritten as:

$$IP - SP = \Delta DCP + CMP - \Delta(PS/GS) - \Delta MQ \quad (6)$$

$$G - T = \Delta NDCG + \Delta(PS/GS) + CMG \quad (7)$$

$$\Delta MQ = \Delta NDC + \Delta NFA \quad (8)$$

$$\Delta NFA = X - M + CM + NFI \quad (9)$$

The new symbols are defined as follows:

CM = the flow of foreign capital into the domestic economy (net)
CMG = foreign capital movements into *GS* (net)
CMP = foreign capital movements into *PS* (net)
DCP = domestic credit to the private sector
IP = private sector investment, i.e., $I_1 + I_2$
M = imports of goods and nonfactor services
MQ = the stock of money and quasi-money (both liabilities of *B*)
NDC = domestic credit of *B*
$NDCG$ = net domestic credit of *B* to *GS*
NFA = the stock of foreign assets (net)
NFI = net factor income from abroad
SP = private sector savings, i.e., $S_1 + S_2$
X = exports of goods and nonfactor services.

Equations of this type may be included in financial models. An example is the Polak model,[3] which will be discussed in "The Polak Model: An Application" (Workshop 5). It may be argued that changes in the composition of a sector's portfolio in any period de-

[3] J. J. Polak, "Monetary Analysis of Income Formation and Payments Problems," *Staff Papers,* Vol. 6 (November 1957), pp. 1–50.

TABLE 6. Summary of Income and Flow-of-Funds Accounts [1]

Item	Sector PS_H Source	Sector PS_H Use	Sector PS_C Source	Sector PS_C Use	Sector *GS* Source	Sector *GS* Use	Sector *B* Source	Sector *B* Use	Sector *FS* Source	Sector *FS* Use	Total Source	Total Use
I. Incomes and Expenditures												
1. Receipts												
Income	Y_1		Y_2						$M($[illegible]$Y_5)$		$Y+M$	
Transfers and taxes	TR				T						TTR	
2. Current expenditure												
Consumption (domestic)		C_1				C_3				C_5		C
Imports		M_1				M_3						M_1+M_3
Transfers and taxes		T_1		T_2		TR						TTR
Wages and salaries						Y_{31}				Y_{51}		$Y_{31}+Y_{51}$
Current account balance												
3. Saving (current account balance)	S_1		S_2		S_3				S_5		S	
4. Investment expenditure		I_1		I_2		I_3				I_5		I
5. Overall position	S_1-I_1		S_2-I_2		S_3-I_3					S_5-I_5		
II. Changes in Financial Balance Sheet												
1. Liabilities or claims												
to or on *B*	$\Delta(B/PS_H)$	$\Delta(PS_H/B)$	$\Delta(B/PS_C)$	$\Delta(PS_C/B)$	$\Delta(B/GS)$					$\Delta(FS/B)$		
to or on *FS*			CMP		CMG			$\Delta(B/FS)$		CM		
to or on PS_H			$\Delta(PS_H/PS_C)$		$\Delta(PS_H/GS)$		$\Delta(PS_H/B)$	$\Delta(B/PS_H)$				
to or on PS_C		$\Delta(PS_H/PS_C)$			$\Delta(PS_C/GS)$		$\Delta(PS_C/B)$	$\Delta(B/PS_C)$				
to or on *GS*		$\Delta(PS_H/GS)$		$\Delta(PS_C/GS)$				$\Delta(B/GS)$				
2. Net financing												

Note: See text for explanation of abbreviations.

pend in part on the amount of readily available funds, which may act as a short-run constraint. It follows that expected flows of funds may influence sectoral behavior, whether financial or nonfinancial.[4]

A financial program may be conceived of as the numerical projection, for the program period, of a flow-of-funds table, which could be linked to a complete matrix of the national accounts. Given the targets of the program, nonfinancial savings or deficits of the economic sectors are first estimated, together with their financing requirements. It would then need to be determined (1) whether these two sets of estimates are consistent with each other among sectors; and (2) whether the banking sector could be induced to mobilize the available savings from the surplus sectors and transfer them, through the creation of appropriate claims, to the deficit sectors, in consistency with the targets set in the program.

Flow-of-funds accounts can also be used in the design and control of development plans. A development plan consists essentially of the control of the flow of available real resources, aiming toward investment to achieve economic growth. The information provided in the flow-of-funds accounts for successive periods of time is useful in determining feasible investment targets for the economic sectors and for the economy as a whole. The relationship between the financing needs of the economic sectors and their expenditures as indicated in the flow-of-funds accounts also suggests the possibility of using financial controls for the implementation of a development plan.

Relations with the Monetary Survey, Government Finance Statistics, and Balance of Payments Statistics

Many countries do not have a comprehensive system of flow-of-funds accounts, in part because of a lack of requisite information. In most cases, data on private sector saving, investment, and financing are so fragmented that the *PS* columns in the summary account of flow of funds are difficult to fill. Nevertheless, a part of this information gap can be closed by making use of the monetary survey, govern-

[4] A. D. Bain, "Flow of Funds Analysis: A Survey," *Economic Journal,* Vol. 83 (December 1973), pp. 1055–93, especially p. 1084.

ment finance statistics, and balance of payments statistics, which are generally available. These data are normally compiled with considerably shorter delays and at more frequent intervals than national income data. The crucial problem is that of achieving an adequate and consistent allocation of the data by sector. In order to show the intersectoral relationships as in a flow-of-funds system, changes in assets and liabilities in these accounting sources must be allocated by sector according to consistent criteria, so that flows originating in one sector and directed to another (as shown in the first sector's statement) are consistent with flows recorded in the second sector (as directed to it from the first).

The monetary survey is a consolidated statement of the banking system, i.e., the monetary authorities and deposit money banks. It does not include other financial intermediaries. In this classification, the nonbank financial intermediaries are lumped together with the private sector. Similarly, when government finance statistics are available only for the central government, municipal and local governments and public enterprises are classified with the private sector. Furthermore, in terms of data classification, there are differences between national income accounts, on the one hand, and balance of payments statistics and government finance statistics, on the other.

The sectoral position for the foreign sector $(X - M)$, which represents net lending to the rest of the world in the national income accounts, is not identical to the net balance on current account in the balance of payments.[5] Among other differences, net lending in the national income accounts classification (1) includes the net purchases of nonfinancial intangible assets, such as leases, (2) excludes earnings reinvested in direct investment enterprises, and (3) excludes shipments of commodities between a parent enterprise and its subsidiary that do not involve a change of ownership. In the balance of payments, (1) net purchases of nonfinancial intangible assets are included in the capital account, (2) the direct investors' share of rein-

[5] International Monetary Fund, *Balance of Payments Manual,* 4th edition (Washington, 1977).

vested earnings is shown as investment income and is balanced by entries in the capital account, and (3) shipments of commodities between a parent enterprise and its subsidiary without a change of ownership are included with merchandise.

Expenditures and revenues of the government in the national income accounts are not identical to those reported in the government finance statistics. A significant difference is that national income accounts adhere to an *accrual basis* of recording, reflecting production and delivery, whereas transactions in the government finance statistics are recorded on a *payments basis.* Other major differences are: (1) resources representing past or future transactions, such as consumption of fixed capital and imputed contributions to unfunded pension schemes, are excluded from the government finance statistics while they are included in the national income accounts; (2) government lending operations undertaken for public policy purposes are classified with expenditure in the government finance statistics rather than with financing (as in national accounts); and (3) banking and monetary authorities' functions performed by government are separated from government in the government finance statistics, while they are grouped with government in the national accounts.[6]

When consistent allocation by sector is made and data are classified appropriately, the monetary survey, the central government budgetary operations, and the balance of payments summary can be used in the columns for *B, GS,* and *FS* in the summary of flow-of-funds accounts (Table 6). Part of the column for *PS,* i.e., a consolidated account for PS_H and PS_C, can then be filled in, even without the national income accounts pertaining to the sector.

National Income Accounts and Flow of Funds of a Hypothetical Economy

The following statistical data on current and financial transactions are assumed for a hypothetical economy during a certain year (year *n*).

[6] International Monetary Fund, *A Manual on Government Finance Statistics: Draft* (Washington, June 1974).

1. The *household sector* spent $9,700 million on consumption and $100 million on housing. Income tax payments amounted to $2,000 million. When the financial transactions of this sector were consolidated, it was found that its currency holdings had increased by $30 million and its deposits with banks had risen by $250 million. Moreover, household holdings of market instruments had risen by $120 million, of which $70 million were in corporate stocks and the remainder were in government bonds. Borrowing from banks had increased by $100 million.

2. The *corporate sector* received $450 million from intra-sector sales of investment goods, $3,100 million from sale of goods and services to the government, and $4,250 million from exports of goods and services. On the other hand, this sector paid $11,100 million to household units for factor services and spent $4,700 million on imports; tax payments to the government amounted to $1,500 million. Its financial assets increased by $450 million ($410 million in demand deposits and $40 million in holdings of government bonds), and its financial liabilities to banks rose by $530 million.

3. The *government sector*'s net tax receipts were insufficient to cover expenditures amounting to $2,900 million on current account ($1,000 million for wages and salaries of government employees and $1,900 million for consumption goods and other services) and $1,200 million on capital goods. In view of the financing requirements, the government issued treasury bonds, which were sold to the public, and borrowed $510 million from the banking system.

4. The *foreign sector* incurred current expenditures (hypothetical economy's exports) equal to $4,000 million, whereas its receipts (hypothetical economy's imports) amounted to $4,700 million. In addition, this sector spent $250 million on investment expenditures. The credit balance that resulted from these transactions was reflected in a credit entry on the consolidated balance sheet of the hypothetical economy's banking system.

5. The balance sheet of the *banking sector,* i.e., the central bank and the commercial banks, recorded the transactions shown in Table 7.

TABLE 7. Summary Balance Sheets of the Central Bank and the Commercial Banks of the Hypothetical Economy
(In millions of U.S. dollars)

Item	End of Year $n-1$	End of Year n	Item	End of Year $n-1$	End of Year n
Summary balance sheet of the central bank					
Net international reserves			Currency issue		
(foreign exchange)	1,250	800	Currency held by banks	420	435
Credit to banks	1,030	1,300	Currency outside banks and *GS*	970	1,000
Credit to government (net)	130	640	Deposits of banks		
			Required reserve deposits	1,020	1,305
Assets	**2,410**	**2,740**	**Liabilities**	**2,410**	**2,740**
Summary balance sheets of commercial banks					
Reserve accounts	1,440	1,740	Credit from central bank	1,030	1,300
Currency in vaults	*420*	*435*	Liabilities to private sector	3,010	3,670
Deposits in central bank	*1,020*	*1,305*	PS_H	*1,010*	*1,260*
Credit to private sector	2,600	3,230	PS_C	*2,000*	*2,410*
PS_H	*600*	*700*			
PS_C	*2,000*	*2,530*			
Assets	**4,040**	**4,970**	**Liabilities**	**4,040**	**4,970**

Note: See text for explanation of abbreviations.

EXERCISES

1. *On the basis of the statistical information provided, construct account tables showing the current transactions and the balance sheet changes of each sector separately (similar to Tables 1–5).*

2. *Show how the constructed account tables can be grouped together to provide a summary of transactions of the hypothetical economic system (similar to Table 6).*

NATIONAL ACCOUNTS AND FLOW OF FUNDS OF KENYA, 1976

Basic income and financial data for Kenya for the years 1975–76 are provided in Tables 8–14. Several points should be mentioned before the flow-of-funds accounts are compiled. First, since no separate data are available for the household and corporate sectors, the transactions of these two sectors vis-à-vis the other sectors of the economy are consolidated into one sector, i.e., the private sector. The format for the current transactions account and for changes in the balance sheet of the private sector is provided in Table 16. Second, insufficient information is available regarding the income and financial transactions of the local governments, other official entities, and the nonbank financial institutions. For this reason and from a practical policymaking point of view, the government sector includes only Budgetary Central Government, while the banking sector comprises the Central Bank and the commercial banks.

Table 15 summarizes the relevant data on income-expenditure and financial transactions, as provided in Tables 8–14, for the compilation of flow-of-funds accounts for Kenya for 1976. Some adjustments have been made for the convenience of the compilation.

TABLE 8. Kenya: Selected National Accounts Data, 1975–76
(In millions of Kenya shillings)

Item	1975	1976
Resources		
GDP at factor cost in current prices	20,560	25,257
Indirect taxes and subsidies	2,783	3,325
GDP at market prices	23,343	28,581
Imports of goods and services	8,358	9,436
Total	**31,701**	**38,017**
Use of resources		
Private fixed investment	2,824	3,390
Public fixed investment	2,026	2,450
Change in stocks	−275	133
Gross investment	**4,576**	**5,973**
Private consumption	15,731	17,542
Public consumption	4,256	4,943
Total consumption	**19,987**	**22,485**
Gross domestic expenditure	24,563	28,457
Exports of goods and services	7,138	9,560
Total	**31,701**	**38,017**
National income		
GDP at factor cost	20,560	25,257
Factor incomes received from abroad	428	352
Factor incomes paid abroad	1,256	1,444
GNP at factor cost	19,732	24,165
Indirect taxes and subsidies	2,783	3,325
GNP at market prices	22,515	27,490

Source: Kenya, *Economic Survey*, 1978.

TABLE 9. Kenya: Summary of Central Government Budgetary Operations, Fiscal Years 1976 and 1977
(In millions of Kenya shillings; year ending June 30)

	Item	1976	1977
1	Current revenue	5,123	6,149
1.1	Tax	4,571	5,297
1.2	Nontax	552	852
2	Capital revenue	—	—
3	Total revenue (1 + 2)	5,123	6,149
4	Grants	201	234
4.1	Current	61	24
4.2	Capital	140	210
5	Total revenue and grants (3 + 4)	5,325	6,383
6	Current expenditure	4,904	5,580
7	Capital expenditure	1,259	1,660
8	Total expenditure (6 + 7)	6,164	7,240
9	Lending minus repayments	870	470
10	Expenditure and lending minus repayments (8 + 9)	7,034	7,710

TABLE 9. Kenya: Summary of Central Government Budgetary Operations, Fiscal Years 1976 and 1977 (concluded)
(In millions of Kenya shillings; year ending June 30)

	Item	1976	1977
11	Current account surplus or saving (without grants) (1 — 6)	219	569
12	Gross fixed capital formation	1,059	1,388
13	Gross capital formation	1,059	1,388
14	Overall deficit/surplus (5 — 10)	—1,709	—1,327
15	Financing (= 14)	1,709	1,327
15.1	Abroad	639	464
15.2	Domestic	1,070	863
15.2.1	Nonbank	670	868
15.2.2	Deposit money banks	350	684
15.2.3	Central Bank	50	—689

Sources: International Monetary Fund, *Government Finance Statistics Yearbook,* Vol. 2 (Washington, 1978), and *International Financial Statistics,* various issues; Central Bank of Kenya, *Annual Report for the Financial Year Ended 30th June, 1977.*

TABLE 10. Kenya: Expenditure and Lending Minus Repayments by Economic Type for Budgetary Central Government, Fiscal Years 1976 and 1977
(In millions of Kenya shillings; year ending June 30)

	Item	1976	1977
I	Total expenditure and lending minus repayments (II + V)	7,034	7,710
II	Total expenditure (III + IV)	6,164	7,240
III	Current expenditure	4,904	5,580
1	Expenditure on goods and services	2,230	2,965
1.1	Wages and salaries	1,295	1,379
1.2-3	Employers' contributions	18	22
1.4	Other purchases of goods and services	918	1,564
2	Interest payments	391	479
3	Subsidies and other current transfers	2,283	2,136
3.3	Transfers to other levels of National Government	1,258	1,365
3.6	Transfers abroad	20	26
IV	Capital expenditure	1,259	1,660
4	Acquisition of fixed capital assets	1,059	1,388
6	Purchases of land and intangible assets	174	272
7	Capital transfers	26	—
7.1	Domestic	26	—
7.1.1	To other levels of National Government	26	—
V	Total lending minus repayments	870	470
8	Domestic	870	470
8.1	To other levels of Government	434	161

Sources: International Monetary Fund, *Government Finance Statistics Yearbook,* Vol. 2 (Washington, 1978); Kenya, *Appropriation Accounts, Other Public Accounts and the Accounts of the Funds for the Year 1975/76* and *1976/77.*

TABLE 11. Kenya: Monetary Survey, December 1974–June 1977
(In millions of Kenya shillings)

Item	1974	1975		1976		1977
	December	*June*	*December*	*June*	*December*	*June*
Net foreign assets	**969**	**854**	**581**	**1,189**	**1,459**	**3,776**
Central Bank[1]	1,061	933	681	1,192	1,449	3,717
Government[2]	4	—	8	9	16	13
Commercial banks	–96	–79	–108	–12	–6	46
Domestic credit	**4,966**	**5,297**	**6,414**	**6,563**	**7,475**	**7,798**
Government (net)	930	1,100	1,767	1,500	1,898	1,495
Claims	*1,036*	*1,183*	*1,789*	*2,279*	*2,043*	*2,787*
Deposits	*106*	*83*	*22*	*779*	*145*	*1,292*
Nongovernment	4,036	4,197	4,647	5,063	5,577	6,303
Official entities	*223*	*221*	*303*	*250*	*215*	*205*
Private sector[3]	*3,813*	*3,976*	*4,344*	*4,813*	*5,362*	*6,098*
Other items (net)	**–18**	**–59**	**180**	**321**	**479**	**622**
Money and quasi-money	**5,819**	**6,077**	**6,814**	**7,432**	**8,454**	**10,952**
Money	4,016	4,052	4,540	4,966	5,674	7,496
Currency outside banks	*1,086*	*1,022*	*1,234*	*1,194*	*1,625*	*1,765*
Demand deposits[4]	*2,930*	*3,030*	*3,306*	*3,772*	*4,049*	*5,731*
Quasi-money	1,803	2,025	2,274	2,466	2,780	3,456
SDR allocations	**134**	**134**	**—**[5]	**—**	**—**	**—**

Sources: Central Bank of Kenya, *Annual Report for the Financial Year Ended 30th June, 1977;* International Monetary Fund, *International Financial Statistics,* July 1978.

1 Foreign liabilities include use of Fund credit.

2 Foreign exchange holdings.

3 Includes Cereals and Sugar Finance Corporation and Agricultural Finance Corporation.

4 Adjusted for "uncleared effects."

5 The domestic counterpart of Kenya's SDR allocation was transferred in September 1975 to treasury deposits with the Central Bank of Kenya.

TABLE 12. Kenya: Summary Accounts of the Monetary Authorities, December 1974–June 1977

(In millions of Kenya shillings)

Item	1974	1975		1976		1977
	December	*June*	*December*	*June*	*December*	*June*
Net foreign assets	**1,065**	**933**	**689**	**1,201**	**1,465**	**3,730**
Foreign assets	1,354	1,380	1,439	1,867	2,309	4,477
Foreign exchange [1]	*1,338*	*1,340*	*1,403*	*1,862*	*2,282*	*4,432*
SDRs	*16*	*40*	*36*	*5*	*27*	*45*
Reserve position in the Fund	—	—	—	—	—	—
Foreign liabilities [2]	289	447	750	666	844	747
Domestic credit	**726**	**872**	**1,205**	**678**	**787**	**—53**
Government (net)	490	586	1,171	636	778	—53
Claims	526	575	1,112	1,295	851	1,100
Advances	*200*	*339*	*543*	*288*	*200*	*200*
Treasury bills	*148*	*87*	*284*	*164*	*20*	—
Government securities	*177*	*149*	*150*	*709*	*497*	*741*
SDR allocations used by Government	—	—	*134*	*134*	*134*	*134*
Trust Fund loans	—	—	—	—	—	*25*
Deposits	36	—11	—59	659	73	1,153
Official entities	—	—	—	—	—	—
Commercial banks	236	286	34	42	9	—
Other items (net) [3]	**—132**	**138**	**281**	**145**	**251**	**287**
Reserve money	**1,789**	**1,533**	**1,613**	**1,734**	**2,001**	**3,390**
Currency outside banks	1,086	1,022	1,234	1,194	1,625	1,765
Currency in commercial banks	253	161	174	189	205	217
Banks' deposits	381	313	131	311	133	1,268
Official entities' deposits	69	37	74	40	38	139
SDR allocations	**134**	**134**	—[4]	—	—	—

Sources: Central Bank of Kenya, *Annual Report for the Financial Year Ended 30th June, 1977;* International Monetary Fund, *International Financial Statistics*, July 1978.

[1] Includes balances with banks abroad and foreign securities.

[2] Includes use of Fund credit.

[3] Includes revaluation account, uncleared effects, and other unclassified assets and liabilities.

[4] The domestic counterpart of Kenya's SDR allocation was transferred in September 1975 to treasury deposits with the Central Bank of Kenya.

TABLE 13. Kenya: Summary Accounts of the Commercial Banks, December 1974–June 1977
(In millions of Kenya shillings)

Item	1974	1975		1976		1977
	December	*June*	*December*	*June*	*December*	*June*
Net foreign assets	**—96**	**—79**	**—108**	**—12**	**—6**	**46**
Foreign assets	304	268	372	352	407	400
Foreign liabilities	400	347	480	364	413	354
Reserves	**514**	**452**	**298**	**475**	**313**	**1,458**
Currency	253	161	174	189	205	217
Deposits with Central Bank	261	291	124	285	108	1,240
Domestic credit	**4,476**	**4,711**	**5,243**	**5,927**	**6,697**	**7,851**
Government (net)	440	514	596	864	1,120	1,548
Claims	510	608	677	984	1,192	1,687
Advances	—	*6*	*4*	*3*	*17*	*3*
Treasury bills	*326*	*424*	*498*	*815*	*1,015*	*1,499*
Government securities	*184*	*177*	*174*	*166*	*159*	*185*
Deposits	70	94	81	120	72	139
Nongovernment	4,036	4,197	4,647	5,063	5,577	6,303
Official entities	*223*	*221*	*303*	*250*	*215*	*205*
Private sector	*3,813*	*3,976*	*4,344*	*4,813*	*5,362*	*6,098*
Other items (net)	**—44**	**—33**	**—109**	**12**	**145**	**135**
Liabilities to Central Bank	**254**	**29**	**19**	**14**	**—**	**—**
Money and quasi-money	**4,684**	**5,088**	**5,523**	**6,364**	**6,859**	**9,220**
Demand deposits	2,881	3,063	3,249	3,898	4,079	5,764
Time and savings deposits	1,803	2,025	2,274	2,466	2,780	3,456

Sources: Central Bank of Kenya, *Annual Report for the Financial Year Ended 30th June, 1977;* International Monetary Fund, *International Financial Statistics,* July 1978.

TABLE 14. Kenya: Balance of Payments Summary, 1976
(In millions of Kenya shillings)

Item	1976		
	Source	*Use*	*Net Source*
Current account	**10,552**	**11,250**	**—698**
Trade balance	6,224	8,158	—1,934
Imports, c.i.f.		*8,158*	*—8,158*
Exports, f.o.b.	*6,224*		*6,224*
Services	3,688	2,722	966
Freight and insurance	*550*	*92*	*458*
Other transportation	*1,516*	*558*	*958*
Foreign travel	*858*	*260*	*598*
International investment income	*310*	*1,262*	*—952*
Government transactions, n.e.s.	*170*	*232*	*—62*
Other services	*284*	*318*	*—34*
Transfers	640	370	270
Private	*144*	*186*	*—42*
Government	*496*	*184*	*312*
Capital account	**1,677**	**237**	**1,440**
Private long-term	512	50	462
Government long-term	702	—8	710
Government corporations long-term	188	86	102
Short-term	275	109	166
Government	—	*12*	*—12*
Government corporations	*6*	*8*	*—2*
Commercial banks	*—35*	*67*	*—102*
Private	*304*	*22*	*282*
Errors and omissions	**—**	**—**	**34**
Overall balance	**—**	**—**	**776**
Financing (increase in assets)	**158**	**934**	**—776**
Gross official reserves	—	870	—870
Use of Fund credit	158	—	158
Other liabilities[1]	—	64	—64

Sources: For the current account and the capital account (except commercial banks), the data are taken from Kenya, *Economic Survey,* 1978. The data for commercial banks and financing are taken from International Monetary Fund, *International Financial Statistics,* July 1978, in order to ensure consistency with the monetary accounts for purposes of financial programming (see Workshop 9: Financial Programming). The adjustment for the resulting discrepancy is contained in the residual item, Errors and omissions.

Note: n.e.s. = not elsewhere specified.

[1] Includes foreign banks' deposits with the Central Bank of Kenya and International Monetary Fund deposits.

TABLE 15. Kenya: Income-Expenditure and Financial Transactions, 1976
(In millions of Kenya shillings; at current prices)

Income-Expenditure Transactions		
Private sector	*Amount*	*Sources*[1]
Imports of goods and nonfactor services	9,436	(8 and 14)
Payments (abroad) for factor services	1,444	(14)
Tax payments	4,934	(9)
Other payments to Government	702	(9)
Transfer payments abroad	347	(10 and 14)
Receipts from the sale of goods and services to Government	4,257	(10)
Exports of goods and nonfactor services	9,560	(8 and 14)
Transfer receipts		
From the Government	2,187	(10)
From abroad	422	(9 and 14)
Receipts from factor services (abroad)	352	(14)
Other income	4,749	(8 and 9)
Intrasector investment (including variation in stocks)	4,749	(8 and 9)
Government sector		
Consumption of goods and services	1,241	(10)
Payments for wages and salaries	1,792	(10)
Government investment	1,224	(9 and 10)
Transfer payments		
To private sector	2,187	(10)
Abroad	23	(10)
Tax revenue	4,934	(9)
Transfer receipts from abroad	218	(9)
Other income	702	(9)
Foreign sector		
Payments for goods and nonfactor services (exports of the domestic economy)	9,560	(8 and 14)
Transfer payments	640	(14)
Payments for factor services	352	(14)
Receipts from the sale of goods and services (imports of the domestic economy)	9,436	(8 and 14)
Transfer receipts	370	(14)
Receipts from factor services	1,444	(14)
Financial Transactions[2]		
Banking sector		
Credit to private sector	930	(11)
Credit to government sector	254	(11)
Foreign assets	905	(12 and 13)
Currency in circulation (outside banks)	391	(11)
Treasury deposits with the banking sector	123	(11)
Demand deposits of the private sector	743	(11)
Time and savings deposits of the private sector	506	(11)
Other liabilities to private sector	299	(11)
Foreign liabilities	27	(12 and 13)

See footnotes at end of table.

TABLE 15. Kenya: Income-Expenditure and Financial Transactions, 1976 (concluded)
(In millions of Kenya shillings; at current prices)

Financial Transactions[2] *(concluded)*		
Other sectors	*Amount*	*Sources*[1]
Private sector's holdings of government securities increased by	600	(9, 11, 14)
Outstanding external debt of Government increased by	552	(9)
Direct foreign investment in the private sector increased by	1,024	(9 and 14)
Government loans to the private sector increased by	670	(9)

[1] Numbers in parentheses refer to Tables 8–14.
[2] These data represent *changes* in assets and liabilities of the private, government, and foreign sectors during 1976.

TABLE 16. Kenya: Transactions and Changes in Balance Sheet of the Private Sector (PS), 1976
(In millions of Kenya shillings)

Item	Source	Use
I. Incomes and Expenditures		
1. Current receipts		
Sales to Government		
Exports		
Factor services		
Other income		
Transfers		
2. Current expenditures		
Imports		
Factor services		
Taxes		
Other payments		
Transfers		
Current account balance		
3. Saving (current account balance)		
4. Investment expenditure		
5. Overall sector position		
II. Changes in Financial Balance Sheet		
1. Claims		
Deposits at banks		
Purchase of government securities		
2. Liabilities		
Loans from the Government		
Borrowing from banks		
Borrowing from foreign sector		
Net financing		

TABLE 17. Kenya: Summary of Income and Flow-of-Funds Accounts, 1976

(In millions of Kenya shillings)

Item	Sector *PS* Source	Sector *PS* Use	Sector *GS* Source	Sector *GS* Use	Sector *B* Source	Sector *B* Use	Sector *FS* Source	Sector *FS* Use	Total Source	Total Use
I. Incomes and Expenditures										
1. Receipts										
Exports										
Transfers										
Taxes										
Other income										
2. Current expenditure										
Consumption										
Imports										
Transfers										
Taxes										
Other										
Current account balance										
3. Saving										
4. Investment expenditure										
5. Overall position										
II. Changes in Financial Balance Sheet										
1. Liabilities (claims)										
to (on) *B*										
to (on) *FS*										
to (on) *PS*										
to (on) *GS*										
2. Net financing										

Note: See text for explanation of abbreviations.

EXERCISES

1. *On the basis of Table 15, construct the current transactions account and compute the saving or dissaving of each sector. The format of Part I of Tables 3, 5, and 16 will facilitate this work. Determine the overall balance or position of each sector.*
2. *Using the financial data in Table 15, show how each sector financed its deficit or disposed of its surplus, i.e., construct the balance sheet of each sector. The format of Part II of Tables 3, 5, and 16 can be used for this purpose. Note that the financial transactions data are given as* changes *in assets and liabilities between the end of 1975 and the end of 1976.*
3. *Construct the balance sheet of the banking sector, using Table 4.*
4. *Summarize the current accounts and balance sheets of all sectors in Table 17. Note that, apart from the consolidation of the household and corporate sectors into one sector, Table 17 is similar in structure to Table 6.*

ISSUES FOR DISCUSSION

1. *The nonbank financial institutions are excluded from the account for the banking/financial sector. What are the implications of this exclusion?*
2. *In what sense can the private sector be a borrower and a lender at the same time? Discuss the changes in the financial assets and liabilities of the private sector in Kenya in 1976.*
3. *Unlike the other sectors of the economy, the claims of the banking sector are always equal to its liabilities, as a consequence of the assumption that this sector is not involved in income-expenditure transactions. However, it is sometimes argued that an active banking sector should, besides stimulating household units to save and corporate units to invest, undertake saving on its own as an economic unit. Is this distinction valid?*

4. *From an analytical point of view, what are the advantages or disadvantages of the summary of flow-of-funds accounts in comparison with accounts provided in other sources (namely, national income accounts, summary of central government finance, monetary survey, and balance of payments summary)? What light do the tables for the individual sectors shed on the allocation of economic resources among the various sectors in Kenya?*

5. *Assume that the summary of income and flow-of-funds accounts (in the form shown in Table 17) is the only data available to the Kenyan authorities for a given year. What types of policy issues can be discussed on the basis of this table? What policy instruments can be identified from the table? Can the effects of the use of these instruments be traced in the table? Would your answer change if these summary accounts could be compiled for a series of years?*

6. *In what way can the summary of income and flow-of-funds accounts be used for the construction of a macroeconomic model? What differences would arise between a model based on a flow-of-funds scheme and one based on market equilibria?*

WORKSHOP 5

The Polak Model: An Application

Since the early 1950s, economists and policymakers have been increasingly preoccupied with the problems of inflation and balance of payments disequilibria. Their preoccupation has led to new approaches to monetary analysis.[1] In this period, there has been a gradual evolution of the so-called monetary approach to the balance of payments, the third major approach; the two best-known earlier approaches are the elasticity (neoclassical) approach and the income absorption (neo-Keynesian) approach.[2]

[1] M. W. Holtrop, "Method of Monetary Analysis Used by De Nederlandsche Bank," *Staff Papers*, Vol. 5 (February 1957), pp. 303–15; Paolo Baffi, "Monetary Analysis in Italy," *Staff Papers*, Vol. 5 (February 1957), pp. 316–22; Ralph A. Young, "Federal Reserve Flow-of-Funds Accounts," *Staff Papers*, Vol. 5 (February 1957), pp. 323–41; Earl Hicks, Graeme S. Dorrance, and Gerard R. Aubanel, "Monetary Analyses," *Staff Papers*, Vol. 5 (February 1957), pp. 342–433; and Harold M. Knight, "A Monetary Budget," *Staff Papers*, Vol. 7 (October 1959), pp. 210–23.

[2] Of several attempted reconciliations of the elasticity and absorption approaches, particular mention may be made of S. C. Tsiang, "The Role of Money in Trade Balance Stability: Synthesis of the Elasticity and Absorption Approaches," *American Economic Review*, Vol. 51 (December 1961), pp. 912–36.

It has often been pointed out that each of the three approaches could in principle produce the right answers if it were correctly applied, that is to say, if proper allowance were made for all the repercussions throughout the economy of the change whose effect is being analyzed. It has, however, proved difficult in practice to set forth a suitable framework for use with either the elasticities approach or the income-absorption approach within which the requisite information would be marshaled in a comprehensive and consistent manner. For applied research and background work for policy discussion on balance of payments problems, the monetary approach suggested itself, therefore, as apparently simpler and more manageable than the other approaches. It is based on the postulates of a stable demand function for money and of a stable process through which the money supply is being generated. The demand for money, it is argued, depends on a relatively small number of economic factors, and the effects of economic changes on the demand for money are therefore easy to assess because they can operate only through one or several of these few factors. A similar argument can be made with respect to the determination of the supply of money. By focusing directly on the relevant monetary aggregates, this approach eliminates the intractable problems associated with the estimation of numerous elasticities of international transactions and of the parameters describing their interdependence, which are inherent in other approaches.

The apparent simplicity of the monetary approach to the balance of payments is, however, somewhat deceptive. Even though for many purposes the demand for money can be conveniently expressed as a function of a small number of variables, it is still just as much the resultant of all the influences that come to bear on the economy as are national income and national expenditure. Again, domestic credit creation, which is often taken as being determined exogenously, may in fact be systematically influenced by factors determining the demand for money or by some of the events whose monetary effects are being examined. These considerations do not invalidate the monetary approach; they merely draw attention to the possibility that it will be seen, on further examination, to be not quite so superior in terms of simplicity of application as had first been thought.[3]

An early exposition of the monetary approach to the balance of payments is contained in a simple, highly aggregative model for-

---

[3] International Monetary Fund, *The Monetary Approach to the Balance of Payments* (Washington, 1977), pp. 3–4.

mulated by J. J. Polak, former Economic Counsellor of the International Monetary Fund.[4] A considerable volume of literature has since been written on the subject.[5]

The Polak model focuses on the relationship between credit expansion and change in foreign assets. In broad terms, the Polak model can be described as a system of four interdependent endogenous variables—namely, the stock of money *(MO)*, nominal income *(Y)*, imports *(M)*, and change in net foreign assets *(ΔNFA)*—whose values change if there is a change in value of at least one of the following exogenous variables: exports *(X)*, capital movements *(CM)*, and change in net domestic credit *(ΔNDC)*. Of the exogenous variables, *ΔNDC* is considered as a policy variable—that is, a variable that can be controlled by the authorities.

In this model, the interest rate plays no role, therefore making the model less complicated and more realistically applicable to developing countries where, because of scarcity of easily marketable financial assets, variations in interest rates do not play a significant role.

[4] The model was originally presented in J. J. Polak, "Monetary Analysis of Income Formation and Payments Problems," *Staff Papers,* Vol. 6 (November 1957), pp. 1–50. It was subsequently modified and applied to several countries, and the results were reported in J. J. Polak and Lorette Boissonneault, "Monetary Analysis of Income and Imports and Its Statistical Application," *Staff Papers,* Vol. 7 (April 1960), pp. 349–415. A more recent version of the model is contained in J. J. Polak and Victor Argy, "Credit Policy and the Balance of Payments," *Staff Papers,* Vol. 18 (March 1971), pp. 1–24. All three of the articles cited here appear in *The Monetary Approach to the Balance of Payments* (see footnote 3).

[5] In addition to the writings cited in the preceding footnotes, the following may be of interest: Jacob A. Frenkel and Harry G. Johnson (eds.), *The Monetary Approach to the Balance of Payments* (London: Allen and Unwin; and University of Toronto Press, 1976); Michael Mussa, "A Monetary Approach to Balance of Payments Analysis," *Journal of Money, Credit and Banking,* Vol. 6 (August 1974), pp. 333–51; Arthur B. Laffer, "Monetary Policy and the Balance of Payments," *Journal of Money, Credit and Banking,* Vol. 4, Part I (February 1972), pp. 13–22; and Robert A. Mundell, *Monetary Theory: Inflation, Interest and Growth in the World Economy* (Pacific Palisades, California: Goodyear Publishing Company, 1971).

Also, because of its simplicity, the few data needed for the application of the model are readily available in most developing countries. Of particular significance is the fact that the Polak model has been estimated for a large number of developing countries with reasonably good results.[6]

In this workshop the parameters of the Polak model are estimated by using statistical data for Kenya. Once the estimates have been made, the model is used to show how to project imports as well as how to find the change in net domestic credit compatible with a preassigned target for the change in net foreign assets.

THE MODEL

The relationships of the Polak model are specified as follows:

$$M_t = mY_t, \; 0 < m < 1 \qquad (1)$$

$$Y_t = \frac{1}{k} MO_t, \; 0 < k < 1 \qquad (2)$$

$$MO_t = \Delta NFA_t + \Delta NDC_t + MO_{t-1} \qquad (3)$$

$$\Delta NFA_t = X_t + CM_t - M_t \qquad (4)$$

The first relation is a behavioral equation, indicating that nominal imports in period t are a constant fraction m of the nominal income of the same period; the coefficient m is called the (average and marginal) propensity to import. Equation (2) implies a constant proportional relationship between nominal income and money stock;[7] the coefficient $1/k$ is the (average and marginal) income velocity of money (Y_t/MO_t). This implies that the increase in income will be

[6] Reference may be made to the following studies: J. Marcus Fleming and Lorette Boissonneault, "Money Supply and Imports," *Staff Papers,* Vol. 8 (May 1961), pp. 227–40; Lorette Boissonneault and Joseph O. Adekunle, "Monetary Analysis of Imports and Income: Further Investigations" (unpublished paper, December 1968); and S. N. Kimaro, "The Polak Model: Empirical Evidence from Selected African Countries," *East African Economic Review,* Vol. 7 (December 1975), pp. 53–107.

[7] Nominal income is taken over a given period, while money stock corresponds to the end of that period.

equal to the increase in the quantity of money times the income velocity of money. Relationships (3) and (4) are definitional equations (identities). The former states that money in this period (MO_t) is equal to money at the end of the previous period (MO_{t-1}) plus the change in net foreign assets (ΔNFA_t) and in net domestic credit of the banking system (ΔNDC_t) in this period. The latter defines the change in the net foreign assets of the banking system as being equal to the overall balance of payments surplus or deficit.

The definition of money in the model can be taken either in the broad sense (currency + demand deposits + quasi-money) or in the narrow sense (currency + demand deposits). Adoption of the broad definition implies that MO_t in equation (3) includes quasi-money and that the income velocity of money $1/k$ is interpreted accordingly.[8]

After combining the two definitional equations to yield the following result:

$$\Delta MO_t = X_t + CM_t - M_t + \Delta NDC_t$$

and after defining

$$A_t = X_t + CM_t + \Delta NDC_t$$

(that is, the sum of the three exogenous variables, including the policy variable), the model may be written as:

$$M_t = mY_t,\ 0 < m < 1 \qquad (1)'$$

$$Y_t = \frac{1}{k}\ MO_t,\ 0 < k < 1 \qquad (2)'$$

$$MO_t = A_t - M_t + MO_{t-1} \qquad (3)'$$

The effects on the endogenous variables M, Y, and MO of a change in one or more exogenous variables can be traced in the above equations. Given the constancy of the parameters m and k, a change in A will affect M through changes in MO and Y. But then a change

---

[8] The original Polak model, as well as the subsequent version, follows the second approach, which implies that quasi-money is exogenous. When choosing between the two definitions of money, the main consideration is whether the assumption of constant income velocity of money is more realistic following the first or the second approach.

in M will inversely affect MO and Y, thus generating a second round of effects, this time in the opposite direction, and so on. The net effects can be computed by taking into account all rounds—that is, by obtaining the reduced form of the model (each endogenous variable expressed in terms of exogenous and lagged endogenous variables).

The model could be used for various purposes if there were numerical values (estimates) of the parameters m and k and if the level of the exogenous variables was known or could be estimated. For instance, imports might be projected in the future; the impact on any endogenous variable of a given increase in net domestic credit could be determined, as well as values for the impact, truncated, and overall (or equilibrium) multipliers. Estimates of the short-run and long-run elasticities of imports with respect to exports and other exogenous variables could be computed. Finally, a target regarding income or foreign assets could be set and the change in net domestic credit, as compatible with the preassigned target, could be determined. In short, the estimated model could be used for forecasting and policy purposes.

These possible uses of the Polak model should take into account its limitations. The reliability of the results of any macroeconomic forecasting exercise may vary, depending on (1) whether the specified relationships in the model depict correctly the actual behavior of the economy, (2) whether the statistical observations are free of measurement errors and correspond to the definition of variables involved in the model, and (3) whether the estimation techniques yield reliable estimates.

DEFINITIONS OF VARIABLES AND ESTIMATION OF PARAMETERS

The parameters of a model can be estimated on the basis of historical data (time series) regarding the variables involved in the model. With the aid of established techniques, these data can yield numerical values of the parameters. The choice of techniques depends on the specification of the model, the nature of the available data, and the purpose of the model. However, before choosing a particular technique and applying statistical inference, it is necessary to identify the concept-variables involved in the model with corresponding observations in the statistical world.

Statistical Definitions of Variables

For the purpose of this workshop, the following definitions are adopted:

1. *Income (Y)* is identified with gross domestic product at market prices.

2. *Net foreign assets (NFA)* represent net foreign assets of the banking system.

3. *Imports (M)* comprise payments for goods and nonfactor services.

4. *Exports (X)* comprise receipts from goods and nonfactor services less net factor payments abroad.

5. *Capital movements (CM)* cover all items of the balance of payments that are not classified as imports, exports, or reserve movements, so that $CM = M - X + \Delta NFA$.

6. *Money (MO)* is defined as the sum of money plus quasi-money.

7. *Net domestic credit (NDC)* is defined as domestic credit extended by the banking system *(DC)* less other items net *(NOI)*: $NDC = DC - NOI$.

Statistical Data on Variables

Statistical data corresponding to the above definitions of the variables are presented in Appendix I. These data consist of annual observations expressed in current prices, covering the period 1968–76. For simplicity's sake, data on stock variables *(MO, NFA,* and *NDC)* are given for the end of the year. To minimize the calculations involved in the estimation of parameters, Appendix II contains the computed ratios M/Y and MO/Y over the sample period.

Estimation of *k* and *m*

The parameters k and m, which are assumed to remain constant over time, can be estimated by calculating for each period the ratios of money/income (MO/Y) and imports/income (M/Y), respectively, and then taking the averages over the sample period (1968–76). This method is used in the present workshop.

Alternatively, these parameters may be estimated using regression analysis. Appendix III contains regression estimates of k and m.

USE OF MODEL FOR FORECASTING AND POLICYMAKING

By combining equations (1)′, (2)′, and (3)′, the reduced form for imports is obtained, as follows:

$$M_t = \alpha A_t + \alpha\beta M_{t-1} \tag{5}$$

where

$$\alpha = \frac{m}{m+k}, \ \beta = \frac{k}{m}$$

This equation is a dynamic one, as the effects on imports of an increase in one of the components of A will be distributed over an infinite number of periods. This is easily seen by writing

$$M_{t-1} = \alpha A_{t-1} + \alpha\beta M_{t-2}$$

$$M_{t-2} = \alpha A_{t-2} + \alpha\beta M_{t-3}$$

and by substituting successively into equation (5).

This then yields

$$M_t = \alpha A_t + \alpha^2\beta A_{t-1} + \alpha^3\beta^2 A_{t-2} + \ldots \tag{6}$$

It may be noted that equation (5), or its equivalent (6), is stable only if $\alpha\beta$ is numerically less than unity. In other words, the effects on imports of a unit increase in one of the components of A will diminish from one period to the next. The total effect will be given by

$$\alpha + \alpha^2\beta + \alpha^3\beta^2 + \alpha^4\beta^3 + \ldots$$

or

$$\alpha\,[1 + \alpha\beta + \alpha^2\beta^2 + \alpha^3\beta^3 + \ldots]$$

If $\alpha\beta$ is numerically less than unity, this total effect (namely, the long-run multiplier) is equal to

$$\frac{\alpha}{1-\alpha\beta} = \frac{m/(m+k)}{1-k/(m+k)} = 1$$

The same result can be obtained if time subscripts are suppressed in equation (5) and rearranged, as follows:

$$M = \alpha A + \alpha\beta M$$

or

$$M = \frac{\alpha}{1-\alpha\beta} A = A \quad (\text{since} \frac{\alpha}{1-\alpha\beta} = 1) \qquad (7)$$

and

$$\Delta M = \frac{\alpha}{1-\alpha\beta} \Delta A = \Delta A$$

Forecasting

After estimates of the parameters m and k, and, therefore, of α and $\alpha\beta$ have been made, equation (5) or equation (6) can be used to forecast the value of imports in period t. However, from a practical point of view, it is more convenient to use equation (5). All that is needed is the level of A in period t and the value of imports in the preceding period. It should be noted that, once it is desired to project imports beyond the sample period, there arises the problem of knowing the levels of the exogenous variables. It is necessary to estimate or obtain information about their levels separately. Often, their past trend is extrapolated. The problem, of course, does not arise for those exogenous variables which are assumed to be policy (or control) variables. Therefore, equation (5) or equation (6) can provide forecasts of imports that are conditioned on the accuracy of the estimates for exogenous variables and parameters.

Monetary Policy

For analyzing monetary policy problems, equation (5) may be written in the following form:

$$M_t = \alpha(X_t + CM_t + \Delta NDC_t) + \alpha\beta M_{t-1} \qquad (8)$$

Equation (8) shows that the authorities, through credit policy, can influence directly the value of imports. For example, a policy of balance of payments equilibrium, equivalent to

$$M_t - X_t - CM_t = 0 \tag{9}$$

will be achieved if credit is set at

$$\Delta NDC_t = \frac{(1-\alpha)}{\alpha}(X_t + CM_t) - \beta M_{t-1} \tag{10}$$

Equation (10) is obtained by substituting from equation (8) into equation (9).

Thus, a monetary policy leading to a balance of payments equilibrium consists, according to the Polak model, of maintaining a fixed relationship between the various elements of monetary expansion. This fixed relationship depends on the velocity of circulation of money and the marginal propensity to import.

EXERCISES

1. Estimates of Parameters and Computation of Multipliers and Elasticities

(*a*) *Using the data provided in Appendix II, make estimates of* m *and* k, *and obtain numerical values for* α *and* β.

(*b*) *What is the impact (first period) multiplier of imports with respect to* ΔNDC? *What are the two-period and three-period truncated multipliers? What is the long-run or equilibrium multiplier? Are these multipliers different from those with respect to exports?*

(*c*) *The short-run (first period) elasticity of imports with respect to capital flows is given by*

$$(e_{M,CM})_t = \frac{\Delta M_t / M_t}{\Delta CM_t / CM_t} = \frac{\Delta M_t \cdot CM_t}{\Delta CM_t \cdot M_t} = \alpha \frac{CM_t}{M_t}$$

This will vary from period to period as the ratio CM_t/M_t *is unlikely to remain constant. A mean elasticity for the sample period can be defined by taking the ratio of the averages* $(\overline{CM}/\overline{M})$.

(i) *Compute this mean elasticity.*

(ii) *What will be the long-run elasticity?*

(iii) *Compare the above elasticities with the corresponding ones for exports.*

2. Forecasting of Imports

(*a*) *Given that*

$$X_{1977} = 11{,}580,\ CM_{1977} = 2{,}282, \text{ and } \Delta NDC_{1977} = 1{,}785,$$

forecast the value of imports and the change in net foreign assets in 1977.

(*b*) *Compare the above forecasts with the following outturn figures:*

$$M_{1977} = 11{,}688 \text{ and } \Delta NFA_{1977} = 2{,}174.$$

Given that

$$Y_{1977} = 36{,}653 \text{ and } MO_{1977} = 12{,}413,$$

analyze the errors of forecast.

3. Monetary Policy

(*a*) *For the values of exports and capital movements given above, what amount of credit would be compatible with the target of achieving balance of payments equilibrium in 1977?*

$$(\Delta NFA_{1977} = 0)$$

(*b*) *Suppose that the Kenyan authorities fix a target for net foreign assets at the end of 1977 equivalent to one month of imports in the preceding year*

$$(NFA_{1977} = \frac{1}{12} M_{1976}).$$

What would be the amount of credit expansion compatible with this target?

(*c*) *Show why*

$$\Delta NDC_t = -\Delta NFA_t$$

corresponds to a situation of no change in imports, income, and money

$$(\Delta M_t = \Delta Y_t = \Delta MO_t = 0).$$

ISSUES FOR DISCUSSION

1. *Comment on the following criticisms of the Polak model:*
   (*a*) *The structure of the economy is described in terms of only two fixed ratios and, hence, the model is oversimplified and not adequate for formulating monetary policy.*
   (*b*) *The model has an essentially short-run orientation.*
2. *What are the implications of using the broader definition of money (including quasi-money) in the model?*
3. *With reference to Appendix II, comment on the stability of the ratios of money/income* (MO/Y) *and imports/income* (M/Y) *over the sample period.*
4. *Discuss in simple economic terms the conclusion in Exercise 3(c).*
5. *Compare the results of the regressions in Appendix III with those obtained in the above exercises.*

APPENDIX I

Kenya: Statistical Data on Variables, 1968–76 [1]

(In millions of Kenya shillings)

t	*Y*	*M*[2]	*X*[2]	*MO*	*NFA*	*NDC*	Δ*NFA*	Δ*NDC*	*CM*[3]	*A*[4]
1968	9,666	2,832	2,389	2,317	789	1,528				
1969	10,417	2,926	2,708	2,748	1,256	1,492	467	—36	685	3,357
1970	11,453	3,512	2,996	3,505	1,617	1,888	361	396	877	4,269
1971	12,703	4,470	3,256	3,770	1,201	2,569	—416	681	798	4,735
1972	14,447	4,323	3,568	4,294	1,358	2,936	157	367	912	4,847
1973	16,761	5,036	3,932	5,356	1,558	3,798	200	862	1,304	6,098
1974	20,343	8,676	6,298	5,819	969	4,850	—589	1,052	1,789	9,139
1975	23,343	8,358	6,310	6,814	581	6,233	—388	1,383	1,660	9,353
1976	28,582	9,436	8,468	8,454	1,459	6,995	878	762	1,846	11,076

Sources: International Monetary Fund, *International Financial Statistics*, May 1978; Kenya, *Statistical Abstract*, 1976; and Kenya, *Economic Survey*, 1976, 1977, and 1978.

[1] See text for definition of variables.

[2] On national accounts basis.

[3] Residual variable obtained from the identity $CM = \Delta NFA + M - X$.

[4] $A = X + \Delta NDC + CM$.

APPENDIX II

Kenya: Ratios of Imports to Income *(M/Y)* and of Money to Income *(MO/Y)*, 1968–76

t	*M/Y*	*MO/Y*
1968	0.293	0.240
1969	0.281	0.264
1970	0.307	0.306
1971	0.352	0.297
1972	0.299	0.297
1973	0.300	0.320
1974	0.426	0.286
1975	0.358	0.292
1976	0.330	0.296
Sum	2.946	2.598

Source: Appendix I.

CHART 1. Time Trends of *M/Y* and *MO/Y*

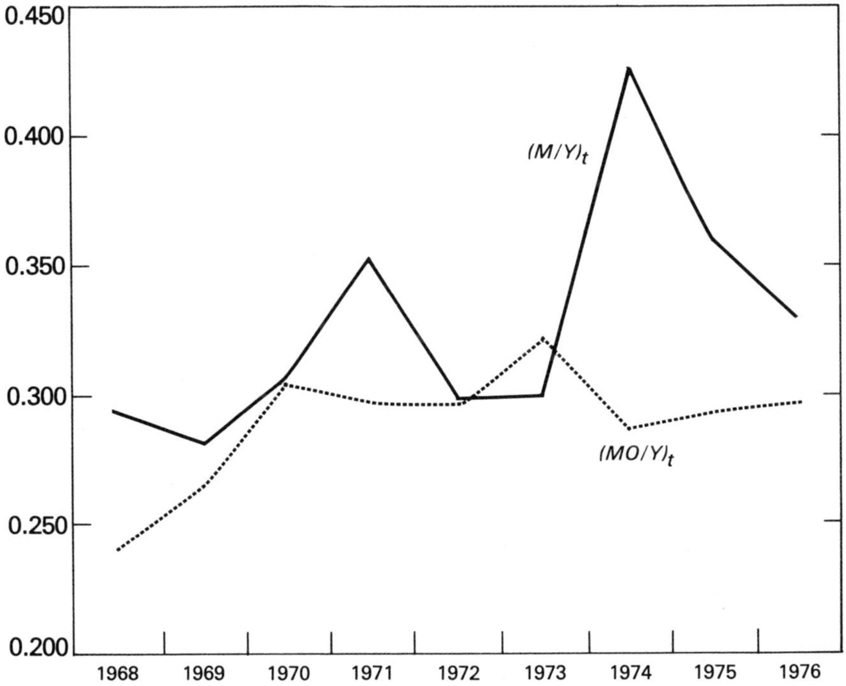

Source: Appendix I.

APPENDIX III

Regression Results, 1968–76

Control Information

Number of Observations: 9
Response Variable: M
Estimation Period: 1968 to 1976

Variable	*Coefficient*	*S.E. Coefficient*	*t*	*t Probability*	*Beta*
Y	0.342438	0.149129E-01	22.9625	1.0000	0.8482

S.E. Estimate	783.37914	Durbin-Watson	1.81557
R^2	0.985054	RHO	0.521875E-01
Adjusted R^2	0.983186	Sum of squares	4909463.0
R	0.992499	F (1, 8)	527.278
R^2 (mean adjustment)	0.910046	F probability	1.000000
Adjusted R^2 (mean adjustment)	0.910046	Condition number	1.00000

Ordinary Prediction Method Used

Observation Number	*Observed*	*Predicted*	*Residual*
1	2832.00	3310.01	−478.008
2	2926.00	3567.18	−641.180
3	3512.00	3921.95	−409.946
4	4470.00	4349.99	120.007
5	4323.00	4947.21	−624.206
6	5036.00	5739.61	−703.608
7	8676.00	6973.07	1702.93
8	8440.00	8004.15	435.848
9	9436.00	9771.82	−335.819

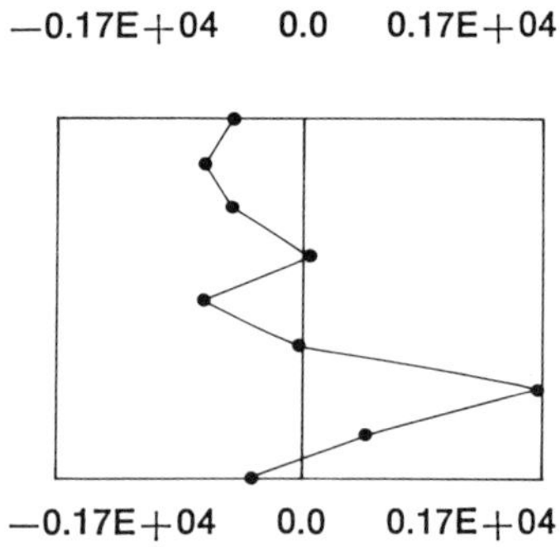

Estimated import equation: $M_t = 0.342438\, Y_t$

Appendix III
Regression Results, 1968–76
(concluded)

Control Information

Number of Observations: 9
Response Variable: MO
Estimation Period: 1968 to 1976

Variable	*Coefficient*	*S.E. Coefficient*	*t*	*t Probability*	*Beta*
Y	0.293491	0.527876E-02	55.5985	1.0000	0.9476

S.E. Estimate	277.29476	Durbin-Watson	1.28043
R^2	0.997419	RHO	0.158272
Adjusted R^2	0.997096	Sum of squares	615139.07
R	0.998709	F (1, 8)	3091.20
R^2 (mean adjustment)	0.980851	F probability	1.000000
Adjusted R^2 (mean adjustment)	0.980851	Condition number	1.00000

Ordinary Prediction Method Used

Observation Number	*Observed*	*Predicted*	*Residual*
1	2317.00	2836.89	–519.888
2	2748.00	3057.30	–309.300
3	3505.00	3361.36	143.643
4	3770.00	3728.22	41.7791
5	4294.00	4240.07	53.9302
6	5356.00	4919.21	436.791
7	5819.00	5976.36	–157.365
8	6814.00	6860.07	–46.0673
9	8454.00	8375.07	78.9302

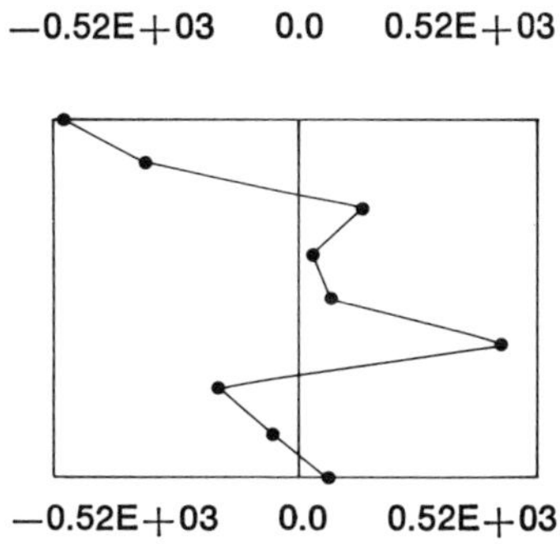

Estimated money-income relationship: $MO_t = 0.293491\ Y_t$

Chapter 8

WORKSHOP 6

Projection of Monetary Aggregates

A forecast of the monetary aggregates is an integral part of any financial program. If economic developments relating to national income, the rate of inflation, balance of payments, unemployment, etc., are unfavorable, government policymakers will desire to take corrective action, including changes in monetary management. Usually, before taking any monetary or credit policy measure, the authorities will need some projections or forecasts in respect of the monetary aggregates concerned so that they can compare the likely outcome with and without the policy measure under consideration. When a policy involves limits on the growth of certain monetary aggregates, projections for all the related monetary aggregates would help in determining the overall consistency and the feasibility of the policy.

Several types of monetary aggregates that appear in the balance sheets of the monetary authorities, the deposit money banks, and the banking system as a whole may be distinguished. Some monetary aggregates, such as net domestic credit of the monetary authorities, are controlled by the monetary authorities themselves. Other monetary aggregates reflect the performances of various sectors of the economy; for example, the change in net foreign assets of the monetary authorities reflects the balance of payments outturn. Still other monetary aggregates usually have close relationships with other variables in the economy; for example, the money stock may be closely related to output and prices.

In order to make the projections realistic, it will be necessary to review the performance of the banking system in the past few years and to observe the outlook or the objectives in relation to the balance of payments and to government budget operations. Developments in output, prices, and possibly other economic aggregates that closely relate to the monetary aggregates would have to be predicted. The projected amounts of monetary aggregates must be consistent with the expected overall economic activity in the future period. Furthermore, the balance sheets that involve the relevant monetary aggregates must be balanced for the forecast period. For example, on the balance sheet of the monetary authorities, the planned expansion of net domestic credit of the monetary authorities plus the desired (or forecast) increase in net foreign assets must be equal to the forecast increase in reserve money. Thus, if this balance sheet identity is not observed, the policy contemplation and the economic objectives are not compatible, given other variables over which the authorities have limited control.

The consolidated monetary account—namely, the monetary survey—is a good basis on which to make monetary projections, as the expected results of government budget operations and of the balance of payments are reflected in this monetary account. Furthermore, monetary policy often involves a restraint on credit expansion. The projected growth of monetary stock (money and quasi-money) consistent with the expected rate of credit expansion can be derived from this account. When the target level for net foreign assets of the banking system, the target rate for growth in income, and other targets are set and the necessary policy measures to achieve these targets are spelled out, the monetary survey in the forecast period becomes a "desired" balance sheet for the banking system and often constitutes a component in a financial program. This will be elaborated in the introduction to Workshop 9 on Financial Programming.

The projections for Kenya to be made in this workshop cover the items in the monetary survey, as well as the demand for monetary stock for December 1977. A simultaneous equation approach to monetary projections is also discussed. This approach implies that both supply and demand factors are at work in determining the levels of monetary stock.

RECENT MONETARY DEVELOPMENTS IN KENYA

After six years of steady growth in international reserves, Kenya experienced its first balance of payments deficit in 1971. The authorities responded by imposing selective credit controls in July 1971 and by instituting an extensive import control system in January 1972. The selective credit controls included absolute ceilings on credit to importers of consumer goods; these were set at 70 per cent of the amounts then outstanding for motor vehicle importers and 95 per cent for importers of other consumer goods. In February 1972, a ceiling of 12 per cent per annum on the growth of commercial bank credit to the private sector was established.

During the 18 months ended June 1973, imports declined and net foreign assets rose by over 60 per cent, while credit to the private sector increased by only 6 per cent. However, credit to the Cereals and Sugar Finance Corporation (CSFC) and to the Agriculture Finance Corporation (AFC) and net credit to the Government of Kenya rose by 64 per cent. Money and quasi-money grew at an annual rate of 20 per cent for this period.

As a result of these improvements in the balance of payments, the ceiling on bank credit expansion was lifted in March 1973, most of the selective credit controls were abolished in April, and import controls were liberalized in July. During the 12 months to July 1974, private sector credit rose by almost 50 per cent, net foreign assets dropped by 20 per cent, money supply increased by 19 per cent, and despite a rapid increase in bank deposits, bank reserves fell by more than 50 per cent. By mid-1974, commercial banks were approaching the minimum liquidity ratio of 15 per cent.

On June 1, 1974, the Central Bank of Kenya forecast a large loss in foreign exchange reserves over the coming 18 months because of the anticipated sharp increase in import prices. Consequently, the following measures were taken. First, a 12 per cent ceiling on the increase in bank credit to the private sector and public enterprises (excluding the CSFC and the AFC) was imposed for the period June 1974 to June 1975. Second, the 15 per cent liquidity ratio was extended to licensed financial institutions, except for housing finance companies. Third, local borrowing for nonresident-controlled companies was further restricted. On July 1, 1974, the Central Bank raised the legal minimum interest rate on time and savings deposits from 3 to 5 per cent and the minimum lending rate from 7 to 8 per cent. The discount rate on crop finance paper was raised from 6.5 per cent to 7 per cent.

From June 1974 to June 1975, money plus quasi-money rose by 6 per cent, owing to an increase of 21 per cent (KSh 908 million) in domestic credit, as net foreign assets fell by KSh 580 million or 40 per cent. Credit to the nongovernment sector increased by only 7 per cent (KSh 274 million) during this period as a result of the more restrictive credit policy. However, net credit to the Government increased sharply by KSh 634 million (Table 1). The composition of money plus quasi-money shifted as the share of quasi-money in the total rose from 28 per cent in June 1974 to 33 per cent in June 1975, mainly because of the increase in the legal minimum interest rate on time and savings deposits.

In mid-1975, in view of the slackened pace of economic activity and a more favorable foreign reserve position than anticipated, the Central Bank sought to encourage a more rapid credit expansion than had been occurring up to that time. The Central Bank expressed willingness to lend to the commercial banks. To promote lending to the agricultural sector, the Central Bank required the commercial banks to increase the share of their deposits lent to the agricultural sector to 17 per cent by end-June 1976, compared with 10 per cent at end-June 1975.

During the second half of 1975, money and quasi-money grew at an annual rate of 24 per cent, owing to the increase in domestic credit, as net foreign assets declined slightly. Net credit to the Government increased sharply by KSh 667 million. The domestic counterpart of Kenya's allocation of special drawing rights (SDRs) by the International Monetary Fund (KSh 134 million) was transferred in September 1975 to treasury deposits with the Central Bank. Credit to the nongovernment sector increased by KSh 450 million, equivalent to an annual rate of 21 per cent during these six months.

In 1976, the balance of payments registered a surplus of KSh 776 million, compared with a deficit of KSh 356 million for the previous year. Export receipts increased by 31 per cent. In anticipation of a rapid growth in bank deposits due to the increase in export receipts, the Central Bank increased the liquidity ratio of commercial banks from 15 per cent to 18 per cent, effective July 1, 1976. Nevertheless, money and quasi-money increased by 24 per cent in 1976. In October, in view of the low rate of credit expansion to the private sector during the first three quarters, the Central Bank informally encouraged the commercial banks to increase their lending to the private sector. Furthermore, effective December 8, 1976, the Central Bank abolished the minimum lending rate of 8 per cent. Accompanying these measures, the Central Bank reduced its discount rates by a half of 1 per cent. For 1976 as a whole, domestic credit increased by 16 per cent (KSh 1,061 million), reflecting partly the response to monetary policies and partly the general economic recovery toward the end of the year.

PROJECTIONS

For 1977, the balance of payments forecasts implied an overall surplus of KSh 2,200 million.[1] Central bank domestic credit for

[1] In January 1977, the official projection for the balance of payments was a surplus of KSh 445 million. The official projection has been revised for the purpose of this workshop.

1977 was to be reduced by KSh 800 million. The overall budget deficit for fiscal year 1978 was estimated at KSh 2,384 million, compared with a deficit of KSh 1,327 million for fiscal year 1977. External borrowing was to finance 29 per cent of the estimated deficit, compared with 35 per cent in the previous fiscal year. Net borrowing from the banking system was expected to be KSh 1,200 million, compared with minus KSh 5 million for the previous fiscal year. The remainder of the budget deficit was to be financed through the nonbank domestic sector.

Supply of Money and Quasi-Money

For the period 1967–76, regression equations for the supply of money and the supply of money plus quasi-money have been estimated as follows:[2]

$$MO_t = \underset{(1.74)}{-910.55} + \underset{(8.04)}{3.0870}\, RM_t \qquad \bar{R}^2 = 0.876 \qquad (1)$$

$$MQ_t = \underset{(1.84)}{-1479.23} + \underset{(7.79)}{4.6052}\, RM_t \qquad \bar{R}^2 = 0.869 \qquad (2)$$

where

MO = money at the end of December, in millions of Kenya shillings

MQ = money plus quasi-money at the end of December, in millions of Kenya shillings

RM = reserve money at the end of December, in millions of Kenya shillings.

The figures in parentheses indicate the t values for the corresponding coefficients.

Demand for Money and Quasi-Money

Demand functions for money and for money plus quasi-money in real terms for Kenya for the period 1967–76 have been estimated as follows:

[2] Selected data for Kenya for the period 1966–76 appear in Table 3.

$$MO_t^* = -1883.91 + 0.3706\, GDP_t - 28.9752\, \dot{P}_t \quad \bar{R}^2 = 0.929 \qquad (3)$$
$$\qquad (3.05) \qquad (6.42) \qquad (1.58)$$

$$MQ_t^* = -2630.84 + 0.5243\, GDP_t - 34.9792\, \dot{P}_t \quad \bar{R}^2 = 0.959 \qquad (4)$$
$$\qquad (3.88) \qquad (8.28) \qquad (1.74)$$

where

MO^* = two-year averages of end-of-year stocks of money, in millions of Kenya shillings, deflated by the gross domestic product (GDP) deflator

MQ^* = two-year averages of end-of-year stocks of money plus quasi-money, in millions of Kenya shillings, deflated by the GDP deflator

$\dot{P}$ = percentage change in the GDP deflator

GDP = GDP at factor cost at constant 1972 prices, in millions of Kenya shillings.

The growth rate in real GDP has been targeted at 7 per cent for 1977, and the corresponding growth rate for nominal GDP has been projected to be 25 per cent.

Projections with a Simultaneous Equation Model

As mentioned earlier in this chapter, the monetary stock can be estimated by using a simultaneous equation model that includes both supply and demand factors. The simplest form of such a model is:

$$MO_t^d = k\, MGDP_t + u_t \qquad (5)$$

$$MO_t^s = m\, RM_t + v_t \qquad (6)$$

$$RM_t = NFA_t^* + NDC_t^* \qquad (7)$$

where

MO^d = demand for nominal stock of money

MO^s = supply of nominal stock of money

$MGDP$ = GDP at current prices

NDC^* = domestic credit of the monetary authorities

NFA^* = net foreign assets of the monetary authorities.

With $MGDP$ and NDC^* exogenous and $MO^d = MO^s = MO$ in equilibrium, the above model determines MO, RM, and NFA^*.

A less aggregative model, which involves estimations of imports, domestic aggregate expenditure, nominal GDP, change in net foreign assets of the banking system, and monetary stock, is provided as follows:

$$M_t^d = a_0 + a_1 AE_t + u_t \tag{8}$$

$$\Delta M_t = \alpha\,[M_t^d - M_{t-1}] \tag{9}$$

$$AE_t^d = b_0 + b_1 MQ_t + b_2 MGDP_t + v_t \tag{10}$$

$$\Delta AE_t = \beta\,[AE_t^d - AE_{t-1}] \tag{11}$$

$$MGDP_t = AE_t + X_t - M_t \tag{12}$$

$$\Delta NFA_t = X_t - M_t + CM_t \tag{13}$$

$$\Delta MQ_t = \Delta NFA_t + \Delta NDC_t \tag{14}$$

This model assumes (1) that import demand (M^d) depends on aggregate expenditure (AE); (2) that change in actual imports (ΔM) adjusts to excess demand for imports; (3) that desired aggregate expenditure (AE^d) depends on nominal GDP $(MGDP)$ and monetary stock (MQ); (4) that change in actual value of aggregate expenditure adjusts to the difference between desired expenditure and actual expenditure; and (5) that change in monetary stock reflects the balance of payments outturn (ΔNFA) and change in domestic credit of the banking system (ΔNDC). Equations (12) through (14) are accounting identities. Exports (X), domestic credit (NDC), and net foreign capital inflows (CM) are treated as exogenous. The structure of the model emphasizes the interrelationships between monetary variables, aggregate expenditure, and the balance of payments.

Using data for Kenya for the period 1967–76, a reduced-form equation for monetary stock derived from the above model is as follows:

$$\begin{aligned} MQ_t = {} & 650.5 - 0.1477\,M_{t-1} - 0.2745\,AE_{t-1} \\ & + 0.8776\,NFA_{t-1} + 0.8122\,X_t + 0.8776\,NDC_t \\ & + 0.8776\,CM_t - 2165.36\,D_t \end{aligned} \tag{15}$$

In estimating this model, a dummy variable (D) has been included in the equations for imports and aggregate expenditure to reflect the exceptionally large increases in imports and inventory accumulations in 1974 due to the speculation of a further sharp increase in import prices.

TABLE 1. Kenya: Monetary Survey, 1973–77
(In millions of Kenya shillings)

Item	1973	1974		1975		1976		1977
	December	*June*	*December*	*June*	*December*	*June*	*December*	*December*
Net foreign assets	**1,558**	**1,434**	**969**	**854**	**581**	**1,189**	**1,459**	
Central Bank [1]	1,584	1,494	1,061	933	681	1,192	1,449	
Government [2]	25	31	4	—	8	9	16	
Commercial banks	—51	—91	—96	—79	—108	—12	—6	
Domestic credit	**3,859**	**4,389**	**4,966**	**5,297**	**6,414**	**6,563**	**7,475**	
Government (net)	479	466	930	1,100	1,767	1,500	1,898	
Claims	*1,019*	*1,008*	*1,036*	*1,183*	*1,789*	*2,279*	*2,043*	
Deposits	*540*	*542*	*106*	*83*	*22*	*779*	*145*	
Nongovernment	3,380	3,923	4,036	4,197	4,647	5,063	5,577	
Official entities	*237*	*176*	*223*	*221*	*303*	*250*	*215*	
Private sector [3]	*3,143*	*3,747*	*3,813*	*3,976*	*4,344*	*4,813*	*5,362*	
Other items (net)	**—69**	**—19**	**—18**	**—59**	**180**	**321**	**479**	
Money and quasi-money	**5,356**	**5,708**	**5,819**	**6,077**	**6,814**	**7,432**	**8,454**	
Money	3,862	4,083	4,016	4,052	4,540	4,966	5,674	
Currency outside banks	*982*	*1,015*	*1,086*	*1,022*	*1,234*	*1,194*	*1,625*	
Demand deposits [4]	*2,880*	*3,068*	*2,930*	*3,030*	*3,306*	*3,772*	*4,049*	
Quasi-money	1,494	1,625	1,803	2,025	2,274	2,466	2,780	
SDR allocations	**130**	**134**	**134**	**134**	—[5]	—	—	

Sources: Central Bank of Kenya, *Annual Report for the Financial Year Ended 30th June, 1977;* and International Monetary Fund, *International Financial Statistics*, July 1978.

[1] Foreign liabilities include use of Fund credit.

[2] Foreign exchange holdings.

[3] Includes Cereals and Sugar Finance Corporation and Agricultural Finance Corporation.

[4] Adjusted for "uncleared effects."

[5] The domestic counterpart of Kenya's SDR allocation was transferred in September 1975 to treasury deposits with the Central Bank of Kenya.

TABLE 2. Kenya: Summary Accounts of the Monetary Authorities, 1973–76

(In millions of Kenya shillings)

Item	1973	1974		1975		1976	
	December	*June*	*December*	*June*	*December*	*June*	*December*
Net foreign assets	**1,609**	**1,525**	**1,065**	**933**	**689**	**1,201**	**1,465**
Foreign assets	1,615	1,559	1,354	1,380	1,439	1,867	2,309
Foreign exchange [1]	*1,371*	*1,305*	*1,338*	*1,340*	*1,403*	*1,862*	*2,282*
SDRs	*142*	*148*	*16*	*40*	*36*	*5*	*27*
Reserve position in the Fund	*102*	*106*	—	—	—	—	—
Foreign liabilities [2]	6	34	289	447	750	666	844
Domestic credit	**—88**	**—31**	**726**	**872**	**1,205**	**678**	**787**
Government (net)	—95	—33	490	586	1,171	636	778
Claims	369	399	526	575	1,112	1,295	851
Advances	*200*	*200*	*200*	*339*	*543*	*288*	*200*
Treasury bills	*60*	*22*	*148*	*87*	*284*	*164*	*20*
Government securities	*109*	*177*	*177*	*149*	*150*	*709*	*497*
SDR allocations used by Government	—	—	—	—	*134*	*134*	*134*
Trust Fund loans	—	—	—	—	—	—	—
Deposits	464	432	36	—11	—59	659	73
Official entities	7	—	—	—	—	—	—
Commercial banks	—	2	236	286	34	42	9
Other items (net) [3]	**—4**	**—40**	**—132**	**138**	**281**	**145**	**251**
Reserve money	**1,395**	**1,400**	**1,789**	**1,533**	**1,613**	**1,734**	**2,001**
Currency outside banks	982	1,015	1,086	1,022	1,234	1,194	1,625
Currency in commercial banks	137	117	253	161	174	189	205
Banks' deposits	221	261	381	313	131	311	133
Official entities' deposits	55	6	69	37	74	40	38
SDR allocations	**130**	**134**	**134**	**134**	— [4]	—	—

Sources: Central Bank of Kenya, *Annual Report for the Financial Year Ended 30th June, 1977;* and International Monetary Fund, *International Financial Statistics,* July 1978.

[1] Includes balances with banks abroad and foreign securities.

[2] Includes use of Fund credit.

[3] Includes revaluation account, uncleared effects, and other unclassified assets and liabilities.

[4] The domestic counterpart of Kenya's SDR allocation was transferred in September 1975 to treasury deposits with the Central Bank of Kenya.

TABLE 3. Kenya: Selected Statistical Data, 1966–76

Year	*MGDP*	*GDP*	*P1*	*P2*	*MO*	*MQ*
1966	7,622	9,125	83.5	57.0	1,333	1,885
1967	8,116	9,546	85.0	58.0	1,410	2,086
1968	8,858	10,282	86.2	58.2	1,627	2,317
1969	9,526	10,941	87.1	58.1	1,927	2,748
1970	10,378	11,673	88.9	59.3	2,410	3,505
1971	11,402	12,330	92.5	61.6	2,589	3,770
1972	13,172	13,172	100.0	65.0	3,029	4,294
1973	14,984	14,066	106.5	71.2	3,862	5,356
1974	17,906	14,350	124.8	83.9	4,016	5,819
1975	20,560	14,523	141.6	100.0	4,540	6,814
1976	25,257	15,405	164.0	111.4	5,674	8,454

Year	*DC*	*DCP*	*RM*	*M*	*X*	*AE*
1966	1,000	1,079	490	2,568	2,696	7,494
1967	1,293	1,339	625	2,586	2,506	8,196
1968	1,341	1,308	784	2,832	2,842	8,848
1969	1,429	1,370	1,133	2,926	3,076	9,376
1970	1,871	1,840	1,263	3,512	3,416	10,474
1971	2,527	2,394	1,152	4,470	3,638	12,234
1972	3,018	2,672	1,264	4,323	4,002	13,493
1973	3,859	3,380	1,395	5,036	4,812	15,208
1974	4,966	4,036	1,789	8,676	7,144	19,438
1975	6,413	4,647	1,613	8,358	7,138	21,780
1976	7,475	5,577	2,001	9,436	9,560	25,133

Sources: *MGDP* = GDP at factor cost at current prices, in millions of Kenya shillings (Kenya, *Economic Survey* and *Statistical Abstract,* various issues).

GDP = GDP at factor cost at constant 1972 prices, in millions of Kenya shillings (Kenya, *Economic Survey* and *Statistical Abstract,* various issues).

P1 = GDP deflator, 1972 = 100, derived from *MGDP* and *GDP.*

P2 = Consumer prices, 1975 = 100 (Kenya, *Statistical Digest,* various issues.

MO = Money, i.e., currency outside banks plus demand deposits, in millions of Kenya shillings *(International Financial Statistics (IFS)).*

MQ = Money plus quasi-money, in millions of Kenya shillings *(IFS).*

DC = Total domestic credit of the banking system, in millions of Kenya shillings *(IFS).*

DCP = Total domestic credit less net credit to the Government, in millions of Kenya shillings *(IFS).*

RM = Reserve money, in millions of Kenya shillings *(IFS).*

M = Imports of goods and nonfactor services, in millions of Kenya shillings (Kenya, *Economic Survey and Statistical Abstract,* various issues).

X = Exports of goods and nonfactor services, in millions of Kenya shillings (Kenya, *Economic Survey* and *Statistical Abstract,* various issues).

AE = Derived as $MGDP + M - X$.

EXERCISES

Exercise A

On the basis of the above information, projections are to be made for domestic credit, net foreign assets, money, and quasi-money for the banking system for December 1977 (Table 1). The following steps may be followed:

1. Net foreign assets. *Information can be obtained from the statement of the balance of payments forecasts for 1977 above. Net foreign assets at the end of 1977 should be equivalent to net foreign assets at the end of 1976, plus the change in net foreign assets reflecting the balance of payments outcome in 1977. Please note that net foreign assets of the commercial banks are not included in official foreign reserves of Kenya.*

2. Money and quasi-money. *Projections for money and quasi-money are to be made using regression equations (1) and (2). The following balance sheet identity is required for the projections:*[3]

   $$\Delta RM_t = \Delta NFA_t^* + \Delta NDC_t^*$$

   The change in net foreign assets for the banking system has been projected in item 1 above. The division between net foreign assets of the monetary authorities and those of the commercial banks may be made on the basis of the situation at the end of December 1976 (Table 1). The level of domestic credit of the monetary authorities at the end of December 1976 can be obtained from Table 2.

3. Other items net. *This item may be assumed to stay the same as in December 1976. Alternatively, a trend ratio between this item and the total liabilities of the banking system may be assumed.*

4. Domestic credit. *This item may be taken to be the difference between money plus quasi-money plus other items (net) and net*

[3] Assuming that other items (net) in the summary accounts of the monetary authorities remain the same.

foreign assets of the banking system. Information about net claims on the Government is contained in a statement concerning the fiscal year 1978 budget in the preceding section. For this exercise, net borrowing from the banking system by the Government for calendar year 1977 may be taken as the average of net borrowing for fiscal years 1977 and 1978. Credit to the non-government sector is to be taken as the difference between total domestic credit and net domestic credit to the Government.

Exercise B

Using regression equations (3) and (4), make a projection for the demand for money and quasi-money for the same date as in Exercise A, based on the targeted income and prices. Historical data for gross domestic product and prices are available in Table 3.

ISSUES FOR DISCUSSION

1. *What are the meanings of the coefficients to reserve money* (RM) *in regression equations (1) and (2)? In relating money or money plus quasi-money to reserve money as in the above equations, the reserve ratios, the ratio between currency and demand deposits, the ratio between time deposits and demand deposits, and the ratio between excess reserves and demand deposits are treated as parameters. How would changes in these ratios affect the coefficients to reserve money in the equations?*

2. *An alternative presentation of the relationship between money and reserve money is to treat the money multiplier as a composite variable. From the following two identities:*

   $$MO = CY + DD$$

   $$RM = CY + Rd + Rt + Re$$

   it follows that

   $$MO = \frac{CY + DD}{CY + Rd + Rt + Re} RM$$

where

CY = *currency outside banks*

DD = *demand deposits*

Rd = *reserves against demand deposits*

Rt = *reserves against time and savings deposits*

Re = *excess reserves.*

The ratio in the above expression is equivalent to the money multiplier.

Compare this approach with the approach implied in equations (1) and (2).

3. *The Kenyan authorities have responded to the balance of payments deficit by imposing credit and import restrictions (1971, 1972, 1974, and 1975). Discuss and evaluate, on the basis of historical data, (a) the effectiveness of the measures in improving the balance of payments and (b) the impact of these measures on real gross domestic product (GDP).*
4. *Comment on the method used to forecast the demand for money. Have important explanatory variables been neglected?*
5. *Compare the projection for money and quasi-money obtained in Exercise B with that in Exercise A and explain the implications of the discrepancy.*
6. *The actual and fitted values for the real money plus quasi-money, based on regression equation (4) are as follows:*

Year	*Actual MQ**	*Fitted MQ**
	(In millions of Kenya shillings)	
1967	2,336	2,311
1968	2,554	2,710
1969	2,908	3,069
1970	3,517	3,417
1971	3,932	3,692
1972	4,032	3,991
1973	4,531	4,516
1974	4,477	4,292
1975	4,461	4,512
1976	4,655	4,892

Was there significant "excess liquidity" or "deficient liquidity" in the economy in any period? Would there be any excess liquidity if no corrective measure was taken in 1977? Explain the implications of the existence of excess liquidity with reference to the case of Kenya (for example, the impact on the balance of payments).

7. *In the model presented in equations (5) through (7), money stock, reserve money, and net foreign assets of the monetary authorities are all determined by the same factors—namely,* MGDP, *which is the determinant of the demand for money, and* NDC*, *which is a policy variable. This approach to net foreign assets is sometimes called the monetary approach. Compare this approach with the approach implied in the model presented in equations (8) through (14).*
8. *Is it possible in the reduced-form equation (15) to identify "demand factor" variables and "supply factor" variables? Explain.*
9. *Discuss the merits and demerits of a forecast based on equation (15) versus forecasts based on Exercises A and B.*

Chapter 9

WORKSHOP 7

Revenue Forecasting

Forecasts of central government revenue are of crucial importance in the formulation of a financial program in order to establish the need for use of other financial resources, such as borrowing and depletion of accumulated reserves. The purpose of the present workshop is to illustrate the practical application to the case of Kenya of some of the principles and techniques involved in forecasting government revenue.[1]

In principle, revenue forecasts should allow for feedbacks between taxes and their bases. For example, different tax rates on income probably affect the size of income itself. If sufficient data and other resources are available, a comprehensive econometric model can be constructed to take these linkages into account. The revenue implications of a particular change in the tax structure can then be

[1] Much of the work on establishing procedures for revenue forecasting in developing countries has been done by the Fiscal Affairs Department of the International Monetary Fund. This workshop draws from several of these unpublished contributions, especially from Roy W. Bahl, "Alternative Methods for Tax Revenue Forecasting in Developing Countries: A Conceptual Analysis" (October 1972); and Sheetal K. Chand, "Some Procedures for Forecasting Tax Revenue in Developing Countries" (October 1975).

worked out for any time period, whether past or future. For most developing countries—and Kenya is no exception—this degree of sophistication is not possible at present. A more practical approach, usually called the partial equilibrium approach, is to estimate the tax functions for different types of taxes and then project revenues on the basis of these functions, assuming given projections of the bases.

In this workshop, a partial equilibrium approach to revenue forecasting is adopted, treating the bases as predetermined variables. The first section provides data on government revenues and on selected bases for the various taxes and also deals with the problem of adjusting tax revenues for the effects of discretionary changes, using the proportional data adjustment method. The second section considers the specification of functional relationships between taxes and their bases, as well as the statistical estimation of a set of parameters that will reflect the current tax structure. The final section contains a series of exercises and issues for discussion. Appendix II presents a summary of the Kenyan tax system.

PREPARATION OF DATA

The first step in the forecasting exercise is to prepare the data on revenues and the bases for statistical estimation.

Tax Revenues and Bases

Since a tax system frequently consists of a large number of minor taxes, selectivity is needed in their disaggregation in order to avoid excessive detail. As a general rule, those taxes that contribute at least 2–5 per cent of revenue on average over the sample period should be isolated for detailed analysis. While the availability of data will determine how far the disaggregation can be carried, the breakdown should attempt, at a minimum, to distinguish between the major tax categories. In the International Monetary Fund's *Government Finance Statistics Yearbook,* taxes are classified into seven major categories[2] according to the nature of the base on which the

[2] See Workshop 2: Government Finance Statistics.

tax is levied. In selecting the appropriate level of disaggregation within each major category, it is necessary to consider the statistical requirements for efficient estimation. A stable functional relationship for a group of taxes will not be established unless the individual taxes in the group exhibit strong correlations. Thus, a group of taxes should be disaggregated if their bases are quite dissimilar, particularly if some of these taxes yield large amounts of revenue. When taxes or groups of taxes involve both specific and ad-valorem rates, it would be appropriate to disaggregate revenue collections accordingly. Greater disaggregation may also help to minimize the number of discretionary changes (legal and administrative) that are present in a single series, because it is quite unlikely that individual taxes will be subject to the same frequency of discretionary changes as will a group of taxes. On the other hand, it is generally true that the more detailed the breakdown of revenue, the greater will be the likelihood that any series will exhibit fluctuations of an increasingly random character. A balance must be struck between these conflicting considerations.

Table 1 presents the time series of Kenya's central government tax revenue, classified as in the *Government Finance Statistics Yearbook,* for the ten-year period covering fiscal years 1968–77 (years ending June 30). A relatively few major types of taxes account for the bulk of tax receipts (see Appendix II for a summary of the tax system). In the three-year period covering fiscal years 1975–77, collections from income tax, sales tax, import duties, and excise duties accounted for some 95 per cent of total tax receipts.

The income tax is the most important source of revenue; in fiscal year 1977 it accounted for some 40 per cent of tax revenue. There are essentially three components of the income tax: (1) taxes on companies, corporations, and enterprises; (2) taxes on individuals; and (3) a capital gains tax. The basic rate on net income for resident companies is 45 per cent, while that for nonresident companies is 52.5 per cent. The income tax structure for individuals is a progressive one, with marginal tax rates ranging from 10 per cent to 70 per cent. The capital gains tax, which was introduced in June

TABLE 1. Kenya: Central Government Tax Revenue, Fiscal Years 1968–77

(In millions of Kenya shillings; year ending June 30)

Tax Revenue Source	1968	1969	1970	1971	1972	1973	1974	1975	1976	1977
1. **Taxes on income, profits, and capital gains**	**467.6**	**502.5**	**632.8**	**809.2**	**937.0**	**1,069.0**	**1,154.6**	**1,531.3**	**1,796.7**	**2,149.3**
1.1 Individual	8.2	30.3	48.8	53.6	36.4	65.0	29.8	...	...	...
Graduated personal tax	*8.2*	*30.3*	*48.8*	*53.6*	*36.4*	*65.0*	*29.8*	—	—	—
1.2 Corporate	459.4	472.2	584.0	755.6	900.6	1,004.0	1,124.8	...	...	...
2. **Social security contributions**	—	—	—	—	—	—	—	—	—	—
3. **Payroll or manpower taxes**	—	—	—	—	—	—	—	—	—	—
4. **Taxes on property**	**7.3**	**6.2**	**6.9**	**6.9**	**10.8**	**8.7**	**10.1**	**11.7**	**8.1**	**11.3**
4.3 Estate duty	7.3	6.2	6.9	6.9	10.8	8.7	10.1	11.7	8.1	11.3
5. **Domestic taxes on goods and services**	**289.3**	**322.4**	**355.9**	**414.1**	**523.7**	**660.5**	**1,182.7**	**1,516.9**	**1,734.2**	**2,028.9**
5.1 Sales tax	—	—	—	—	—	54.1	639.8	937.3	1,185.5	1,308.4
5.2 Excises	247.7	275.9	307.3	357.6	434.6	501.5	429.0	461.6	420.9	574.1
5.4 Taxes on specific services	3.6	3.4	2.5	7.9	20.3	30.6	35.0	40.5	41.9	48.0
5.5 Taxes on use of, or permission to use, goods or to perform activities	38.0	43.1	46.1	48.6	68.8	74.3	78.9	77.5	85.9	98.4
6. **Taxes on international trade and transactions**	**407.2**	**443.6**	**495.0**	**584.1**	**638.9**	**553.5**	**795.4**	**842.2**	**983.6**	**1,057.2**
6.1 Import duties	399.0	436.6	487.0	574.4	630.1	539.9	795.4	842.2	983.6	1,057.2
6.2 Export duties	8.2	7.0	8.0	9.7	8.8	13.6	—	—	—	—
7. **Other taxes**	**15.8**	**18.2**	**21.4**	**25.6**	**26.8**	**26.7**	**44.3**	**41.3**	**48.5**	**50.1**
7.2 Stamp duties	15.8	18.2	21.4	25.6	26.8	26.7	44.3	41.3	48.5	50.1
IV. **Tax revenue**	**1,187.2**	**1,292.8**	**1,512.0**	**1,839.9**	**2,137.2**	**2,318.4**	**3,187.1**	**3,943.4**	**4,571.1**	**5,296.8**

Sources: International Monetary Fund, *Government Finance Statistics Yearbook,* Vol. 1 (1977) and Vol. 2 (1978); and Kenya, *Statistical Abstract,* 1973 and *Appropriation Accounts, Other Public Accounts and the Accounts of the Funds for the Year 1967/68 to 1970/71.*

1975, is levied on the transfer of land, other property, and marketable securities. Companies are taxed at their corporation tax rate, and individuals are taxed at their income tax rate up to a maximum rate of 35 per cent.

The second most important tax is the sales tax, which was introduced in April–May 1973. It contributed 25 per cent of tax collections in fiscal year 1977. The sales tax is a single-stage tax levied on most manufactured goods, whether produced domestically or imported, and on electricity. The tax consists primarily of ad-valorem rates, ranging from 10 per cent to 30 per cent. Specific rates are levied on electricity as well as on a few commodities, such as petroleum products and beer. Exemptions include most animal and vegetable products, pharmaceuticals, fertilizers, certain raw materials, intermediate goods, and capital goods.

Import duties, the third most important source of tax revenue, were equivalent to about 20 per cent of tax receipts in fiscal year 1977. The import duty structure usually uses ad-valorem rates, ranging from 10 per cent to 150 per cent. However, specific duties are levied on some relatively important imports, including petroleum products, alcoholic beverages, and tobacco products. Duty-free items include live animals, pharmaceuticals, and fertilizers. Also, customs duties are refunded on the inputs of certain domestic industries—a rebate of increasing importance.

Excise duties provided 10 per cent of tax receipts in fiscal year 1977, but their significance has declined sharply since the introduction of the sales tax. Presently, excise taxes, which are levied at specific rates, are applied to domestically produced tobacco products, alcoholic beverages, and sugar, as well as to the purchase of second-hand motor vehicles.

There are four minor taxes or tax categories, none of which contributed more than 2 per cent of total tax revenue on average over the sample period. These include: (1) taxes on use of, or permission to use, goods or to perform activities; (2) taxes on specific services; (3) stamp duties; and (4) estate duty.

Effective July 1, 1977, export duties were imposed on coffee and tea.[3] In 1976 exports of these commodities accounted for almost 40 per cent of exports. The basic rate of duty for both coffee and tea is 15 per cent of the export price exceeding KSh 20,000 per metric ton.

After the appropriate revenue classification is selected and the series of tax receipts have been obtained, quantitative information on the bases should be collected. While it would be desirable to obtain data corresponding to the legal tax bases, such information is often either unavailable or available in an unusable form. As a consequence, it may be necessary to select proxies for the legal bases. Frequently, some taxes or tax categories have more than one possible proxy base. In this case, time series should be collected on each alternative and should be studied through the use of statistical and other criteria, so as to facilitate the choice. The selection of the most appropriate proxy base would also depend on whether or not projections of a particular base are available for the period for which revenue forecasts are to be made.

Since the major tax categories often define bases that cover large parts of the economic activity of a country, proxy bases may be found among the variables comprising the national accounts and the balance of payments. These accounts are usually available in both value terms and volume terms. Furthermore, the use of the projections of these accounts makes it possible to examine the revenue forecasts from the viewpoint of overall consistency. Of course, when a particular tax category is highly selective in coverage, it is desirable to find a narrower proxy base that will reflect more adequately fluctuations in the legal base.

Some suggestions on the selection of proxy bases for tax revenues in Kenya appear in Table 2, and data on these are presented in Table 3. These rather aggregative proxy bases reflect to a large extent the lack of relevant disaggregate data for the major categories of revenue. For example, if data had been available on personal and

---

[3] A previous system of export duties was terminated, effective June 15, 1973.

corporate income taxes, it would have been more appropriate to select narrower bases for these taxes. For personal income tax payments, it might have been wages and salaries; and for corporate income tax payments, it might have been the operating surplus of enterprises. But in the case of Kenya, published information on such a breakdown of income taxes is not available for the most recent years.

For import duties and excise duties, revenue collections are grouped by end-use categories and excisable-commodity categories, respectively.[4] However, the disaggregate data are not presented on a fiscal-year basis, and, more importantly, no corresponding disaggregate estimates are published for the revenue effects of discretionary tax measures.[5]

TABLE 2. Kenya: Suggested Proxy Bases for Tax Revenues

	Tax Revenue Source	Suggested Proxy Base
1.	Taxes on income, profits, and capital gains	Gross domestic product at factor cost at current prices
4.3	Estate duty	Gross domestic product at factor cost at current prices
5.1	Sales tax	Private consumption at current prices
5.2	Excises	Private consumption at constant prices
5.4	Taxes on specific services	Private consumption at current prices
5.5	Taxes on use of, or permission to use, goods or to perform activities	Gross domestic product at factor cost at constant prices
6.1	Import duties	Value and volume of imports
7.2	Stamp duties	Gross domestic product at factor cost at constant prices

[4] These data are published in Kenya, *Economic Survey* and *Statistical Abstract,* on a calendar-year basis.

[5] The adjustment of tax revenue for the effects of discretionary measures is discussed below.

TABLE 3. Kenya: Data on Proxy Bases, Calendar Years 1967–77[1]

Proxy Base	1967	1968	1969	1970	1971	1972	1973	1974	1975	1976	1977
Gross domestic product at factor cost at current prices[2]	8,116	8,858	9,526	10,378	11,402	13,172	14,984	17,906	20,560	25,257	32,404
Gross domestic product at factor cost at 1972 prices[2]	9,546	10,282	10,941	11,673	12,330	13,172	14,066	14,350	14,523	15,405	16,536
Private consumption expenditure at current prices[2]	5,864	6,248	6,538	6,894	8,212	9,003	10,848	12,554	15,731	17,542	21,338
Private consumption expenditure at 1975 prices[2, 3]	10,110	10,735	11,253	11,626	13,331	13,851	15,236	14,963	15,731	15,747	16,670
Imports c.i.f. (customs basis) at current prices[2]	2,401	2,541	2,575	3,160	4,001	3,957	4,571	7,677	7,252	8,141	10,630
Imports c.i f. (customs basis) at 1972 prices[2]	3,078	3,217	3,219	3,901	4,496	3,957	3,841	4,313	3,223	3,119	3,783
GDP price deflator (1972 = 100)	85.0	86.2	87.1	88.9	92.5	100.0	106.5	124.8	141.6	164.0	196.0
Consumer price index (1975 = 100)	58.0	58.2	58.1	59.3	61.6	65.0	71.2	83.9	100.0	111.4	128.0
Import price index (1972 = 100)	78	79	80	81	89	100	119	178	225	261	281

Sources: Kenya, *Economic Survey*, *Statistical Abstract*, and *Statistical Digest*, various issues.

[1] National accounts and relevant customs data are available only on a calendar-year basis.

[2] In millions of Kenya shillings.

[3] Deflated by the consumer price index.

For the sales tax, a breakdown of revenue collections is available on revenue from tax on domestically produced and imported manufactures.[6] But this is not a particularly useful grouping from the viewpoint of estimation. And again, no disaggregate estimates are published for the revenue effects of discretionary tax measures.

Adjustment of Tax Revenue to Current Structure Basis

To estimate forecasting equations associated with a given tax structure, it is necessary to separate those changes in revenue that took place automatically in response to growth in the tax base from changes in revenue that occurred as a result of discretionary changes, whether legal or administrative. To do this, methods must be employed that convert the actual revenue data into a series that shows what revenues would have been if there had been no discretionary changes relative to the current year's tax system.

Two methods may be applied to generate such a "clean" revenue series.[7] The first is the constant rate structure method, which consists of applying the current year's tax rates to the base values in the earlier years, thus simulating a revenue series that corresponds to the current year's structure.[8] Unfortunately, when applied properly, this procedure requires much information; for each tax category, it is necessary to have detailed information on rates, on the base, and on the distribution of the base by brackets or rate categories. Furthermore, the method depends on the assumption that changes in the tax structure do not affect the magnitudes of the subtax bases, which implies that resource allocation is not affected by changes in the

---

[6] The data can be obtained from Kenya, *Appropriation Accounts, Other Public Accounts and the Accounts of the Funds for the Year* (annual).

[7] When discretionary changes are few relative to the number of observations, their effects on the structure can be estimated by the technique of dummy variables.

[8] For an application of this method and a discussion of some of the issues involved in using it, see Nurun N. Choudhry, "A Study of the Elasticity of the West Malaysian Income Tax System, 1961–70," *Staff Papers,* Vol. 22 (July 1975), pp. 494–509.

relative prices. Because of the very heavy requirement of data and the restrictive assumptions, the constant structure method has found little practical application.

The other method is the proportional data adjustment method, which permits adjustment of a tax revenue series without any information on the tax base. Apart from data on the actual revenue collections, the only additional information required in applying this method is estimates of the quantitative impact on revenue of discretionary changes for the years in which the changes took place.[9] Assume the following series of actual revenue collection in years *1* through *n:*

$$T_1, T_2, \ldots, T_{n-1}, T_n,$$

where *n* is the last or the current year.

Let the estimated revenue effect of discretionary changes in the years in which they occurred be as follows: [10]

$$D_2, \ldots, D_{n-1}, D_n.$$

Let us now construct an adjusted series of revenue equal to those revenues that would pertain if the current year's tax structure had been in operation throughout the period under analysis:

$$AT_1, AT_2, \ldots, AT_{n-1}, AT_n.$$

Since the current year *(n)* is the reference year, the actual and adjusted revenue for that year would be the same

$$AT_n = T_n.$$

---

[9] This method has been applied in a number of Fund studies; see, for example: Charles Y. Mansfield, "Elasticity and Buoyancy of a Tax System: A Method Applied to Paraguay," *Staff Papers,* Vol. 19 (July 1972), pp. 425–46; Hessel J. Baas and Daryl A. Dixon, "The Elasticity of the British Tax System, 1950/51–1970/71" (unpublished paper, September 1974); and Sheetal K. Chand, "Tax Revenue Forecasting: An Approach Applied to Malaysia" (unpublished paper, March 1975).

[10] Note that the first discretionary change occurs in year *2,* since year *1* is the first year in the time series.

However, actual revenue collection in years $n-1, n-2, \ldots, 2, 1,$ must be corrected for discretionary changes in subsequent years. Under the proportional adjustment hypothesis, the series of adjusted revenue, with n as the reference year, becomes as follows:[11]

$$AT_{n-1} = T_{n-1}\left(\frac{T_n}{T_n - D_n}\right)$$

$$AT_{n-2} = T_{n-2}\left(\frac{T_n}{T_n - D_n}\right)\left(\frac{T_{n-1}}{T_{n-1} - D_{n-1}}\right)$$

$$\vdots$$

$$AT_2 = T_2\left(\frac{T_n}{T_n - D_n}\right)\left(\frac{T_{n-1}}{T_{n-1} - D_{n-1}}\right)\cdots\left(\frac{T_3}{T_3 - D_3}\right)$$

$$AT_1 = T_1\left(\frac{T_n}{T_n - D_n}\right)\left(\frac{T_{n-1}}{T_{n-1} - D_{n-1}}\right)\cdots\left(\frac{T_3}{T_3 - D_3}\right)\left(\frac{T_2}{T_2 - D_2}\right)$$

which can be expressed by the general formula:

$$AT_{n-j} = T_{n-j}\left(\frac{AT_{n-j+1}}{T_{n-j+1} - D_{n-j+1}}\right), j = 1, 2, \ldots, n-2, n-1.$$

It may be helpful to provide a numerical illustration of the method. Let the actual revenue collections in years *1* through *5* be as follows:

$$T_1 = 100, T_2 = 140, T_3 = 170, T_4 = 250, T_5 = 320.$$

Assume that discretionary changes occurred only in years *2* and *4,* with

$$D_2 = 20, D_3 = 0, D_4 = 30, D_5 = 0.$$

Let us now construct an adjusted revenue series with year *5* as reference year. The effect of the discretionary action in year *4* was to raise revenue collections in that year by 13.64 per cent:

$$\frac{T_4}{T_4 - D_4} = \frac{250}{250 - 30} = 1.1364.$$

[11] The assumption that discretionary actions affect revenue proportionately implies that the built-in elasticity of the particular tax is unaffected. Thus, the effects of discretionary actions are equivalent to multiplicative shifts in the relationship of the tax to the base.

If this discretionary action had been taken at the beginning of the data period, the proportional adjustment hypothesis would imply a corresponding proportionate increase in revenue collections in all years preceding year *4*. Similarly, the effect of the discretionary action in year *2* was to raise revenue in that year by 16.67 per cent:

$$\frac{T_2}{T_2 - D_2} = \frac{140}{140 - 20} = 1.1667.$$

Only revenue in year *1* needs to be corrected for the change in year *2*. Thus, if both discretionary actions had been taken at the beginning of the data period, the revenue series would have become as follows under the proportional adjustment hypothesis:

$$AT_5 = T_5 = 320$$

$$AT_4 = T_4 = 250$$

$$AT_3 = T_3 \left(\frac{T_4}{T_4 - D_4}\right) = 170 \times 1.1364 = 193.2$$

$$AT_2 = T_2 \left(\frac{T_4}{T_4 - D_4}\right) = 140 \times 1.1364 = 159.1$$

$$AT_1 = T_1 \left(\frac{T_4}{T_4 - D_4}\right)\left(\frac{T_2}{T_2 - D_2}\right) = 100 \times 1.1364 \times 1.1667 = 132.6.$$

This workshop applies the proportional data adjustment method to generate a "clean" revenue series, showing what the revenues would have been if there had been no discretionary changes relative to the current year's tax structure. In Kenya, estimates of the revenue effects of discretionary measures are prepared at the time the budget is formulated and are published in the budget speech. As can be seen from Table 4, discretionary changes have occurred very frequently for all major tax categories, thus effectively ruling out the application of the dummy variable technique to the raw revenue data. Since the actual revenue effect of discretionary changes may well differ from the *ex ante* budget estimates, an attempt should be made to update these estimates. In Kenya, however, no *ex post* revision of the initial estimates is provided. One possible approach to correcting the *ex ante* budget estimates would be to apply the ratios

TABLE 4. Kenya: Budget Estimates of the Revenue Effects of Discretionary Tax Measures, Fiscal Years 1969–77

(In millions of Kenya shillings; year ending June 30)

Tax Revenue Source	1969	1970	1971	1972	1973	1974	1975	1976	1977
1. Taxes on income, profits, and capital gains[1]	—	—	—	—	–5.0	–19.0	70.0	64.0	1.0
4.3 Estate duty	—	—	—	—	1.6	—	—	—	—
5.1 Sales tax	—	—	—	—	. . .[2]	440.0	152.0	69.0	32.0
5.2 Excises	8.0	3.0	—	58.0	57.0	–177.0	7.0	–25.0	102.0
5.4 Taxes on specific services	—	—	2.6	10.0	4.0	—	1.6	—	2.0
5.5 Taxes on use of, or permission to use, goods or to perform activities	—	—	–3.6	14.0	—	—	—	—	—
6.1 Import duties	6.0	1.0	6.8	7.5	40.4	2.6	–2.0	242.0	86.0
7.2 Stamp duties	—	—	—	—	—	5.0	—	—	—
IV. Tax revenue[3]	**14.0**	**4.0**	**5.8**	**89.5**	**98.0**	**251.6**	**228.6**	**350.0**	**223.0**

Source: Kenya, *Financial Statements*, 1968/69 to 1976/77.

[1] Excluding the graduated personal tax, which was abolished December 31, 1973.

[2] The sales tax was introduced in April–May 1973, and no budget estimate was available for fiscal year 1973.

[3] Excluding the graduated personal tax, which was abolished December 31, 1973, and the export duties that were removed June 15, 1973.

of actual to estimated overall yield of each tax, on the assumption that the percentage error in estimating the revenue effect of a discretionary change of a particular tax would be the same as the percentage error in forecasting the overall yield of that same tax. This assumption may not be entirely appropriate, but it is reasonable, at least.[12] Table 5 provides data on the ratios of actual to estimated tax revenue, which can be applied to the *ex ante* budget estimates to obtain *ex post* estimates of the revenue effect of discretionary changes in the years in which they occurred. These revised estimates may be used to construct the adjusted revenue series.

Nontax Revenue

Data on central government nontax revenue, classified as in the *Government Finance Statistics Yearbook,* are presented in Table 6 for the six-year period of fiscal years 1972–77. In fiscal year 1977, nontax revenue contributed almost 14 per cent of total revenue. The two most important categories are (1) property income, which takes the form of dividends, interest, rents, royalties, or withdrawal from entrepreneurial income; and (2) administrative fees, charges, and nonindustrial sales.

Systematic relationships may be found for certain components of nontax revenue, such as administrative fees, but in other instances, such as profits of the Central Bank, there may be considerable volatility in the time series. Of necessity, the method of projection must be ad hoc in many cases. Sometimes a forecast is made of total nontax revenue by applying the last year's ratio of total nontax revenue to gross domestic product (GDP) to the projected value of GDP. However, rather than relying on a mechanistic projection of the aggregate, it might be feasible to allow for expected changes in

[12] If some of the estimates of the revenue effect of discretionary action seem excessively unreliable, it may be possible, under certain circumstances, to estimate their effects on the tax structure by applying the technique of dummy variables in conjunction with the proportional data adjustment method.

TABLE 5. Kenya: Ratios of Actual to Estimated Tax Revenue, Fiscal Years 1969–77

(In per cent; year ending June 30)

Tax Revenue Source	1969	1970	1971	1972	1973	1974	1975	1976	1977
1. Taxes on income, profits, and capital gains[1]	108.6	113.5	118.4	110.7	119.7	125.9	121.5	110.9	110.8
4.3 Estate duty	112.0	115.7	108.3	146.9	72.2	100.8	117.0	80.9	80.6
5.1 Sales tax	—	—	—	—	...[2]	145.4	110.3	109.8	102.2
5.2 Excises	111.6	108.9	113.0	100.7	92.8	118.7	100.5	77.5	108.5
5.4 Taxes on specific services	97.1	70.2	120.7	102.5	114.8	119.6	98.4	102.0	102.1
5.5 Taxes on use of, or permission to use, goods or to perform activities	114.3	116.0	120.4	100.1	106.2	107.3	104.0	104.3	105.8
6.1 Import duties	112.2	115.0	120.7	108.6	97.1	121.9	100.1	84.3	97.9
7.2 Stamp duties	113.9	130.7	116.4	116.5	95.4	138.4	103.2	89.8	100.0
IV. Tax revenue[3]	**110.7**	**113.2**	**118.0**	**107.6**	**105.6**	**126.7**	**110.3**	**99.4**	**105.3**

Source: Kenya, *Appropriation Accounts, Other Public Accounts and the Accounts of the Funds for the Year 1968/69* to *1976/77.*

1 Excluding the graduated personal tax, which was abolished December 31, 1973.

2 The sales tax was introduced in April–May 1973, and no budget estimate was available for fiscal year 1973.

3 Excluding the graduated personal tax and export duties.

TABLE 6. Kenya: Central Government Nontax Revenue, Fiscal Years 1972–77
(In millions of Kenya shillings; year ending June 30)

Nontax Revenue Source	1972	1973	1974	1975	1976	1977
V. Current nontax revenue	**493.3**	**497.6**	**438.1**	**403.4**	**551.8**	**851.8**
9. Property income	214.2	219.1	156.8	144.1	238.0	305.6
10. Administrative fees and charges and nonindustrial sales	177.8	207.5	201.4	160.7	194.8	382.8
11. Fines and forfeits	16.4	15.8	18.6	20.0	27.1	48.6
13. Other	84.9	55.2	61.3	78.6	91.9	114.9
VI. Capital revenue	—	**1.3**	—	**0.2**	**0.4**	**0.5**
Total nontax revenue	**493.3**	**498.9**	**438.1**	**403.6**	**552.2**	**852.3**

Source: International Monetary Fund, *Government Finance Statistics Yearbook*, Vol. 1 (1977) and Vol. 2 (1978).

relevant factors through judgmental adjustments in the individual components.

STATISTICAL ESTIMATION

Having adjusted the actual revenue series for the effects of discretionary changes, the major steps in the forecasting procedure consist of specifying functional relationships between the taxes and the selected proxy bases, estimating a set of parameters reproducing the current tax structure, and applying these estimates to forecast tax revenues for given values of the bases.

Specification of Functional Relationships

Choosing the proxy bases suggested in Table 2, the following relationships were specified for the individual taxes or tax categories.

Taxes on Income, Profits, and Capital Gains

$$ATI_t = a + bY_t + cDA_t \quad (1)$$

$$Ln\, ATI_t = a + b\, Ln\, Y_t + c\, Ln\, DB_t \quad (2)$$

where

ATI = adjusted revenue from taxes on income, profits, and capital gains

Y = gross domestic product at factor cost at current prices.

DA and *DB* are dummy variables for changes in the timing of the payment of income taxes:[13]

$$DA_t = \begin{cases} 0 \text{ for fiscal years 1968–70} \\ 1 \text{ for fiscal years 1971–77} \end{cases}$$

$$Ln\, DB_t = \begin{cases} 0 \text{ for fiscal years 1968–70} \\ 1 \text{ for fiscal years 1971–77.} \end{cases}$$

Sales Tax

$$ATS_t = a + b\, CP_t \qquad (3)$$

$$Ln\, ATS_t = a + b\, Ln\, CP_t \qquad (4)$$

where

ATS = adjusted revenue from sales tax

CP = private consumption expenditure.

Import Duties

$$ATM_t = a + b\, M_t + c\, \overline{M}_t \qquad (5)$$

$$Ln\, ATM_t = a + b\, Ln\, M_t + c\, Ln\, \overline{M}_t \qquad (6)$$

where

ATM = adjusted revenue from import duties

M = imports (customs basis) at current prices

$\overline{M}$ = imports (customs basis) at constant prices.

Excise Duties

$$ATE_t = a + b\, \overline{CP}_t \qquad (7)$$

$$Ln\, ATE_t = a + b\, Ln\, \overline{CP}_t \qquad (8)$$

where

ATE = adjusted revenue from excise duties

$\overline{CP}$ = private consumption expenditure deflated by the CPI.

---

[13] The revenue effects of these changes are not taken into account in Table 4. Actually, the changes produced both permanent and windfall gains in tax revenue, but the specification of equations (1) and (2) attempts to estimate the permanent effect on the tax structure.

Minor Taxes

Estimating equations were specified for three of the four minor taxes as follows:

$$Ln\,ATUP_t = a + b\,Ln\,\overline{Y}_t \qquad (9)$$

$$Ln\,ATSD_t = a + b\,Ln\,\overline{Y}_t \qquad (10)$$

$$Ln\,ATSS_t = a + b\,Ln\,CP_t \qquad (11)$$

where

$ATUP$ = adjusted revenue from taxes on use of, or permission to use, goods or to perform activities

$ATSD$ = adjusted revenue from stamp duties

$ATSS$ = adjusted revenue from taxes on specific services

$\overline{Y}$ = gross domestic product at factor cost at constant prices.

Estimation Results

Since data on the bases were not available on a fiscal-year basis, it was decided to regress tax revenue in fiscal year t on two alternative bases: [14]

(a) LB_t = lagged, calendar-year base;
for example, LB_{1968} is equal to calendar-year 1967 base; and

(b) MB_t = mean of two calendar-year bases;
for example, MB_{1968} is equal to the mean of the bases in the two calendar years 1967 and 1968.

The parameters were estimated by the method of ordinary least squares. The estimation results are shown below with t values in parentheses.[15] Given the limited number of observations, considerable care is needed in the evaluation of the regression estimates; in

[14] Note that fiscal year 1968 covers the period July 1, 1967–June 30, 1968.

[15] The predicted values for some of the equations are presented in Table 7, together with the actual revenue series adjusted for the effects of discretionary tax measures.

particular, for the sales tax, there are only four observations to estimate the two parameters of the regression equation.

Taxes on Income, Profits, and Capital Gains

Estimation period: fiscal years 1968–77

$$ATI_t = -257.07 + 0.09049\, LY_t + 165.63\, DA_t \qquad (1a)$$
$$(6.94) \quad (28.44) \quad (4.45)$$
$$\bar{R}^2 = 0.995 \qquad D\text{-}W = 2.50$$

$$ATI_t = -154.96 + 0.07570\, MY_t + 184.56\, DA_t \qquad (1b)$$
$$(3.33) \quad (21.00) \quad (3.71)$$
$$\bar{R}^2 = 0.990 \qquad D\text{-}W = 2.23$$

$$Ln\, ATI_t = -3.68010 + 1.09750\, Ln\, LY_t + 0.26426\, Ln\, DB_t \qquad (2a)$$
$$(6.98) \quad (18.95) \quad (5.78)$$
$$\bar{R}^2 = 0.992 \qquad D\text{-}W = 3.08$$

$$Ln\, ATI_t = -2.99441 + 1.01734\, Ln\, MY_t + 0.26577\, Ln\, DB_t \qquad (2b)$$
$$(5.61) \quad (17.42) \quad (5.36)$$
$$\bar{R}^2 = 0.991 \qquad D\text{-}W = 2.79$$

Sales Tax

Estimation period : fiscal years 1974–77

$$ATS_t = 163.23 + 0.06622\, LCP_t \qquad (3a)$$
$$(1.76) \quad (10.29)$$
$$\bar{R}^2 = 0.972 \qquad D\text{-}W = 2.19$$

$$ATS_t = 172.30 + 0.06002\, MCP_t \qquad (3b)$$
$$(1.52) \quad (8.31)$$
$$\bar{R}^2 = 0.958 \qquad D\text{-}W = 2.31$$

$$Ln\, ATS_t = -\ 1.28589 + 0.86750\, Ln\, LCP_t \qquad (4a)$$
$$(1.59) \quad (10.22)$$
$$\bar{R}^2 = 0.972 \qquad D\text{-}W = 2.30$$

$$Ln\, ATS_t = -\ 1.32644 + 0.86375\, Ln\, MCP_t \qquad (4b)$$
$$(1.58) \quad (9.88)$$
$$\bar{R}^2 = 0.970 \qquad D\text{-}W = 2.29$$

Import Duties

Estimation period: fiscal years 1968–77

$$ATM_t = 157.59 + 0.07183\, LM_t + 0.11081\, L\overline{M}_t \qquad (5a)$$
$$(0.71) \qquad (5.14) \qquad (1.87)$$
$$\bar{R}^2 = 0.769 \qquad D\text{-}W = 2.89$$

$$ATM_t = -23.98 + 0.07018\, MM_t + 0.15341\, M\overline{M}_t \qquad (5b)$$
$$(0.10) \qquad (6.51) \qquad (2.44)$$
$$\bar{R}^2 = 0.833 \qquad D\text{-}W = 2.17$$

$$Ln\, ATM_t = 0.38600 + 0.40020\, Ln\, LM_t + 0.37235\, Ln\, L\overline{M}_t \qquad (6a)$$
$$(0.20) \qquad (5.40) \qquad (1.53)$$
$$\bar{R}^2 = 0.791 \qquad D\text{-}W = 2.74$$

$$Ln\, ATM_t = -0.74410 + 0.40859\, Ln\, MM_t + 0.49701\, Ln\, M\overline{M}_t \qquad (6b)$$
$$(0.37) \qquad (7.11) \qquad (2.05)$$
$$\bar{R}^2 = 0.862 \qquad D\text{-}W = 2.37$$

Excise Duties

Estimation period: fiscal years 1968–77

$$ATE_t = -236.72 + 0.04959\, L\overline{CP}_t \qquad (7a)$$
$$(3.80) \qquad (10.67)$$
$$\bar{R}^2 = 0.926 \qquad D\text{-}W = 2.20$$

$$ATE_t = -269.84 + 0.05083\, M\overline{CP}_t \qquad (7b)$$
$$(4.11) \qquad (10.63)$$
$$\bar{R}^2 = 0.926 \qquad D\text{-}W = 1.74$$

$$Ln\, ATE_t = -8.95805 + 1.57886\, Ln\, L\overline{CP}_t \qquad (8a)$$
$$(7.19) \qquad (12.00)$$
$$\bar{R}^2 = 0.941 \qquad D\text{-}W = 2.26$$

$$Ln\, ATE_t = -9.70251 + 1.65294\, Ln\, M\overline{CP}_t \qquad (8b)$$
$$(7.73) \qquad (12.52)$$
$$\bar{R}^2 = 0.945 \qquad D\text{-}W = 1.82$$

Minor Taxes

Taxes on Use of, or Permission to Use, Goods or to Perform Services

Estimation period: fiscal years 1968–77

$$Ln\, ATUP_t = -10.70870 + 1.58136\, Ln\, L\overline{Y}_t \qquad (9a)$$
$$(14.15) \qquad (19.71)$$

$$\bar{R}^2 = 0.977 \qquad D\text{-}W = 1.43$$

$$Ln\, ATUP_t = -11.26880 + 1.63591\, Ln\, M\overline{Y}_t \qquad (9b)$$
$$(21.91) \qquad (30.11)$$

$$\bar{R}^2 = 0.990 \qquad D\text{-}W = 1.76$$

Stamp Duties

Estimation period: fiscal years 1968–77

$$Ln\, ATSD_t = -15.99393 + 2.06526\, Ln\, L\overline{Y}_t \qquad (10a)$$
$$(11.88) \qquad (14.47)$$

$$\bar{R}^2 = 0.959 \qquad D\text{-}W = 2.79$$

$$Ln\, ATSD_t = -16.54503 + 2.11742\, Ln\, M\overline{Y}_t \qquad (10b)$$
$$(11.03) \qquad (13.36)$$

$$\bar{R}^2 = 0.952 \qquad D\text{-}W = 2.71$$

Taxes on Specific Services

Estimation period: fiscal years 1971–77

$$Ln\, ATSS_t = -4.33160 + 0.84651\, Ln\, LCP_t \qquad (11a)$$
$$(3.50) \qquad (6.36)$$

$$\bar{R}^2 = 0.868 \qquad D\text{-}W = 0.98$$

$$Ln\, ATSS_t = -4.33701 + 0.83950\, Ln\, MCP_t \qquad (11b)$$
$$(3.70) \qquad (6.73)$$

$$\bar{R}^2 = 0.881 \qquad D\text{-}W = 0.82$$

TABLE 7. Kenya: Actual and Predicted Values for Selected Equations, Fiscal Years 1968–77[1]

(In millions of Kenya shillings)

Year Ending June 30	*ATI*	Predicted[2] (1a)	(1b)	*ATM*	Predicted[2] (6a)	(6b)
1968	493.1	477.3	487.4	618.0	659.7	633.4
1969	506.9	544.5	540.8	666.0	686.0	649.5
1970	626.9	604.9	598.4	741.1	689.8	715.6
1971	811.1	847.6	853.9	861.6	804.2	850.6
1972	966.8	940.3	959.7	933.0	931.9	890.6
1973	1,084.2	1,100.5	1,095.3	741.3	884.7	880.4
1974	1,240.5	1,264.4	1,274.4	1,087.8	926.9	1,043.7
1975	1,595.1	1,528.8	1,485.5	1,154.5	1,191.0	1,088.1
1976	1,797.6	1,769.0	1,763.8	1,068.7	1,044.5	1,011.3
1977	2,149.3	2,194.0	2,212.0	1,057.2	1,080.7	1,143.8
Year Ending June 30	***ATE***	**Predicted[2] (8a)**	**(8b)**	***ATS***	**Predicted[2] (4a)**	**(4b)**
1968	269.7	270.7	267.8			
1969	290.7	297.6	292.4			
1970	320.4	320.6	312.3			
1971	372.8	337.5	360.6			
1972	392.2	418.9	415.2			
1973	404.8	445.0	464.4			
1974	515.9	517.3	494.1	853.9	875.4	866.7
1975	546.7	502.7	507.6	1,027.0	993.7	1,020.8
1976	521.4	544.1	529.2	1,215.9	1,208.4	1,174.6
1977	574.1	545.0	555.5	1,308.4	1,328.2	1,343.6

[1] Series under the variable name are actual tax revenues adjusted for the effect of discretionary tax measures, as defined in the text. The numbers in parentheses indicate the equations from which the predictions were obtained.

[2] See text for an explanation of the variables and the equations.

EXERCISES AND ISSUES FOR DISCUSSION

Exercises

1. *Use the proportional adjustment method to construct adjusted revenue series, with fiscal year 1977 as reference year, for the four major tax categories: (1) taxes on income, profits, and capital gains; (2) sales tax; (3) excise duties; and (4) import duties. The necessary data for the calculations are given in Tables 1, 4, and 5, and a sample worksheet for the proportional adjustment method is provided in Appendix I. Note that revenue from the graduated personal tax, which was abolished on December 31, 1973, must be deducted from taxes on income, profits, and capital gains, as presented in Table 1. For the sales tax, which was introduced in April–May 1973, construct an adjusted series of revenue for fiscal years 1974–77.*

2. *Examine the relationships of tax to base as specified and estimated in the section on Statistical Estimation. In particular:*
   (a) *What is the significance of the dummy variables in equations (1) and (2)? Use one of the estimated regression equations (2a) or (2b) to test the hypothesis that the elasticity of taxes on income, profits, and capital gains with respect to GDP at factor cost at current prices is equal to unity.*
   (b) *Comment on the problems that may arise in the estimation of equations (5) and (6). What are the elasticities of import duties in equation (6a) or (6b) with respect to import volume and import price?*
   (c) *Compare the estimation results with a lagged, calendar-year base* (LB) *to those with an average of two calendar-year bases* (MB).

3. *For each tax or tax category, use one of the estimated regression equations with a lagged base to make a forecast for fiscal year 1978. Data on the bases for calendar year 1977 are provided in Table 3 and budget estimates of the revenue effect of discretionary measures in fiscal year 1978 are shown in Table 8. For estate*

TABLE 8. Kenya: Revenue Estimates of Discretionary Tax Measures, Fiscal Year 1978
(In millions of Kenya shillings; year ending June 30)

1.	Taxes on income, profits, and capital gains	—90
5.1	Sales tax	205
5.2	Excises	—32
5.4	Taxes on specific services	10
6.1	Import duties	100
6.2	Export duties	300

Source: Kenya, *Financial Statement*, 1977/78.

duties that do not exhibit any clear trend, make a forecast by taking the average of the last three years.

4. *On the basis of the forecasts made in Exercise 3 for the individual taxes or tax categories for fiscal year 1978, calculate:*
   (a) *the expected built-in elasticity of total tax revenue with respect to lagged, calendar-year GDP at factor cost at current prices; and*
   (b) *the expected overall elasticity of total tax revenue with respect to lagged, calendar-year GDP at factor cost at current prices.*
5. *Compare the forecasts made in Exercise 3 for each tax or tax category with the budget estimates of tax revenue for fiscal year 1978 shown in Table 9. Where do the major differences lie and what factors may account for the differences?*

TABLE 9. Kenya: Budget Estimates of Tax Revenue, Fiscal Year 1978
(In millions of Kenya shillings; year ending June 30)

1.	Taxes on income, profits, and capital gains	2,400
4.3	Estate duty	8
5.1	Sales tax	1,660
5.2	Excises	530
5.4	Taxes on specific services	61
5.5	Taxes on use of, or permission to use, goods or to perform activities	82
6.1	Import duties	1,300
6.2	Export duties	300
7.2	Stamp duties	60
IV.	**Tax revenue**	**6,401**

Source: Kenya, *Estimates of Revenue*, 1977/78.

6. *Make a forecast of total nontax revenue for fiscal year 1978 by applying the ratio of nontax revenue in fiscal year 1977 to GDP at factor cost at current prices in calendar year 1976 to the value of GDP at factor cost at current prices in calendar year 1977.*

Issues for Discussion

1. *Comment on the classification of tax revenue data presented in Table 1. Are there tax categories for which a further breakdown would have been desirable? Identify minor taxes or tax categories that may be forecast together rather than on a tax-by-tax basis.*
2. *Provide reasons for the choices of proxy bases suggested in Table 2. In particular, why would it be inappropriate to choose a common base for domestic taxes on goods and services?*
3. *Discuss the assumptions and possible limitations of the proportional data adjustment method.*
4. *Comment on the data on budget estimates and outturns provided in Table 5. In particular, what factors may account for the systematic underestimation of taxes on income, profits, and capital gains?*
5. *What criteria would you apply in choosing between the various specifications of the tax functions from the point of view of revenue forecasting?*
6. *Discuss how an increase in domestic prices would affect the built-in elasticity of tax revenue with respect to GDP at factor cost at current prices.*
7. *Comment on the time series of nontax revenues presented in Table 6. Indicate what kind of information would be desirable for forecasting the major components.*

APPENDIX I

Kenya: Worksheet for Proportional Adjustment Method
(Reference year: Fiscal Year 1977)

t	T_t	BD_t	R_t	$D_t = R_t \times BD_t$	$T_t - D_t$	$AF_t = \frac{AT_{t+1}}{T_{t+1} - D_{t+1}}$	$AT_t = AF_t \times T_t$
1977							
1976							
1975							
1974							
1973							
1972							
1971							
1970							
1969							
1968							

Notation:

t = Fiscal year

T_t = Actual revenue

BD_t = *Ex ante* budget estimate of the revenue effect of discretionary action in the year in which it was taken

R_t = Ratio of actual to estimated tax revenue

D_t = *Ex post* estimate of the revenue effect of discretionary action in the year in which it was taken

AF_t = Adjustment factor with 1977 as reference year (Note that $AF_t = 1$ for $t = 1977$.)

AT_t = Adjusted revenue with 1977 as reference year (Note that $AT_t = T_t$ for $t = 1977$.)

APPENDIX II

Kenya: Summary of Tax System, July 1977

Tax	Nature of Tax	Exemptions and Deductions	Rates
1. Taxes on net income and profits			
1.1 *Taxes on companies, corporations, and enterprises* Income Tax Act, 1973 (No. 16 of 1973); the 1974 Finance Bill	Tax is charged on income accruing in the Partner States of the East African Community (EAC) or, for nonresidents, on income accrued in Kenya.	Incomes of specified agricultural produce boards, certain cooperatives, approved pension schemes and provident funds, all EAC corporations, etc., are exempt. Income deriving from interest on government tax reserve certificates and on specified loans to government and public authorities, etc., is exempt, as are dividends from companies of which the recipient controls more than 12.5 per cent of the voting stock. Annual depreciation allowances as per cent of written down value are as follows: buildings, 2.5 per cent (hotels, 4 per cent); machinery, 12.5 per cent; mining opera-	Resident companies, 45 per cent. The tax rate is 27.5 per cent for income from mining of specified materials for the first four years during which a company is liable to tax. The rate for life insurance business of resident insurance companies is 40 per cent. For nonresident companies the rate is 52.5 per cent. Dividend and interest payments to residents are subject to withholding tax at a rate of 15 per cent and 12.5 per cent, respectively, which is credited against tax payable. Payments to nonresidents are taxed at the following rates:

Kenya: Summary of Tax System, July 1977 (continued)

Tax	Nature of Tax	Exemptions and Deductions	Rates	
1. **Taxes on net income and profits** (continued)		tions, 10 per cent of the capital investment; agricultural land improvements, 20 per cent; agricultural machinery, 37½ per cent. In addition to the annual allowances, an initial "Investment deduction" of 20 per cent is granted for new investment in buildings (including hotels) and equipment outside the municipalities of Nairobi and Mombasa.		*(In per cent)*
			Management or professional fees	20.0
			Royalties	20.0
			Dividends	15.0
			Interest	12.5
		In ascertaining total income, all expenditure incurred wholly and exclusively in the production of income is deductible, including, inter alia, preproduction business expenditures, capital expenditure on farm land for the purpose of preventing soil erosion or for clearing and planting permanent or semipermanent crops, and interest on money em-		

		ployed in the production of income. Resident companies are entitled to relief by way of tax credits for taxes paid to other EAC states on income derived from that Partner State.	
1.2 *Taxes on individuals* Income Tax Act, 1973 (No. 16 of 1973); the 1974 Finance Bill	Tax is charged on income accruing in the EAC Partner States, or, for nonresidents, on income accrued in Kenya. The income of a married woman living with her husband is deemed to be her husband's income for tax purposes. Losses can be offset against other sources of income and can be carried forward indefinitely. A pay-as-you-earn (PAYE) system is in operation for employees.	The President of Kenya is exempted from taxes on his salary, etc., as are allowances of Members of Parliament. Interest on post office savings bank deposits and interest on tax reserve certificates and on specified government securities held by nonresidents are exempt. Interest on amounts not exceeding KSh 200,000 borrowed for the purchase or improvement of owner-occupied housing may be deducted. In ascertaining total income, all expenditure incurred wholly and exclusively in the production of income is deductible, including inter alia: capi-	*Taxable Income* *(In per cent)* On the first KSh 24,000 10 On the next KSh 24,000 15 On the next KSh 24,000 25 On the next KSh 24,000 35 On the next KSh 24,000 45 On the next KSh 24,000 50 On the next KSh 48,000 60 On income in excess of KSh 180,000 70 Dividends and interest payments to resident individuals are subject to withholding tax at a rate of 15 per cent and 12.5 per cent, respectively, which is credited against tax payable. Tax on payments to nonresidents:

Kenya: Summary of Tax System, July 1977 (continued)

Tax	Nature of Tax	Exemptions and Deductions	Rates	
1. **Taxes on net income and profits** (concluded)				
		tal expenditure on farm land for the purpose of preventing soil erosion or for clearing and planting permanent or semipermanent crops; interest on money employed in the production of income; for professionals, a housing deduction equal to 15 per cent of the gains or profits from the profession or KSh 14,000, whichever is less.		*(In per cent)*
			Management or professional fees	20
			Royalties	20
			Dividends	15
			Interest	12.5
			Pension annuities	5
		Personal reliefs, which are set off against tax payable, are as follows: (a) "family relief" of KSh 1,680 for any married taxpayer; (b) "single relief" of KSh 600; (c) "special single relief" of KSh 720 per single person with children; (d) maximum amount that can be claimed as insurance relief is KSh 480.		
		Residents are entitled to relief		

		by way of tax credits for taxes paid to other EAC states on income derived from that Partner State. Income in kind or "perquisites" provided by employers are included in taxable income.	
1.3 *Capital gains tax*	(a) Transfer of land and property; (b) Transfer of marketable securities. Transfer includes sale, exchange, conveyance, and gift. The tax base is reduced, depending upon the length of time property has been held.	The following transfers are exempt: (a) One owner-occupied house held for more than three years; (b) Rural land less than 100 acres or KSh 30,000 in transfer value.	Companies are taxed at the normal corporation tax rate, while individuals are taxed at their normal income tax rate up to a maximum of 35 per cent.
2. **Social security contributions** The National Social Security Fund Act, 1965 (No. 28 of 1965)		Persons in the public service covered by the Pensions Act are exempt, as are members of the armed forces, police force, prison services, and National Youth Service. However, temporary staff which do not enjoy government pension benefits are covered by the social security plan.	The employer and employee contribute 5 per cent each of the salary, up to a maximum of KSh 80 per month each.
3. **Payroll taxes** (other than social security contributions)	None.		

Kenya: Summary of Tax System, July 1977 (continued)

Tax	Nature of Tax	Exemptions and Deductions	Rates
4. **Taxes on property**			
4.1 *Real estate taxes*	There are no central government taxes on land and urban property.		
4.2 *Net wealth taxes*	None.		
4.3 *Death and gift taxes Estate duty*	Levied on dutiable estates of deceased persons. Gifts in excess of KSh 10,000 to any one donee made three years or less before the death of the deceased are included in the estate.	Exemptions include immovable property situated outside the country and bequests to the Government or for specified public purposes. Duties may be reduced in cases of quick succession. Estates under KSh 50,000 are exempt.	Rates of tax increase from 1 per cent on estates between KSh 50,000 and KSh 100,000 to 50 per cent on estates in excess of KSh 20 million.
4.4 *Property transfer taxes*	None.		
4.5 *Nonrecurrent taxes on property (e.g., capital)*	None.		
4.6 *Other*	None.		

5. **Taxes on goods and services**

5.1 *Sales tax*
Sales Tax Act, 1973 (No. 7 of 1973); the 1974 Finance Bill

The sales tax is a single-stage tax levied on all manufactured goods (except those which are specifically exempted), whether locally produced or imported, and on electricity. It is collected from registered manufacturers and importers.

Provision is made for discretionary remission of taxes on goods that are exported.

Exemptions include animal and vegetable products, pharmaceuticals and fertilizers (but not dried vegetables, bread, and margarine), specified items of raw materials, intermediate goods, and capital goods. Sales tax is rebated on exports (and the rebate acts as a subsidy when applied to goods which have not suffered domestic sales tax). Tax can also be waived by the Minister of Finance.

10 per cent on the sale price, or in the case of imports, 10 per cent on the customs duty value plus the amount of the customs duty.

15 per cent on wines and spirits; watches; travel goods; domestic appliances such as washing machines, refrigerators, etc.; cars; cameras, gramophones, tape recorders, etc.

The sales tax on cigarettes and tobacco is 30 per cent, levied on the value excluding excise.

The following products are subject to specific rates:

(a) Petroleum	KSh 605 per 1,000 liters
(b) Diesel	KSh 0.10 per liter
(c) Beer	KSh 2.22 per liter
(d) Electricity	KSh 0.01 per kwh

Kenya: Summary of Tax System, July 1977 (continued)

Tax	Nature of Tax	Exemptions and Deductions	Rates
5. **Taxes on goods and services** (continued)			
5.2 *Selective excises*			
5.21 *Tobacco* The Excise Tariffs Act (Chapter 474 of the Laws of Kenya); East African Customs and Excise Tariffs; East African Excise Management Act (Chapter 28 of the Laws of the Community); the 1974 Finance Bill	Levied on the ex-factory price of cigarettes, cigars, etc., pipe tobacco, and snuff.	. . .	The rate for cigarettes varies from 90 to 105 per cent depending on the price. The rate for pipe tobacco is 80 per cent. The following are subject to specific rates: Cigars, etc. KSh 42.33 per kg. Snuff KSh 15.87 per kg.
5.22 *Liquor*			
5.221 *Excise duty on beer* The Excise Tariffs Act	Levied on locally brewed beer	. . .	KSh 1.50 per liter of light beer KSh 2.25 per liter of heavy beer (stout)

	(Chapter 474 of the Laws of Kenya); East African Customs and Excise Tariffs; East African Excise Management Act (Chapter 28 of the Laws of the Community)			
5.222	*Excise duty on spirits and wines* The Excise Tariffs Act (Chapter 474 of the Laws of Kenya); East African Customs and Excise Tariffs; East African Excise Management Act	Levied on locally produced products	. . .	KSh 40 per proof liter of spirits KSh 1.32 per liter of still wine KSh 3.96 per liter of sparkling wine

Kenya: Summary of Tax System, July 1977 (continued)

Tax	Nature of Tax	Exemptions and Deductions	Rates
5. **Taxes on goods and services** (continued) (Chapter 28 of the Laws of the Community)			
5.24 *Other excises*			
5.241 *Secondhand motor vehicle purchase tax*	Levied on purchases of secondhand motor vehicles	Ambulances, etc.	KSh 60 for vehicles with less than four raised wheels and KSh 400–800 for all other vehicles depending upon the engine capacity
5.242 *Other* The Excise Tariffs Act (Chapter 474 of the Laws of Kenya); East African Customs and Excise Tariffs; East African Excise Management Act	Specific duties are levied on certain locally manufactured products; payable by the producer.	. . .	*Sugar:* KSh 100 per 100 kg.

(Chapter 28 of the Laws of the Community)			
5.4 *Taxes on specific services*			
5.41 *Hotel accommodation tax* The Hotel Accommodation Tax Act, 1971 (No. 23 of 1971) and amendment and regulations	Levied on hotel room occupancy charges	Premises run by the Government, the EAC, charitable organizations, etc.	Where charges include only room or room and breakfast, 10 per cent; in all other cases, 7.5 per cent.
5.42 *Air passenger tax* Air Passenger Tax Act, 1970 (No. 21 of 1970); Air Passenger Tax (Amendment) Act, 1973 (No. 8 of 1973)	Collected by airlines from all passengers embarking at an airport on an external ticket	Children under two years	KSh 40 per passenger
5.43 *Betting and gaming tax* The Betting,	Levied on (1) all bets made with a bookmaker other than at an authorized race meet-	. . .	(1) *Bets made with a bookmaker* (a) on losing bets, 7.5 per cent of stake; (b) on

Kenya: Summary of Tax System, July 1977 (continued)

Tax	Nature of Tax	Exemptions and Deductions	Rates
5. **Taxes on goods and services** (concluded)			
Lotteries and Gaming Act, 1966 (No. 9 of 1966) (Chapter 131 of the Laws of Kenya)	ing; (2) totalizators; (3) pool betting; and (4) gaming in public premises		winning bets, 7.5 per cent of winnings. (2) *Totalizators:* 5 per cent of the authorized commission. (3) *Pool betting:* 20 per cent of gross stakes. (4) *Gaming:* 5 per cent of authorized commission.
5.44 *Entertainment tax* The Entertainments Tax Act, 1950 (Chapter 479 of the Laws of Kenya)	Levied on entrance charges	Exemptions include charitable and sporting events.	*Entrance Charge (in KSh)* — *Tax Payable (in KSh)* 0 – 1.15 — — 1.16 – 2.25 — 0.15 2.26 – 4.50 — 0.30 4.51 – 7.00 — 0.75 7.01 – 10.00 — 1.25 10.01 – 20.00 — 2.00 20.01 and above — 3.00
5.5 *Taxes on use of, or permission to use, goods or to perform activities*			
5.51 *Business and professional licenses*			

5.511 *Business license fees*	All firms are required to have a license for all categories of business in which they are engaged. Fees vary according to the type of business and are graduated according to whether a business is located in a general business area or elsewhere in city and rural areas.	. . .	License fees range from KSh 50 to KSh 400 per annum.
5.512 *Liquor license fees*	Firms engaged in the sale of beer, wine, and spirits are required to obtain an annual liquor license. Licenses are in three broad categories: general licenses, off-licenses, and on-licenses; fees vary with the location of the business and the specific form of licenses.	. . .	License fees range up to KSh 2,000.
5.52 *Motor vehicle taxes*	Annual fees vary with the weight and type of vehicle. The rates for diesel-driven vehicles are twice those for gasoline-driven vehicles.	. . .	*Type of Vehicle* — *Fee (in KSh)* Cars weighing —less than 1,000 kilos — 200 —between 1,000–1,250 kilos — 250 —between 1,251–1,500 kilos — 350

Kenya: Summary of Tax System, July 1977 (continued)

Tax	Nature of Tax	Exemptions and Deductions	Rates
6. **Taxes on international trade and transactions**			
6.1 *Taxes on imports* The Customs Tariffs Act, Chapter 472, Revised Edition 1972, Updated to 1977	There are both specific and ad-valorem duties; the latter are determined on the basis of a price which includes, inter alia, cost of freight and insurance to the port or place of importation. Only one half of the cost of air freight, however, is included in the tax base.	Exemptions include goods purchased for the use of the President and by religious bodies and approved educational institutions. The legislation provides for refund of customs duties to certain local industries, which is generally granted to individual companies with respect to specific imports and for a limited period. Waiver can be granted by the Minister of Finance. (Note: Imports are also subject to exchange control licenses and quotas, and a charge of 1 per cent c.i.f. is levied for such applications.)	Ad-valorem duties predominate in the tariff, and the rates range from zero to 150 per cent. Selected ad-valorem rates include: Duty free: Live animals, medicine, fertilizers, industrial electric motors, tanning machinery, rolling mills, machine tools, weaving machines, milling machinery, agricultural machinery, boilers, pharmaceuticals 10 per cent: Welding equipment, electric hand tools, measuring instruments, grinding machinery, and pig iron 20–30 per cent: Majority of goods

33⅓ per cent	Polishes
37½ per cent	Television parts
40 per cent	Musical instruments, watches, electric lights, typewriters, carpets, automobiles (not exceeding 1,200 cc)
50 per cent	Scent, toys, meat extracts
55 per cent	Gramophone records
60 per cent	Hessian and sacking, radio and television sets
65 per cent	Matches
70 per cent	Scarves, corsets, outer garments
150 per cent	Automobiles (over 2,250 cc)

Specific duties apply to a number of goods, e.g.:

Beer	KSh 4 per liter
Wine	KSh 5 per liter
Liquor	KSh 60 per proof liter
Cigarettes	KSh 180 per kg.

Kenya: Summary of Tax System, July 1977 (concluded)

Tax	Nature of Tax	Exemptions and Deductions	Rates
6. **Taxes on international trade and transactions** (concluded)			
6.1 *Taxes on imports* (concluded)			Cigars: KSh 200 per kg. Petroleum products: KSh 600 per cubic meter Kerosene: KSh 140 per cubic meter Motor fuel: KSh 600 per cubic meter In some cases alternative specific and ad-valorem duties are prescribed, and in those cases the rate chargeable is that which results in the higher duty.
6.2 *Export duty* June 1977	(a) Coffee sold at Nairobi Auction, including commission for more than KSh 20,000 per ton; (b) Coffee entered for export which Commissioner has reason to believe has not been sold through Nairobi Auction;	Price under KSh 20,000 per ton—duty is nil.	15 per cent of the difference between KSh 20,000 per ton and higher price KSh 6,000 per ton or 10 per cent of the f.o.b. value, whichever is the greater

	(c) Tea: rates over KSh 20,000 per ton.	Value under KSh 20,000 per ton—duty is nil.	15 per cent of the difference between KSh 20,000 per ton and higher price
7. **Other taxes**			
7.1 *Poll taxes*	None		
7.2 *Stamp duties*	Duty is levied on a range of specified instruments, including agreements, articles of association of a company, bills of exchange, bills of sale, deeds, leases, certain insurance policies and transfers.	General exemptions include instruments on which duty would be paid by the Government and certain savings bank and building societies' documents.	Rates of duty vary widely according to the nature of the instruments, the matter to which it relates, and the value thereof.
7.3 *Other taxes*	None		

Source: Information provided by the Kenyan authorities.

Chapter 10

WORKSHOP 8

Balance of Payments Forecasting

This workshop provides background information and discusses possible techniques for forecasting balance of payments developments in Kenya during the period of a hypothetical financial program.[1] Balance of payments forecasting is particularly important in developing countries with large foreign sectors[2] and potentially unstable export receipts. Further, forecasting the possible need for balance of payments assistance and the impact of proposed adjustment policies represents a crucial element of financial programs linked to the use of the International Monetary Fund's resources.

One of the more difficult parts of an overall macroeconomic forecast is the balance of payments. By definition, the external sector involves interrelationships with the rest of the world and therefore necessitates assumptions about developments in other countries.

[1] The present workshop utilizes data up to the end of 1976 and presents forecasting exercises for 1977. Data are also provided, however, for the actual outcome for 1977, in order to allow comparison with the results of the forecasting exercise and to aid in the completion of the hypothetical financial program for 1978 presented in Workshop 9.

[2] Exports and imports (national accounts basis) averaged 33 per cent of gross domestic product in Kenya during the period 1971–76.

Items entering the balance of payments of one country must be recorded in the balance of payments of another.[3] Even apart from the need to consider developments in other countries, the diversity of balance of payments components complicates analysis and considerable differences may be expected in the types of behavorial relationships used to explain items in the trade, services, or capital accounts. Further, the development of stable behavioral relationships for specific items may be particularly difficult in countries with some form of import or foreign exchange controls.

Reflecting these difficulties, the workshop provides material for an eclectic approach to balance of payments forecasting. The first section contains information on the structure of Kenya's external sector and recent economic developments affecting balance of payments. The second section presents a general analysis of factors that might influence developments in the external sector. The final section gives some guidelines for forecasting balance of payments developments.

THE EXTERNAL SECTOR IN KENYA

Analysis of the structure of the foreign sector, knowledge of the major policy measures significantly affecting it, and data on recent balance of payments developments are a prerequisite of any forecasting exercise.

Structure of the Foreign Sector

Imports disaggregated according to economic category are presented in Table 1. About 85 per cent of Kenya's 1976 imports

[3] There are some exceptions to this principle, such as the purchase of gold from the private sector by domestic monetary institutions (see Workshop 3: Balance of Payments Statistics). The interrelationships between external sectors have led to the development of consistent models for forecasting the balance of payments for a group of countries. See, for example, Michael C. Deppler and Duncan M. Ripley, "The World Trade Model: Merchandise Trade," *Staff Papers,* Vol. 25 (March 1978), pp. 147–206.

TABLE 1. Kenya: Total Imports by Economic Category, 1973–77

Item	1973	1974	1975	1976	1977	1973	1976
	(In millions of Kenya shillings)					*(In per cent)*	
Consumer goods	**833**	**1,195**	**906**	**1,164**	**1,376**	**18**	**14**
Passenger cars	95	190	125	168	248	2	2
Food and beverages	246	299	155	291	200	6	3
Other nondurables	186	249	260	233	318	4	3
Semidurables	198	313	260	332	429	4	4
Other durables	108	144	106	140	181	2	2
Intermediate goods	**2,416**	**4,902**	**4,289**	**4,794**	**5,908**	**53**	**59**
Primary industrial inputs	204	239	249	238	321	4	3
Processed industrial inputs	1,766	3,032	2,124	2,478	3,244	39	30
Fuels and lubricants	446	1,631	1,916	2,078	2,343	10	26
Capital goods	**1,313**	**1,558**	**2,044**	**2,164**	**3,333**	**29**	**27**
Transport equipment	183	253	381	339	770	4	4
Other machinery and equipment	792	778	1,126	1,285	1,829	17	16
Parts and accessories	338	527	537	540	734	8	7
Other goods	**9**	**23**	**13**	**18**	**12**	**—**	**—**
Total imports, customs basis	**4,571**	**7,678**	**7,252**	**8,140**	**10,629**	**100**	**100**
Adjustment to balance of payments basis	...	18	72	18	73		
Total imports, balance of payments basis	**...**	**7,696**	**7,324**	**8,158**	**10,702**		
Memorandum item:							
All imports except fuels and lubricants	4,125	6,047	5,336	6,062	8,286	90	74

Source: Kenya, *Economic Survey,* 1977 and 1978.

were intermediate and capital goods, with industrial inputs and fuels each representing about a third of this total. Consumer goods imports were relatively unimportant, accounting for only 14 per cent of the 1976 imports. Western Europe supplies about 45 per cent of imports, with the United Kingdom and to a lesser extent the Federal Republic of Germany as the major sources (Table 2). Reflecting the increased price of oil, the share of Middle Eastern countries in total imports has risen sharply.

Imports are influenced by both economic forces and the system of trade and exchange controls. All nongovernment imports require a license by the Central Bank of Kenya, but this approval is granted automatically for imports on open general license. In addition,

Kenya maintains four import schedules. Goods under Schedules I and II require specific import licenses to be issued by the Director of Trade and Supplies. Foreign exchange approval is granted freely

TABLE 2. Kenya: Direction of Trade, 1973–77

(As percentage of total)

Country or Region	1973	1974	1975	1976	1977
Destination of exports					
Western Europe	**34.8**	**32.5**	**30.4**	**40.5**	**51.5**
United Kingdom	11.4	7.9	9.5	10.5	12.7
Germany, Fed. Rep. of	7.5	7.6	8.1	12.2	17.1
Other European Community	9.8	12.0	8.0	11.8	16.5
Other Western Europe	6.1	4.9	4.7	6.1	5.2
Eastern Europe	**1.2**	**1.3**	**1.0**	**1.0**	**3.0**
United States and Canada	**5.7**	**4.8**	**5.7**	**7.1**	**7.2**
Africa	**39.9**	**40.7**	**39.9**	**31.3**	**22.0**
East African Community	28.7	27.8	25.8	19.3	12.3
Other Africa	11.3	12.8	14.1	12.0	9.7
Far East	**9.2**	**8.8**	**7.6**	**7.2**	**5.0**
Japan	2.8	2.3	2.7	1.3	1.0
Other Far East	6.4	6.6	4.9	5.9	3.9
Middle East	**2.0**	**2.0**	**2.3**	**1.7**	**2.5**
Other countries [1]	**3.3**	**4.0**	**5.3**	**4.4**	**2.7**
Aircraft and ships' stores	**3.9**	**6.0**	**7.8**	**6.9**	**6.2**
Total [2]	**100.0**	**100.0**	**100.0**	**100.0**	**100.0**
Origin of total imports					
Western Europe	**51.9**	**46.8**	**45.0**	**44.9**	**48.4**
United Kingdom	25.0	18.5	20.9	18.9	17.9
Germany, Fed. Rep. of	9.2	10.0	8.0	10.1	10.9
Other European Community	12.6	12.9	11.1	11.1	14.3
Other Western Europe	5.2	5.3	5.0	4.8	5.3
Eastern Europe	**2.6**	**2.8**	**1.0**	**0.9**	**0.8**
United States and Canada	**9.2**	**6.3**	**8.6**	**7.4**	**6.7**
Africa	**6.9**	**4.9**	**3.5**	**4.1**	**1.5**
East African Community	5.9	3.8	2.9	3.2	0.4
Other Africa	1.0	1.1	0.6	0.8	1.1
Far East	**18.5**	**18.4**	**14.1**	**18.1**	**20.5**
Japan	11.9	10.9	8.7	11.1	12.3
Other Far East	6.6	7.4	5.4	7.0	8.1
Middle East	**8.7**	**18.6**	**23.1**	**23.9**	**17.0**
Other countries [1]	**2.2**	**2.2**	**4.8**	**0.8**	**5.1**
Total [2]	**100.0**	**100.0**	**100.0**	**100.0**	**100.0**

Source: Kenya, *Economic Survey,* 1977 and 1978.

[1] Including Australia.

[2] Components may not add to totals because of rounding.

for goods under Schedule I and, on the basis of quotas reflecting past imports, for goods under Schedule II. Imports under Schedule III are generally prohibited; for goods on Schedule IV no specific import license is required, but foreign exchange is allocated on a quota basis. Goods listed under Schedules I, II, and III are items produced locally, and the lists were introduced to protect local producers. Items under Schedule IV are not produced locally, and the foreign exchange allocation was introduced for balance of payments reasons. Schedules II, III, and IV cover approximately 25 per cent of the 1973 imports. About 11 percentage points of this total reflect an expansion in coverage introduced in June 1974 and a further 4 percentage points arose from changes in June 1975.[4] No major changes were made in the system of exchange control in 1976. In addition to changes in the list of restricted items, the effective tightness of controls can be influenced by administrative decisions on the allocation of quotas for goods under Schedules II and IV.[5]

Exports are dominated by primary products, of which the most important are coffee and tea (Table 3). Although these two commodities account for over 45 per cent of non-oil exports, Kenya has only a small share of total world exports.[6] Kenya refines imported crude oil for export to neighboring countries and for sale as fuel for aircraft and ships. Oil products accounted for about 20 per cent of 1976 exports. In 1976 the United Kingdom was the market for only 10 per cent of Kenya's exports, which was a little less than the share of the Federal Republic of Germany. African countries, and

[4] In June 1974 the Central Bank of Kenya also restricted foreign-owned firms, except in certain sectors, from borrowing domestically more than 20 per cent of their local capital requirements.

[5] For a description of exchange restrictions on other items in Kenya's balance of payments, see International Monetary Fund, *Twenty-Eighth Annual Report on Exchange Restrictions* (Washington, 1977), pp. 277–80.

[6] Kenya accounts for about 2 per cent of world coffee exports and about 6 per cent of world tea exports. The latter share makes Kenya the world's third largest exporter of tea.

particularly the East African Community (EAC),[7] represented important export markets. In part reflecting oil exports, Kenya had a substantial trade surplus with the EAC countries.

Kenya has in recent years benefited from a substantial surplus in the service account, and in 1976 receipts represented 59 per cent of exports while payments represented 33 per cent of imports. Major receipts arise from port services and tourism, while investment income represents the most important debit item. The balance of

TABLE 3. Kenya: Composition of Exports, 1973–77

Type of Export	1973	1974	1975	1976	1977	1973	1976
	(In millions of Kenya shillings)					*(In per cent)*[1]	
Non-oil exports	**3,062**	**3,660**	**3,438**	**5,314**	**8,152**	**85**	**77**
External exports	2,192	2,642	2,633	4,486	. . .	61	65
Coffee	*716*	*768*	*704*	*1,866*	*4,087*	*20*	*27*
Tea	*339*	*388*	*459*	*635*	*1,436*	*9*	*9*
Hides and skins	*104*	*89*	*108*	*171*	*160*	*3*	*2*
Meat	*75*	*90*	*100*	*166*	. . .	*2*	*2*
Pyrethrum extract	*58*	*91*	*70*	*114*	*100*	*2*	*2*
Sisal	*96*	*339*	*147*	*84*	*82*	*3*	*1*
Other	*804*	*877*	*1,045*	*1,450*	. . .	*22*	*21*
Exports to Uganda	481	571	340	289	. . .	13	4
Exports to Tanzania	389	447	465	539	. . .	11	8
Oil exports[2]	**426**	**912**	**1,172**	**1,394**	**1,664**	**12**	**20**
External exports[3]	260	618	747	890	. . .	7	13
Exports to Uganda	110	222	319	374	. . .	3	5
Exports to Tanzania	56	72	106	130	. . .	2	2
Total exports, customs basis	**3,614**	**4,714**	**4,760**	**6,902**	**10,036**	**100**	**100**
External exports	2,452	3,260	3,380	5,376	8,578	68	78
Exports to Uganda	591	793	659	663	1,041	16	9
Exports to Tanzania	445	519	571	669	197	13	10
Re-exports[4]	126	142	150	194	220	3	3
Adjustment to balance of payments basis[3]	**. . .**	**—192**	**—2**	**—676**	**—618**		
Total exports, balance of payments basis	**. . .**	**4,522**	**4,758**	**6,226**	**9,418**		

Sources: Kenya, *Economic Survey,* 1978 and *Statistical Abstract,* 1977.

[1] Non-oil and oil exports do not total 100 per cent because of the exclusion of re-exports.
[2] Includes petroleum by-products.
[3] Includes aircraft and ships' stores.
[4] Consists of imported goods re-exported in the same form to countries outside the East African area.

[7] Composed of Tanzania, Uganda, and Kenya.

payments is also affected by substantial long-term capital inflows (Table 4).

On October 27, 1975, Kenya adopted a new central rate of KSh 9.66=SDR 1, a depreciation of 12.4 per cent from the exchange

TABLE 4. Kenya: Balance of Payments Summary, 1973–77
(In millions of Kenya shillings)

Item	1973	1974	1975	1976	1977
A. Goods, services, and unrequited transfers	**—882**	**—2,154**	**—1,488**	**—698**	**482**
Exports, f.o.b.	3,290	4,522	4,758	6,224	9,418
Imports, c.i.f.	—4,384	—7,696	—7,324	—8,158	—10,702
Trade balance	**—1,094**	**—3,174**	**—2,566**	**—1,934**	**—1,284**
Freight and insurance	228	370	384	458	486
Other transportation	286	892	880	958	1,136
Travel	266	278	448	598	844
Investment income	—714	—722	—840	—952	—1,190
Government (not included elsewhere)	—106	—58	—56	—62	—154
Other services	42	36	2	—34	54
Total services	**2**	**796**	**818**	**966**	**1,176**
Private transfers	6	16	—20	—42	70
Government transfers [1]	204	208	280	312	520
Unrequited transfers	**210**	**224**	**260**	**270**	**590**
B. Capital (excluding reserves)	**1,001**	**1,599**	**1,280**	**1,440**	**1,813**
Private nonbank	732	1,040	544	744	616
Central Government [1]	282	348	596	698	664
Other public sector	—	166	128	100	460
Commercial banks	—13	45	12	—102	73
C. Errors and omissions [2]	**68**	**11**	**—168**	**34**	**—48**
D. Overall balance	**187**	**—544**	**—376**	**776**	**2,247**
E. Financing (increase in assets —)	**—187**	**544**	**376**	**—776**	**—2,247**
Gross official reserves	—172	261	—85	—870	—1,973
Use of Fund credit	—	280	383	158	—361
Other liabilities	—15	3	78	—64	87

Sources: For Items A and B (except commercial banks), the data for 1976 and 1977 are taken from Kenya, *Economic Survey,* 1978; the data for 1974 and 1975 from Kenya, *Economic Survey,* 1977; and the data for 1973 from Kenya, *Economic Survey,* 1976. The data for commercial banks (in Item B) and financing (Item E) are taken from International Monetary Fund, *International Financial Statistics,* July 1978, in order to ensure consistency with the monetary accounts for purposes of financial programming (see Workshop 9: Financial Programming). The adjustment for the resulting discrepancy is contained in the residual item, errors and omissions (Item C).

[1] Data have been adjusted to include capital grants in government transfers and exclude them from capital movements.

[2] Includes valuation changes.

rate prevailing at that time. The Kenya shilling was then pegged to the SDR rather than to the U.S. dollar, as it had been previously.

Recent Balance of Payments Developments

There was a sharp deterioration in the balance of payments situation in 1974 as a result of an approximate tripling of the trade deficit. Imports grew by about 68 per cent, with the value of oil imports rising to 3.5 times the 1973 level and non-oil imports increasing by nearly 50 per cent. To an important extent, these increases reflected higher import prices, but there was also a substantial rise in the import volume of intermediate goods for stockbuilding purposes (Charts 1 and 2). Exports grew by more than 30 per cent, with much of the rise occurring in oil exports. The deterioration in the trade balance was partially offset by a substantial rise in the surplus in services. This largely resulted from the increased value of sales of fuel for ships and airplanes (Chart 3). There was also a substantial inflow of capital; net private nonbank borrowing in 1974 increased by 42 per cent, in part reflecting trade credits for the higher imports and in part due to the effect of the restrictions introduced in June on foreign company borrowing in the Kenyan market (Chart 4). The overall balance of payments position changed from a surplus of KSh 187 million in 1973 to a deficit of KSh 544 million in 1974, or about 3 per cent of the nominal GDP in 1974.

In 1975, the trade deficit declined by 19 per cent to KSh 2,566 million, owing to a reduction in imports of about 25 per cent in volume and 6 per cent in value. In part this decline reflected an adjustment from the high level of inventory accumulation in 1974, but there may also have been some administrative tightening in the system of import controls. The value of exports grew by only 2 per cent, with a rise in oil exports more than offsetting the decline in non-oil exports. This latter development reflected the impact of drought on coffee exports, a sharp decline in the volume and price of sisal exports, and a reduction in exports to Uganda. The surplus on services remained at about the same level as 1974. There was a decline in net capital inflow, with an increase in net public sector

CHART 1. Kenya: Import Ratios, 1970–77 [1]

(As percentage of GDP)

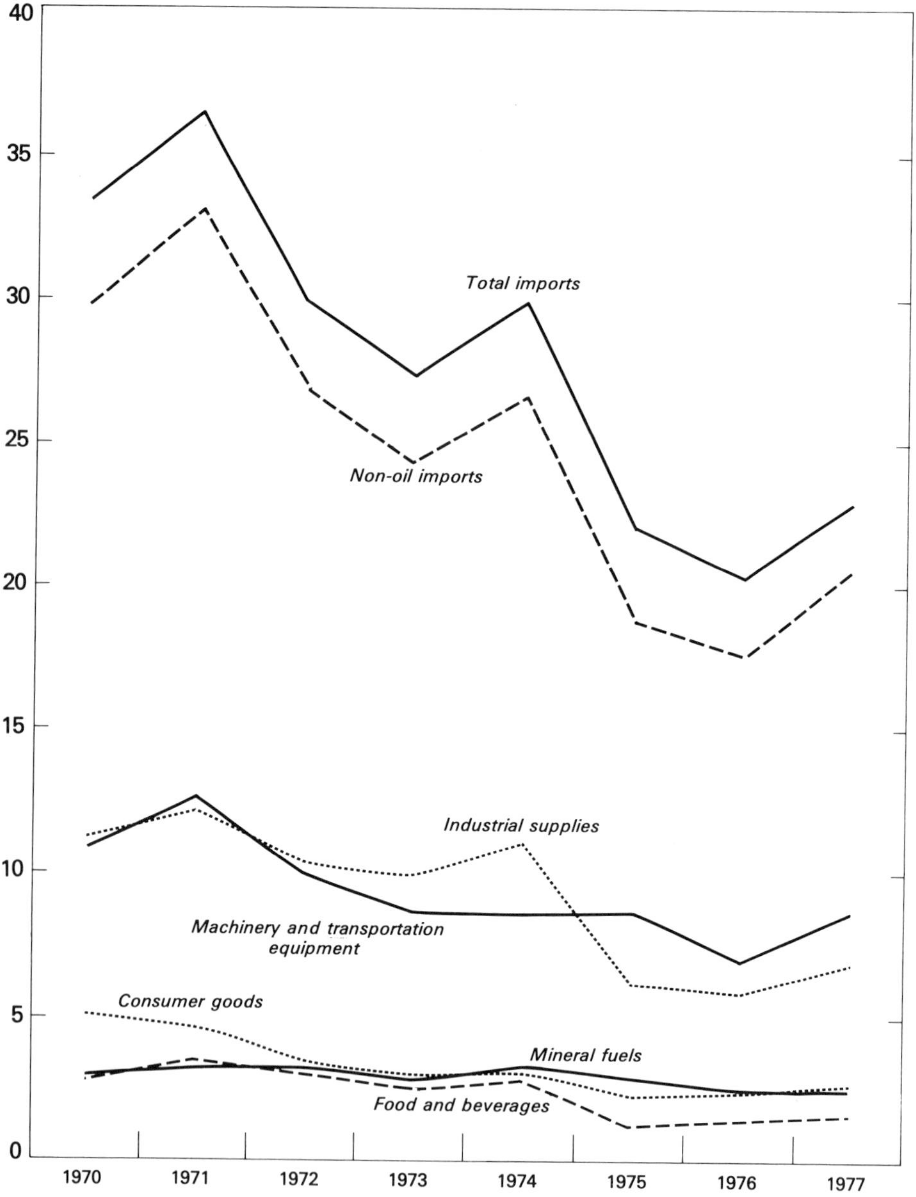

[1] Imports and gross domestic product at factor cost, measured at constant 1972 prices.
Note: Derived from the data in the Appendix.

CHART 2. Kenya: Import Prices, 1970–77

(1969 = 100)

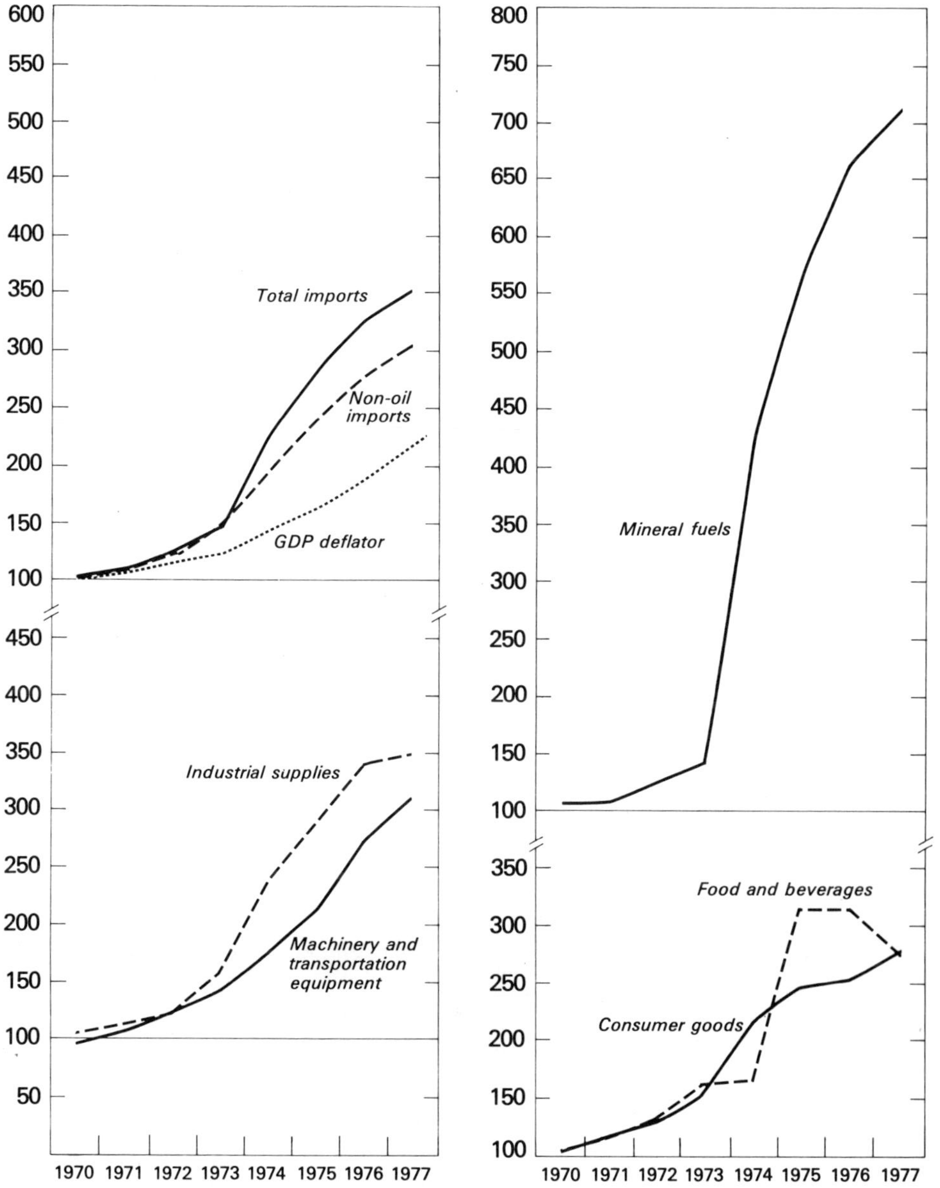

Note: Derived from the data in the Appendix.

CHART 3. Kenya: Services and Unrequited Transfers, 1970–77
(In millions of Kenya shillings)

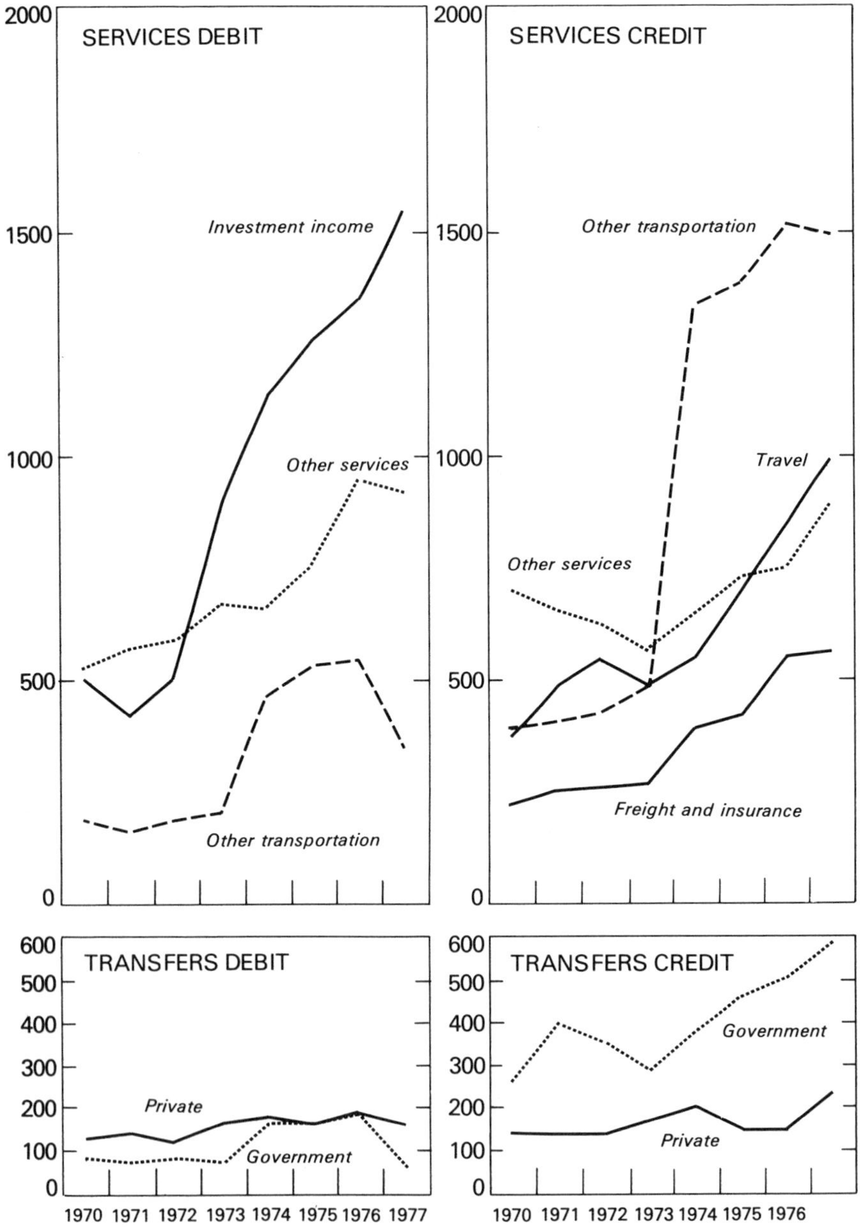

Note: Derived from the data in the Appendix.

CHART 4. Kenya: Nonmonetary Capital Flows, 1973–77
(In millions of Kenya shillings)

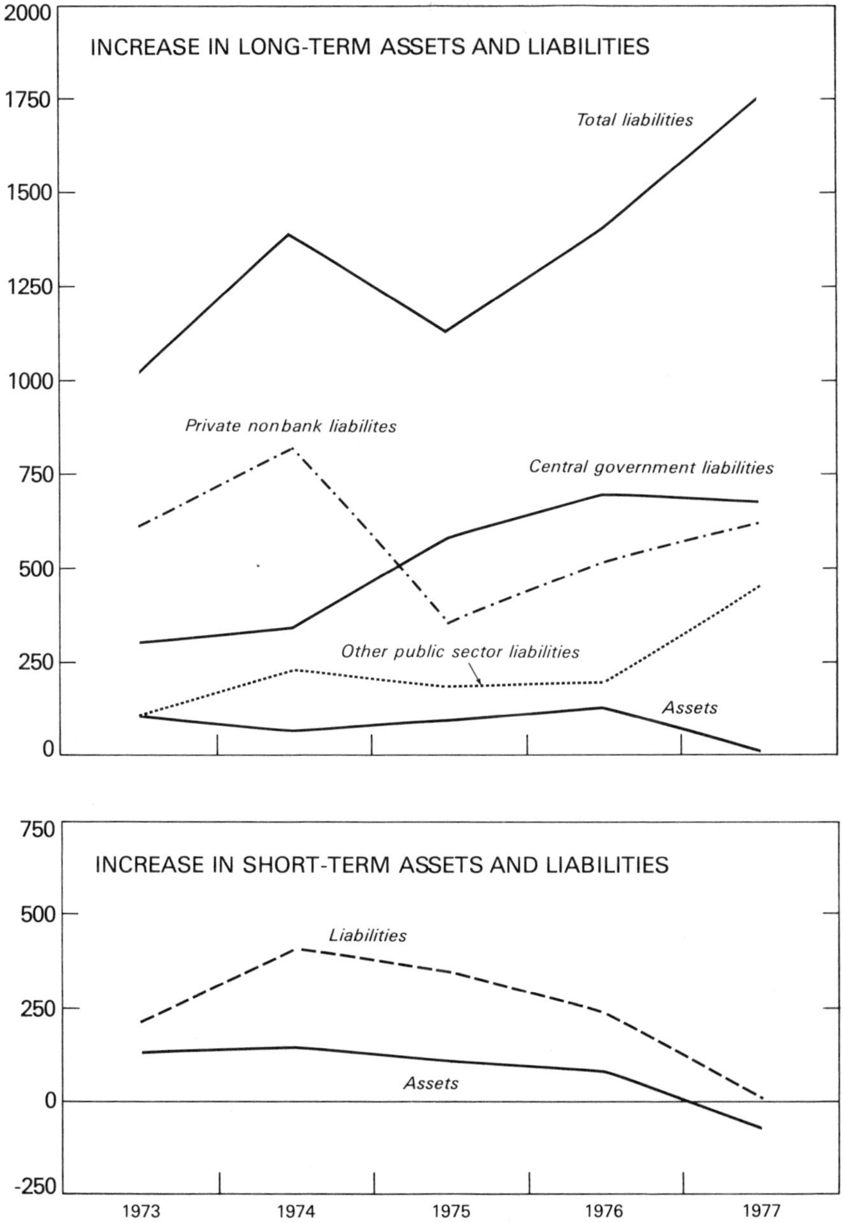

Note: Derived from the data in the Appendix.

borrowing failing to offset a fall in net private foreign borrowing. The overall deficit in 1975 declined to KSh 376 million, or about 1.8 per cent of nominal GDP.

There was a sharp turnaround in the balance of payments situation in 1976, and a substantial overall surplus emerged.[8] In large part this improvement was due to a reduction in the trade deficit as a result of a 130 per cent rise in the export price of coffee.[9] The 31 per cent rise in the value of exports also reflected higher tea prices and the impact of improved weather conditions on coffee and tea production. Imports grew in nominal terms by only 11 per cent, while in real terms they continued to decline. There was a further rise in the surplus on services, with higher receipts from tourism and transportation offsetting a rise in investment income outflows; the "current account" deficit was more than halved. An increase in net capital inflow allowed an overall surplus of KSh 776 million, equivalent to about 3 per cent of nominal GDP.

METHODOLOGY FOR BALANCE OF PAYMENTS FORECASTING[10]

For a financial program, forecasting the balance of payments may start from the definitional relationship between changes in net foreign assets *(NFA)* and the other items in the balance of payments:

$$\Delta NFA_t = X_t - M_t + INV_t + CM_t \quad (1)$$

[8] Quarterly data for 1976 and 1977 on the trade component of the balance of payments and on changes in net foreign assets are provided in Appendix Table A.

[9] In July 1975 a severe frost destroyed a substantial part of Brazil's coffee crop. Brazil during 1974–75 accounted for 31 per cent of exportable coffee production. See Horst J. Struckmeyer, "Coffee Prices and Central America," *Finance and Development,* Vol. 14 (September 1977), pp. 28–31.

[10] A rigorous survey of the technical problems involved in forecasting imports and exports is presented by George McKenzie, "Imports and Exports," in David F. Heathfield (ed.), *Topics in Applied Macroeconomics* (London: Macmillan, 1976), pp. 144–63.

where

$$\Delta NFA = \text{change in net foreign assets}$$
$$X = \text{export receipts}$$
$$M = \text{import payments}$$
$$INV = \text{net invisibles, i.e., services and unrequited transfers}$$
$$CM = \text{net capital inflow.}$$

The exact definitions adopted and the level of aggregation for each variable should depend on the availability of data and the development of stable behavioral relationships. For exports and imports a separate determination of unit price and volume may be desired. Although the currency used to obtain the initial forecasts may vary, an eventual aim should be to produce an estimate of *NFA* in domestic currency for inclusion in the monetary survey.

Imports

A simple equation for forecasting the volume of imports could take the following form:

$$\left(\frac{M}{PM}\right)_t = a_0 + a_1 Y_t - a_2 \left(\frac{PM}{PD}\right)_t \qquad (2)$$

where

$$M = \text{value of imports}$$
$$PM = \text{unit value of imports}$$
$$Y = \text{domestic real income}$$
$$PD = \text{domestic price level.}$$

This equation is based on the hypothesis that real import demand depends on domestic income and on the ratio of import to domestic prices as an indicator of possible substitution between domestic and imported goods.

Estimation of the equation in this form involves several important assumptions. In order to predict imports by using only a demand equation, it is necessary to employ the so-called small-country assumption that supply elasticity is infinite or sufficiently large to enable the effect of changing demand on price to be ignored. To the extent that this assumption is not warranted, explicit consideration needs to be given to the supply equation.[11] A corollary of the small-country assumption is that import prices need to be determined from an analysis of world markets and developments in particular trading partners. For a country such as Kenya, the small-country approach would seem reasonable. The specification of equation (2) also assumes that actual imports adjust to the desired level within the observation period. Full adjustment may not, however, occur within one period because of the costs involved in short-run changes in the level of imports or because of limitations imposed by contractual arrangements. The following partial adjustment specification may then be more appropriate:

$$\left(\frac{M}{PM}\right)_t - \left(\frac{M}{PM}\right)_{t-1} = \delta\left(\left(\frac{M}{PM}\right)_t^* - \left(\frac{M}{PM}\right)_{t-1}\right) \quad (3)$$

$$\left(\frac{M}{PM}\right)_t^* = b_0 + b_1 Y_t - b_2\left(\frac{PM}{PD}\right)_t \quad (4)$$

where

$$\left(\frac{M}{PM}\right)^* = \text{desired import volume}$$

and

$$0 < \delta < 1.$$

Substitution of equation (4) in equation (3) and rearrangement yields:

$$\left(\frac{M}{PM}\right)_t = \delta b_0 + \delta b_1 Y_t - \delta b_2\left(\frac{PM}{PD}\right)_t + (1 - \delta)\left(\frac{M}{PM}\right)_{t-1} \quad (5)$$

where the coefficients δb_1 and δb_2 represent the first period effect of real income and relative prices, respectively.[12]

---

[11] See Mohsin S. Khan, "Import and Export Demand in Developing Countries," *Staff Papers,* Vol. 21 (November 1974), pp. 678–93.

[12] The long-run effects are b_1 and b_2.

A further question concerns the appropriate degree of disaggregation for imports. Recent international developments suggest that a disaggregation into oil imports and non-oil imports may be warranted. Such a disaggregation could be further pursued by breaking down non-oil imports according to the major commodity flows. Particular commodity flows could then be related to specific rather than general indicators—for example, import of capital goods as related to domestic investment. Even if imports are not disaggregated, it might be necessary to make allowance for differences in the marginal propensity to import among different demand components. Such an analysis is likely to be especially important when significant changes are expected in the structure of demand. Particular attention may need to be paid to possible changes in imports demanded for stock-building.

An alternative specification of the import equation assumes that there is excess demand for imports at current incomes and prices and that the effective constraint on imports is the availability of credit. It might be argued further that this constraint operates only on the private sector.[13] An equation of the following form could be tested:

$$(M_t - MG_t) = c_0 + c_1 \Delta DCP_t \tag{6}$$

where

MG = value of government imports
DCP = domestic credit to the private sector.

[13] In principle, allowance should also be made for trade credit from abroad. Accurate data on such credit are, however, often difficult to obtain (see Major Sources of Data in Workshop 3: Balance of Payments Statistics). A further hypothesis that may be applicable in some developing countries is that imports are constrained by the availability of foreign exchange reserves or the purchasing power in terms of imports of export receipts. See William L. Hemphill, "The Effect of Foreign Exchange Receipts on Imports of Less Developed Countries," *Staff Papers,* Vol. 21 (November 1974), pp. 637–77.

Exports

For a small primary product exporting country such as Kenya, the small-country assumption is that exports are essentially determined by supply and that changes in exportable output do not affect world market prices. Forecasting of exports should, in these circumstances, be closely linked with the projections of the appropriate items of domestic production. Exports would still be affected by world market prices to the extent that there are variations in output or in the relationship between domestic consumption and exports. The relevant price determining production incentives is the price received by the producer. In Kenya, nearly all the coffee export price has accrued to the producer. In principle, the relative movement of export and domestic prices could influence export supply. The proportion of the main export crops consumed domestically in Kenya is, however, very limited.[14] In the long run, coffee prices would affect domestic production and exports through their impact on coffee plantings. Some short-run price responsiveness may also occur through the intensity of cultivation.[15] For many primary producing countries, the central problem is to obtain a forecast of the world market price for their major export commodities.[16]

---

[14] Domestic consumption of coffee is less than 3 per cent of total production.

[15] Coffee plantings have a gestation period of about 5 years, mature in 7–10 years, and have an economic life of about 40 years. Newer hybrids mature, however, somewhat sooner. Heavy picking of coffee beans in one year may adversely affect output in the following year. See Shamsher Singh, and others, *Coffee, Tea and Cocoa: Market Prospects and Development Lending,* World Bank Staff Occasional Paper No. 22 (Baltimore: Johns Hopkins University Press, 1977).

[16] Such forecasts might be obtained from agencies specializing in the commodity concerned or from various international organizations. For an approach based on a time series technique, see Ke-Young Chu, "Short-Run Forecasting of Commodity Prices: An Application of Autoregressive Moving Average Models," *Staff Papers,* Vol. 25 (March 1978), pp. 90–111.

In cases where it may be appropriate to forecast exports using a demand equation, the following type of specification may be used:[17]

$$\left(\frac{X}{PX}\right)_t = d_0 + d_1 VYW - d_2 \left(\frac{PX}{PW}\right)_t \qquad (7)$$

where

X = value of exports
PX = unit value of exports
VYW = real world income
PW = world price level.

Many of the problems of estimation encountered in the use of the above equation are similar to those mentioned earlier in the case of the import equation. Particular aggregation problems exist, however, in developing adequate indicators of world prices and incomes.[18]

Other Items

Determination of services, unrequited transfers, and capital flows would usually require more eclectic methods, and the scope for econometric analysis is probably limited.[19] Some items of the service

---

[17] See Khan (cited in footnote 11), pp. 683–84. Particularly for short-run analysis, the indicator of world demand might be weighted according to market shares. In some cases, industrial production might be a more appropriate variable than income. Consideration might also be given to the cyclical position in the domestic economy and the prospective markets. Publications such as the Organization for Economic Cooperation and Development, *Economic Outlook,* and United Kingdom, National Institute of Economic and Social Research, *National Institute Economic Review,* provide forecasts of short-run developments in industrial countries.

[18] See, for example, Jacques R. Artus and Susana C. Sosa, "Relative Price Effects on Export Performance: The Case of Nonelectrical Machinery," *Staff Papers,* Vol. 25 (March 1978), pp. 25–47.

[19] See, however, Marian E. Bond, "A Model of International Investment Income Flows," *Staff Papers,* Vol. 24 (July 1977), pp. 344–79, and "The World Trade Model: Invisibles," *Staff Papers,* Vol. 26 (June 1979), pp. 257–333.

account, such as transportation and merchandise insurance, may be related in a fairly stable manner to trade flows. Other items, such as travel and investment income, may be forecast by using sample survey and other detailed information provided by the relevant government department. Balance of payments forecasts of unrequited transfers of the government should utilize, and be consistent with, budgetary estimates of foreign grants.

Capital flows may, particularly in a country with a well-developed financial market, reflect interest rate differentials and expected changes in exchange rates.[20] In many developing countries, changes in the system of exchange control are also important. Direct investment may be influenced by the provision of tax incentives or other incentives, and forecasts of this component should take into account development plans and policy. Similarly, information on official capital flows may be obtained from development plans and the budget. Sample survey and banking data may be sources for forecasts of private capital movements. Provisions of trade credit may be related to trade flows.

GUIDELINES FOR FORECASTING BALANCE OF PAYMENTS IN KENYA

This section provides some empirical estimates for the equations discussed in the preceding section. In addition, some indicators of developments in the program period and other background information are presented. The purpose is to stimulate discussion of the issues and exercises pertaining to balance of payments forecasting and to provide a starting point for development of the workshop

[20] Where a forward market exists, the covered interest rate differential may be important. This differential represents the difference between the foreign and domestic interest rate, plus the forward premium or discount on the foreign currency.

participants' own estimates during the financial programming exercise.[21]

Trade Account

Several formulations of the import demand equation were estimated.[22] The actual and predicted values for some of the equations are presented in Table 5.

$$MR = \underset{(3.602)}{2164.256} + \underset{(3.607)}{0.3046}\, GDP - \underset{(2.805)}{2076.471}\left(\frac{PM}{PGDP}\right) \tag{8}$$

$$\bar{R}^2 = 0.501 \qquad D\text{-}W = 2.152 \qquad 1965\text{–}76$$

$$MR = \underset{(8.816)}{2471.379} + \underset{(6.264)}{0.2495}\, GDP - \underset{(5.534)}{1886.755}\left(\frac{PM}{PGDP}\right) + \underset{(5.9)}{860.072}\, DM1 \tag{9}$$

$$\bar{R}^2 = 0.895 \qquad D\text{-}W = 2.651 \qquad 1965\text{–}76$$

---

[21] It should be emphasized that, given the limited number of observations and the complexity of the factors affecting the various balance of payments components, considerable care and judgment are needed in interpreting the regression equations. Where commodity patterns are changing, the measured price indices may be sensitive to the weighting system used. Import and export unit values in Kenya are calculated using a "Fisher Ideal Index." See Kenya, *Statistical Digest* (June 1977).

[22] Import data based on customs information have a slightly different coverage than data from the balance of payments. To use the customs data for balance of payments forecasting, the projected percentage change may be applied to the last observation of imports calculated from balance of payments sources. The sources of the data and a full listing of the definitions of the variables appear in the Appendix. Considerable splicing of series and some approximations were necessary to obtain the time series for the various import price indices. The data and the derived constant price series should therefore be interpreted cautiously.

$$Ln\,MR = \underset{(0.478)}{0.5779} + \underset{(6.235)}{0.8093}\,Ln\,GDP - \underset{(5.134)}{0.6011}\,Ln\left(\frac{PM}{PGDP}\right) + \underset{(5.116)}{0.2231}\,DM1 \qquad (9')$$

$$\bar{R}^2 = 0.913 \qquad D\text{-}W = 2.395 \qquad 1965\text{–}76$$

$$MRL = \underset{(10.617)}{3202.041} + \underset{(5.903)}{0.263}\,GDP - \underset{(5.625)}{3178.603}\left(\frac{PL}{PGDP}\right) + \underset{(5.698)}{798.489}\,DM1 \qquad (10)$$

$$\bar{R}^2 = 0.917 \qquad D\text{-}W = 2.082 \qquad 1965\text{–}76$$

$$MR3 = \underset{(3.018)}{104.337} + \underset{(7.259)}{0.021}\,GDP + \underset{(2.931)}{52.461}\,DM1 \qquad (11)$$

$$\bar{R}^2 = 0.897 \qquad D\text{-}W = 2.22 \qquad 1965\text{–}76$$

where

MR = total imports at constant 1972 prices on a customs basis (in millions of Kenya shillings)

GDP = GDP at factor cost at constant 1972 prices (in millions of Kenya shillings)

PM = price index (unit value) for total imports (1972 = 100)

$PGDP$ = GDP deflator (1972 = 100)

$DM1$ = dummy for inventory accumulation (1971 and 1974 = 1)

MRL = non-oil imports at constant 1972 prices on a customs basis (in millions of Kenya shillings)

PL = prices of non-oil imports (1972 = 100)

$MR3$ = mineral fuel imports at constant 1972 prices on a customs basis (in millions of Kenya shillings).

In addition, the disaggregated import equations presented in Table 6 were estimated.[23]

[23] The adjustment model presented in equation (5) was rejected because of the negative and insignificant coefficient on the lagged endogenous variable.

TABLE 5. Kenya: Actual and Predicted Values for Selected Equations, 1965–76 [1]
(In millions of Kenya shillings)

Year	*MR*	*PR*(8)	*PR*(9)	*MRL*	*PR*(10)	*MR3*	*PR*(11)	*M*	*PR*(12)
1965	2,686	2,717	2,755	2,438	2,458	264	273		
1966	3,251	3,054	3,031	2,935	2,710	293	296		
1967	3,078	3,167	3,122	2,794	2,834	309	305	2,326	2,924
1968	3,217	3,392	3,306	2,840	2,955	334	321	2,412	1,803
1969	3,219	3,589	3,467	2,853	3,123	327	335	2,434	1,986
1970	3,901	3,828	3,665	3,494	3,341	347	350	3,052	3,606
1971	4,496	3,922	4,592	4,069	4,150	394	416	3,930	4,585
1972	3,957	4,100	3,871	3,539	3,488	418	382	3,746	3,830
1973	3,841	4,124	3,868	3,438	3,313	395	400	4,384	5,431
1974	4,313	3,570	4,217	3,827	3,746	481	459	7,696	6,648
1975	3,223	3,286	3,095	2,751	2,664	424	410	7,324	8,209
1976	3,119	3,551	3,311	2,696	2,892	389	428	8,158	6,438

Source: Appendix.

[1] Definition of variables is as in the text. Series under the variable name indicate the actual value, while *PR* refers to the predicted value obtained from the equation. The number in parentheses indicates the relevant equation in the text.

TABLE 6. Kenya: Estimated Import Equations [1]

Item (Per cent) [2]	Constant	Estimated Elasticity with Respect to GDP	Estimated Elasticity with Respect to Prices	Coefficient on Dummy Variable	$\bar{R}^2$	D-W
Total imports (100)	1.305	0.894**	—0.333**	0.206**	0.899	2.419
Non-oil imports (74)	1.088	0.965**	—0.456**	0.214**	0.884	2.026
Mineral fuels (26)	—1.057	0.747**	—0.016	0.121*	0.899	2.346
Industrial supplies (30)	—0.239	1.016**	—0.482**	0.296**	0.746	1.876
Machinery and transportation (29)	—5.921	1.684**	—0.617**		0.81	1.959
Food and beverages (6)	1.038	0.818	—0.632*		0.303	1.152
Consumer goods (9)	3.245	0.608	—0.607**		0.644	2.791

Source: Appendix.

[1] From equation $LnMR = a + bLnGDP + cLnPM + dDM1$
where MR = imports for the respective categories at constant 1972 prices
GDP = gross domestic product at factor cost in 1972 prices
PM = import price deflator (unit value) for the appropriate import category
$DM1$ = dummy variable, taking the values *1* in 1971 and 1974 and *0* in all other years. (This variable is excluded for some import categories.)

[2] Figures in parentheses show the percentage share in the value of total imports in 1976.

** and * show that the coefficients are significant at the 99 per cent and 95 per cent levels, respectively. The equations were estimated for the period 1965–76.

The credit constraint hypothesis was tested:[24]

$$M = 1583.792 + 4.575\,\Delta NDC \quad (12)$$
$$\quad (2.881) \qquad (6.51)$$
$$\bar{R}^2 = 0.84 \qquad D\text{-}W = 2.45 \qquad 1967\text{–}76$$

where

M = imports, c.i.f., on a balance of payments basis (in millions of Kenya shillings)

NDC = total domestic credit of the banking system (in millions of Kenya shillings).

In the preceding section, under Exports, it was suggested that forecasts for Kenya's major export commodities should be closely linked to projections of domestic production.[25] Data on production and exports for some of the major export crops are presented in Table 7. Coffee exports are higher than production in a number of years, mainly because of changes in stocks. Indicators of possible price and market developments for the major export crops are presented in Table 8.

Other Items

As indicated in the preceding section, under Other Items, there is usually only limited scope in a financial programming exercise for a rigorous behavioral analysis of items outside the trade account. Rather, items in the services and capital accounts would usually be determined in an ad hoc manner, with considerable reliance on the

[24] Data are not available for imports net of central government imports. Consequently, *NDC* rather than *DCP* was used as the explanatory variable. Empirically, a lower level of explanation was found when using the latter variable.

[25] An analysis of factors affecting coffee and tea supply and world market prices is presented in Shamsher Singh, and others (cited in footnote 15).

TABLE 7. Kenya: Agricultural Production and Exports, 1973–76
(In thousands of metric tons)

Item	1973	1974	1975	1976
Production for sale				
Clean coffee	71.2	70.1	66.2	80.3
Tea	56.6	53.4	56.7	62.0
Sisal	58.1	86.5	43.6	33.6
Exports				
Coffee, unroasted	75.3	71.7	67.6	77.5
Tea	51.5	49.6	52.5	59.3
Sisal	44.8	72.1	42.7	29.4
Share of agricultural output [1]				
Coffee	26.6	21.8	20.2	38.7
Tea	12.6	11.9	13.1	12.2
Sisal	5.3	11.3	4.0	1.6

Source: Kenya, *Statistical Abstract,* 1977.

[1] Value of gross marketed production divided by total output at current prices.

TABLE 8. Kenya: Semiannual Indicators of Developments in Program Period, 1976–78 [1]

Forecasts	1976 I	1976 II	1977 I	1977 II	1978 I	1978 II
	(In market prices in terms of U.S. dollars; 1968–70 = 100)					
Primary commodity prices						
Coffee	279.3	393.1	663.9	478.9	437.3	384.7
Tea	133.0	163.5	300.5	218.9	212.7	191.4
Meat	154.7	149.9	153.3	151.0	173.7	180.0
Sisal	253.3	282.5	291.0	294.7	300.0	300.0
Hides	255.3	264.6	293.0	279.2	294.3	302.1
	(Percentage change from previous period)					
Total OECD prices and incomes [2]						
Real GNP	6.50	3.00	4.00	3.25	4.00	3.00
GNP deflator	7.00	7.75	7.25	7.25	7.00	7.00
Export prices	2.00	9.25	9.75	7.25	7.75	5.00
Export prices of manufactures	2.50	11.00	9.50	7.50	7.50	6.00

Sources: Commodities Division of the International Monetary Fund's Research Department and Organization for Economic Cooperation and Development, *Economic Outlook,* December 1977.

[1] Actual data for 1976 and 1977 and forecasts for 1978.

[2] Seasonally adjusted at annual rates. Export prices represent average values in terms of U.S. dollars.

forecasts of the relevant government departments. The use of such methods should, however, be based on a careful analysis of the structure of services and capital flows, any trends in the behavior of the major items, and available information on the factors affecting particular components.[26]

The major credit items in the service account are freight and insurance, other transportation, and travel—accounting, respectively, for 15 per cent, 41 per cent, and 23 per cent of service receipts. Freight and insurance receipts can be related through a simple regression to exports, f.o.b.:

$$SC1 = \underset{(3.497)}{59.335} + \underset{(15.803)}{0.0756}X \qquad (13)$$

$$\bar{R}^2 = 0.969 \qquad D\text{-}W = 1.426 \qquad 1968\text{–}76$$

where

$SC1$ = freight and insurance credit (in millions of Kenya shillings)
X = exports, f.o.b. (in millions of Kenya shillings).

In 1976, two thirds of Kenya's receipts from other transportation were from port disbursements, and the remainder was from passenger fares. More than half of the port services were for fuel and ships' stores, with a further 30 per cent representing port dues. Receipts from port services are to a large extent dependent on trade flows. Kenya's receipts from such services may, however, be generated by carriers involved in imports, exports, or trade with third countries. In view of the importance of fuel and ships' stores, the forecast for other transportation should take into account the projections for import prices of fuel.

Receipts from travel largely result from tourist expenditure. Such receipts can be related to the number of tourists and their aver-

[26] Reference should be made to Charts 3 and 4 and to the Appendix, Tables B and C, for an indication of the trend developments in the services and capital accounts.

age length of stay.[27] A relationship of this type, however, only shifts the problem to forecasting the number of tourists and does not deal with the average expenditure of visitors. Nearly two thirds of the visitors to Kenya in 1976 came from Europe and North America. Projections of receipts from travel should therefore consider the cyclical position in those countries and possible changes in air fares.

Investment income represented 46 per cent and other transportation accounted for 21 per cent of total payments for services.[28] The former category covers retained profits, other direct investment income, and other investment income. The shares of these components in 1976 were 18 per cent, 44 per cent, and 38 per cent, respectively. In principle, investment income payments should be related to the actual rate of return for each type of investment and the value of asset holdings.[29] The information necessary for such a sophisticated approach is not, however, available for Kenya or for most developing countries. Insofar as foreign direct investment takes place largely in the export sector, some relationship may be expected between direct investment flows and exports.[30] Allowance should also be made for the definitional relationship between investment

[27] For example:

$$SC3 = \underset{(0.264)}{-27.723} + \underset{(5.36)}{0.1384}\, TO$$

$$\bar{R}^2 = 0.776 \qquad D\text{-}W = 0.7 \qquad 1968\text{–}76$$

where

$SC3$ = travel credit (in millions of Kenya shillings)
TO = total stay of departing visitors (in thousands of days).

[28] Imports are treated on a c.i.f. basis.
[29] See Bond (cited in footnote 19), p. 348.
[30] For example:

$$SD1 = \underset{(1.192)}{81.42} + \underset{(10.615)}{0.2046}\, X$$

$$\bar{R}^2 = 0.933 \qquad D\text{-}W = 2.434 \qquad 1968\text{–}76$$

where

$SD1$ = investment income debit (in millions of Kenya shillings)
X = exports, f.o.b. (in millions of Kenya shillings).

income and direct investment arising from the convention of treating retained profits as distributed and reinvested.[31] Payments for other transportation would be affected by the same type of factors as those that were discussed for receipts from this source. For payments, however, passenger fares are relatively important, accounting in 1976 for 46 per cent of other transportation debits, with the remainder represented by port services.

Government receipts are the major item in unrequited transfers. The forecast for such receipts should be consistent with the projection for grants as shown in the government budget.

Increases in long-term liabilities represent the major nonmonetary capital flows. In 1976, the Central Government, other public sector, and the private nonbank sector accounted for 50 per cent, 13 per cent, and 37 per cent, respectively, of the increase in long-term liabilities. Projections for the public sector components should be consistent with budgetary projections and policy. A substantial backlog of undisbursed loans exists, and the size of the inflow in a particular period should be linked to the expected timing of major capital projects. In 1976, about 60 per cent of the private sector inflows were direct investment. Projections for such inflows should reflect government policy toward direct investment as well as any changes in the availability of domestic credit. Forecasts for short-term capital flows should allow for changes in trade credit to finance imports and for the availability of domestic credit.

EXERCISES AND ISSUES FOR DISCUSSION

1. *The first section (on the External Sector) presents information on Kenya's balance of payments structure and developments for the period 1973–76. On the basis of this information, what do you see as the major problems involved in forecasting balance of payments developments for 1977?*

[31] See Workshop 3: Balance of Payments Statistics.

2. *Compare and contrast the various import equations, utilizing the information on actual and predicted values presented in Table 5. In particular:*
   (a) *Compare equations (8) and (9). Why do you think the addition of the dummy variable improves the fit of the equation? Consider alternative ways of allowing for the effects of inventory accumulation.*
   (b) *Should imports be disaggregated according to oil imports and non-oil imports?*
   (c) *To what extent do the results appear consistent with the credit constraint hypothesis?*
   (d) *Do the data used adequately approximate the variables suggested by the theoretical specification of the import models?*
   (e) *The specification of the partial adjustment equation (equation 5) imposes the same lag structure on the income and the price variable. Do you consider this appropriate?*
   (f) *What alternative specifications of the aggregate import equations might you want to consider?*

3. *Assume that for 1977 import prices increase (in terms of Kenya shillings) by 7.7 per cent, the GDP deflator rises (in terms of Kenya shillings) by 19.5 per cent, and real GDP increases by 7.34 per cent. (These were the 1977 actual increases.) On the basis of equation (9):*
   (a) *Forecast the percentage change in the volume and the value (in terms of Kenya shillings) of imports in 1977. Comment on whether you find the forecast plausible.*
   (b) *How might your forecast be affected by a 5 per cent currency devaluation in 1977?*
   (c) *Compute the income and price elasticities of imports for 1977, using 1976 as a base, and compare them with the corresponding elasticities in equation (9′). Comment on the plausibility of these price and income elasticities.*
   (d) *Comment on how you might allow for an expected liberalization of import controls in 1977.*

(e) *How might your forecast for 1977 depend upon what you assume about inventory accumulation for that year?*

4. *Comment on the disaggregated import equations presented in Table 6. Do you consider the price and income elasticities plausible? How would you improve the specification of the individual commodity equations? Do you consider this degree of disaggregation warranted?*

5. *Discuss possible methods of forecasting exports in Kenya. In particular:*

   (a) *To what extent would it be reasonable to forecast exports using only a demand equation?*

   (b) *How would you attempt to estimate exports, using the small-country assumption that demand is infinitely elastic? In this context what use would you make of the information in Tables 7 and 8? Would the price of exports still have an important role?*

6. *Utilize the information in Charts 3 and 4 and in the Appendix, Tables B and C, to analyze the pattern of invisibles and capital flows. What methods might you use for forecasting these items?*

APPENDIX

Kenya: Selected Variables Influencing Balance of Payments, 1965–77

Variable	Definition and Unit of Measure
MGDP	GDP at factor cost at current prices (in millions of Kenya shillings)
GDP	GDP at factor cost at constant 1972 prices (in millions of Kenya shillings)
PGDP	GDP deflator (1972 = 100)
NDC	net domestic credit of the banking system (in millions of Kenya shillings)
M	imports, c.i.f., on a balance of payments basis (in millions of Kenya shillings)
MR	total imports at constant 1972 prices on a customs basis (in millions of Kenya shillings)
MRL	non-oil imports at constant 1972 prices on a customs basis (in millions of Kenya shillings)
MR1	food and beverage imports at constant 1972 prices on a customs basis (in millions of Kenya shillings)

Kenya: Selected Variables Influencing Balance of Payments, 1965–77
(concluded)

Variable	Definition and Unit of Measure
MR2	industrial supplies imports at constant 1972 prices on a customs basis (in millions of Kenya shillings)
MR3	mineral fuel imports at constant 1972 prices on a customs basis (in millions of Kenya shillings)
MR4	machinery and transportation equipment at constant 1972 prices on a customs basis (in millions of Kenya shillings)
MR5	consumer goods imports at constant 1972 prices on a customs basis (in millions of Kenya shillings)
PM	price index for total imports *(MR)* (1972 = 100)
PL	price index for non-oil imports *(MRL)* (1972 = 100)
P1	price index for food and beverages imports *(MR1)* (1972 = 100)
P2	price index for industrial supplies imports *(MR2)* (1972 = 100)
P3	price index for mineral fuel imports *(MR3)* (1972 = 100)
P4	price index for machinery and transport equipment *(MR4)* (1972 = 100)
P5	price index for consumer goods imports *(MR5)* (1972 = 100)
X	exports, f.o.b., on a balance of payments basis (in millions of Kenya shillings)
PX	index of export prices in Kenya shillings (1972 = 100)
R	exchange rate (in Kenya shillings per U.S. dollar)
VYW	total OECD income at constant 1970 prices and 1970 exchange rates (in billions of U.S. dollars)
YW	total OECD income at current prices and current exchange rates (in billions of U.S. dollars)
DM1	dummy for inventory accumulation (1971 and 1974 = 1)
SD1	investment income debit (in millions of Kenya shillings)
SD2	other transportation debit (in millions of Kenya shillings)
SD3	other services debit (in millions of Kenya shillings)
SC1	freight and insurance credit (in millions of Kenya shillings)
SC2	other transportation credit (in millions of Kenya shillings)
SC3	travel credit (in millions of Kenya shillings)
SC4	other services credit (in millions of Kenya shillings)
UD1	private unrequited transfers debit (in millions of Kenya shillings)
UD2	government unrequited transfers debit (in millions of Kenya shillings)
UC1	private unrequited transfers credit (in millions of Kenya shillings)
UC2	government unrequited transfers credit (in millions of Kenya shillings)
TO	total stay of departing visitors (in thousands of days)

Kenya: Data on Selected Variables Influencing Balance of Payments, 1965–77 [1]

Year	*MGDP*	*GDP*	*PGDP*	*NDC*	*M*	*MR*	*MRL*	*MR1*	*MR2*
1965	6,610	8,015	82			2,686	2,438	315	993
1966	7,622	9,125	84	1,000		3,251	2,935	352	1,101
1967	8,116	9,546	85	1,293	2,326	3,078	2,794	301	956
1968	8,858	10,282	86	1,341	2,412	3,217	2,840	319	1,109
1969	9,526	10,941	87	1,429	2,434	3,219	2,853	247	1,129
1970	10,378	11,673	89	1,871	3,052	3,901	3,494	328	1,322
1971	11,402	12,330	92	2,527	3,930	4,496	4,069	434	1,499
1972	13,172	13,172	100	3,018	3,746	3,957	3,539	390	1,370
1973	14,984	14,066	107	3,859	4,384	3,841	3,438	452	1,391
1974	17,906	14,350	125	4,966	7,697	4,313	3,827	403	1,603
1975	20,560	14,523	142	6,414	7,324	3,223	2,751	180	897
1976	25,257	15,405	164	7,475	8,158	3,119	2,696	221	905
1977	32,404	16,536	196	9,255	10,702	3,783	3,382	264	1,140

Year	*MR3*	*MR4*	*MR5*	*PM*	*PL*	*P1*	*P2*	*P3*	*P4*	*P5*
1965	264	613	458	75	74	90	74	80	76	70
1966	293	938	523	76	76	80	76	82	79	71
1967	309	1,047	444	78	77	74	79	81	81	73
1968	334	925	542	79	80	71	79	81	83	74
1969	327	1,034	482	80	81	76	81	81	81	77
1970	347	1,274	591	81	82	80	86	85	78	80
1971	394	1,571	579	89	90	88	95	86	86	90
1972	418	1,322	457	100	100	100	100	100	100	100
1973	395	1,223	425	119	120	124	128	113	115	118
1974	481	1,240	439	178	158	126	191	339	141	166
1975	424	1,261	338	225	194	238	234	452	172	189
1976	389	1,065	371	261	225	238	274	534	219	195
1977	407	1,432	439	281	245	208	282	575	250	214

See footnote at end of table.

Kenya: Data on Selected Variables Influencing Balance of Payments, 1965–77[1]
(concluded)

Year	*X*	*PX*	*R*	*VYW*	*YW*	*DM1*	*SD1*	*SD2*	*SD3*
1965		88	7.1429	1,673	1,380	0			
1966		88	7.1429	1,764	1,507	0			
1967	1,580	83	7.1429	1,829	1,610	0			
1968	1,676	85	7.1429	1,928	1,739	0	452	170	408
1969	1,804	86	7.1429	2,018	1,904	0	438	174	502
1970	2,040	94	7.1429	2,079	2,079	0	500	186	514
1971	2,098	90	7.1429	2,158	2,311	1	422	170	578
1972	2,410	100	7.1429	2,277	2,680	0	504	186	600
1973	2,290	115	7.0012	2,415	3,243	0	902	198	686
1974	4,522	152	7.1429	2,422	3,594	1	996	454	688
1975	4,758	175	7.3432	2,409	4,019	0	1,154	524	754
1976	6,224	238	8.3672	2,535	4,361	0	1,262	558	902
1977	9,418	337	8.2766	2,630	4,903	0	1,542	354	876

Year	*SC1*	*SC2*	*SC3*	*SC4*	*UD1*	*UD2*	*UC1*	*UC2*	*TO*
1965									
1966									
1967									
1968	182	302	346	474	118	88	118	266	2,440
1969	206	342	334	632	114	80	132	224	2,352
1970	222	374	370	712	128	74	136	248	2,973
1971	240	412	478	656	138	76	138	492	3,734
1972	242	422	546	640	128	84	136	348	4,768
1973	262	484	486	556	162	78	168	282	4,435
1974	390	1,346	540	658	180	166	196	374	4,406
1975	420	1,404	688	738	164	164	144	444	4,963
1976	550	1,516	858	764	186	184	144	496	5,308
1977	566	1,490	994	898	160	70	230	590	5,101

Sources: Data for imports, exports, and gross domestic product are taken from Kenya, *Economic Survey,* 1978 and *Statistical Abstract,* 1977 and also from earlier issues of these publications. Monetary and exchange rate data are from International Monetary Fund, *International Financial Statistics,* July 1978. World income data are from Organization for Economic Cooperation and Development (OECD), *National Accounts,* 1976 and *Main Economic Indicators,* May 1978.

[1] For definitions of variables and units of measure, see above table on Kenya: Selected Variables Influencing Balance of Payments, 1965–77.

TABLE A. Kenya: Quarterly Changes in Balance of Payments Components, 1976–77

Component	1976 I	II	III	IV	1977 I	II	III	IV
	(Percentage change)[1]							
Value								
Total exports[2]	26.3	71.0	75.5	35.1	93.3	76.8	51.1	30.1
Coffee	*110.7*	*275.0*	*239.4*	*61.6*	*273.4*	*97.1*	*80.8*	*67.6*
Tea	*14.2*	*25.3*	*50.5*	*60.7*	*89.4*	*410.1*	*143.4*	*19.3*
Total imports, c.i.f.[2]	11.3	24.0	20.7	11.6	29.7	18.9	41.5	50.3
Crude petroleum	36.2	3.8	32.4	—22.3	19.0	4.7	18.7	—17.3
Volume of exports								
Coffee	9.0	43.7	29.2	—29.3	46.8	—18.1	31.3	63.1
Tea	10.7	28.4	4.7	12.7	11.9	55.8	31.1	—7.7
Unit value of exports								
Coffee	93.3	159.5	162.6	130.8	155.2	141.3	37.3	2.0
Tea	4.0	—1.0	44.8	44.0	68.6	224.8	84.9	28.5
Memorandum item:	*(In millions of Kenya shillings)*							
Change in net foreign assets[3]	287	321	347	—77	1,262	1,055	461	—604

Source: International Monetary Fund, *International Financial Statistics,* July 1978.

[1] Growth over the same quarter of the previous year. Value and prices based on data in Kenya shillings.

[2] Excludes exports to and imports from Tanzania and Uganda. Prior to 1976, imports also include transfers from Tanzania and Uganda of foreign goods.

[3] Change from previous quarter in millions of Kenya shillings. Data are taken from the monetary survey.

TABLE B. Kenya: Services and Transfers, 1973–77
(In millions of Kenya shillings)

Item	1973	1974	1975	1976	1977
Total services	2	796	818	966	1,176
Debit	*—1,786*	*—2,138*	*—2,432*	*—2,722*	*—2,772*
Credit	*1,788*	*2,934*	*3,250*	*3,688*	*3,948*
Freight and insurance	228	370	384	458	486
Debit [1]	*—34*	*—20*	*—36*	*—92*	*—80*
Credit	*262*	*390*	*420*	*550*	*566*
Other transportation	286	892	880	958	1,136
Debit	*—198*	*—454*	*—524*	*—558*	*—354*
Credit	*484*	*1,346*	*1,404*	*1,516*	*1,490*
Travel	266	278	448	598	844
Debit	*—220*	*—262*	*—240*	*—260*	*—150*
Credit	*486*	*540*	*688*	*858*	*994*
Investment income	—714	—722	—840	—952	—1,190
Debit	*—902*	*—996*	*—1,154*	*—1,262*	*—1,542*
Credit	*188*	*274*	*314*	*310*	*352*
Government (not included elsewhere)	—106	—58	—56	—62	—154
Debit	*—208*	*—214*	*—212*	*—232*	*—344*
Credit	*102*	*156*	*156*	*170*	*190*
Other services	42	36	2	—34	54
Debit	*—224*	*—192*	*—266*	*—318*	*—302*
Credit	*266*	*228*	*268*	*284*	*356*
Unrequited transfers	210	224	260	270	590
Debit	*—240*	*—346*	*—328*	*—370*	*—230*
Credit	*450*	*570*	*588*	*640*	*820*
Private	6	16	—20	—42	70
Debit	*—162*	*—180*	*—164*	*—186*	*—160*
Credit	*168*	*196*	*144*	*144*	*230*
Government [2]	204	208	280	312	520
Debit	*—78*	*—166*	*—164*	*—184*	*—70*
Credit	*282*	*374*	*444*	*496*	*590*

Source: Same as Table 4.
[1] Consistent with imports on a c.i.f. basis.
[2] Includes capital grants.

TABLE C. Kenya: Nonmonetary Capital Flows, 1973–77
(In millions of Kenya shillings)

Item	1973	1974	1975	1976	1977
Capital (excluding reserves)	**1,001**	**1,599**	**1,280**	**1,440**	**1,813**
Long-term	908	1,332	1,032	1,274	1,744
Assets	*—106*	*—60*	*—92*	*—128*	*—6*
Liabilities	*1,014*	*1,392*	*1,124*	*1,402*	*1,750*
Short-term	93	267	248	166	69
Assets	*—117*	*—138*	*—100*	*—77*	*65*
Liabilities	*210*	*405*	*348*	*243*	*4*
Private nonbank	**732**	**1,040**	**544**	**744**	**616**
Long-term	626	832	306	462	616
Assets	*16*	*6*	*—42*	*—50*	*—12*
Liabilities	*610*	*826*	*348*	*512*	*628*
Short-term	106	208	238	282	—
Assets	*—12*	*—14*	*—24*	*—22*	—
Liabilities	*118*	*222*	*262*	*304*	—
Central Government[1]	**282**	**348**	**596**	**698**	**664**
Long-term	282	348	596	710	664
Assets	*—16*	*8*	*8*	*8*	*—14*
Liabilities	*298*	*340*	*588*	*702*	*678*
Short-term	—	—	—	—12	—
Assets	—	—	—	*—12*	—
Liabilities	—	—	—	—	—
Other public sector	**—**	**166**	**128**	**100**	**460**
Long-term	—	152	130	102	464
Assets	*—106*	*—74*	*—58*	*—86*	*20*
Liabilities	*106*	*226*	*188*	*188*	*444*
Short-term	—	14	—2	—2	—4
Assets	—	*—42*	*—8*	*—8*	*—8*
Liabilities	—	*56*	*6*	*6*	*4*
Commercial banks	**—13**	**45**	**12**	**—102**	**73**
Short-term	—13	45	12	—102	73
Assets	*—105*	*—82*	*—68*	*—35*	*73*
Liabilities	*92*	*127*	*80*	*—67*	—

Source: Same as Table 4.
[1] Excludes capital grants.

Chapter II

WORKSHOP 9

Financial Programming

A financial program is a set of coordinated policy measures—mainly in the monetary, fiscal, and balance of payments fields—intended to achieve certain economic targets in a relatively short period of time. The task of setting economic targets, choosing policy instruments, and quantifying the appropriate magnitudes of the instruments required to reach the targets is described as financial programming.

NATURE OF FINANCIAL PROGRAMMING

Financial programming is based on the assumption that there is a relatively stable relationship between financial variables (such as money and domestic credit), on the one hand, and nonfinancial variables (such as real national income and prices), on the other hand, and that the monetary authorities can control some of the financial variables so as to affect the real side of the economy. Although financial variables are emphasized, nonfinancial policy measures are also often included in financial programs.

A financial program such as the one described below for Kenya is prepared with the purpose of achieving or maintaining a desirable balance between real income and real absorption.[1] Consideration is also given to changes in prices, international reserves, and the exchange rate. The desirable balance between real income and real absorption and the desirable level of prices, international reserves, and the exchange rate are policy objectives that must be set by the authorities of a country. If the program assumes a substantial inflow of capital from abroad, then the policies must be attuned to this objective as well.

Financial programs that cover a short period of time, such as 12 months, and that are designed to reduce the imbalance between real income and real absorption with reasonable price stability and a given target of international reserves, usually focus on eliminating the most serious distortions that have held back output and on restraining the rate of increase of absorption. Even in such short-run programs, however, attention is given to stimulating the rate of growth through a better allocation of financial and physical resources. In a financial program covering an extended period, such as three years, the authorities consider longer-run policies to bring about a balance between real income and real absorption in order to keep inflation within acceptable limits and to promote a sustainable rate of growth. These could include policies to eliminate structural imbalances, measures to stimulate investment, adjustment of exchange rate and pricing policies to bring about a more desirable resource allocation, measures to promote financial markets, and a reform of the fiscal system.

Financial programming is used in a number of countries, even when the economic situation is satisfactory, in order to ensure further economic progress. However, it is essential to undertake financial programming when, for example, the domestic use of resources or real absorption tends to exceed real income by more than the desired amount and there are excessive price increases or large payments imbalances.

---

[1] Absorption is defined as consumption plus investment, both private and public.

Techniques for Formulating a Financial Program

Various techniques, in principle, may be used to formulate a financial program. If adequate data are available, as well as computing facilities and time, a large-scale econometric model could be built; and if the model is sufficiently reliable (that is, the statistical tests were satisfactory and simulation showed that the model "tracked" quite well over the sample period), it could be used to prepare a financial program. The procedure would be to fix the targets to be achieved in a specified period of time and, after inserting the forecast values for the exogenous variables, the required values of the policy instruments could then be calculated either by solving or by simulating the model.

The computed values of the policy instruments would be subject to various errors associated with this type of analysis—namely, errors in the statistical data used, in the specification of the model, in the estimation procedure, and in forecasting exogenous variables. Furthermore, the stability of the behavioral relationships that are the linkages between variables in the model cannot be taken for granted outside the sample period; this is especially true for a developing economy undergoing rapid structural change. Hence, in the ultimate analysis, judgmental considerations would influence the final decision on the precise values of the policy instruments. Some of the problems associated with prediction on the basis of an econometric model are discussed in the Introduction to Workshops (Chapter 1).

The desirability of having a comprehensive econometric model arises, in part, because a simple model may not accurately portray the structure of the economy and, in part, because the authorities of a country may be concerned with more objectives than the simple model can handle. Even in financial programs where the major objective is a reduction in the balance of payments deficit, the measures aimed at achieving it (such as credit restriction, reduction of the budget deficit, and a change in the exchange rate) usually involve costs in terms of disposable real income that may severely affect certain groups or sectors. The authorities may, therefore, use other policy instruments to minimize these costs—that is, they may utilize multiple policy instruments to achieve multiple targets simultaneously. A comprehensive econometric model will permit the investigation of the effects on all relevant variables of the policy measures that may be used.

When the construction of a comprehensive econometric model is not feasible, it may be necessary to adopt a more pragmatic approach. Nevertheless, the approach must be one that permits judgment of the likely effects of proposed policy actions. On the basis of this pragmatic approach, the authorities should be able to decide on a mix of politically acceptable policy actions that permit the attainment of the primary objectives. One of the various possible methods, which is presented only as an illustration, is described below.

Steps in the Financial Programming Exercise

As a starting point, the values of the exogenous variables needed for the preparation of a financial program may be estimated for the program period—say, the next 12 months. These variables are those over which the current economic policy of the country has relatively little influence during that period, such as the foreign demand for its exports. The next step is to fix tentatively the values of the target variables and to "envisage" the policy actions that may be necessary to achieve such targets, given the values of the exogenous variables. At the outset, a decision must be made whether an adjustment in the exchange rate (a key ingredient in the envisaged policy "mix") is required in the light of recent, as well as expected, changes in either domestic prices and costs or external factors. If a policy mix is found to be inadequate to achieve the desired targets without an exchange rate adjustment, such an adjustment may have to be envisaged; in this event, a new set of policies consistent with the new exchange rate would be formulated. After this preliminary work, it is necessary to check whether the envisaged policy actions are appropriate to achieve the results expected of the financial program.

A convenient procedure is to estimate the values, for the next 12 months, of the various items appearing in a monetary or financial survey (see Workshop 1), as has been done in Workshop 6:

Projection of Monetary Aggregates. These estimates should be made on the basis of the assumed values for the target variables and the exogenous variables. Thus, starting with the monetary survey, "net foreign assets" may be taken as a target variable on the basis of a given exchange rate. This is likely to be the procedure followed in financial programs for countries that have a deficit in the balance of payments and have a low level of international reserves. Accordingly, a value that is desirable in view of the circumstances is assigned to this item.

The next step is to estimate "money." This is done on the basis of a demand for money function. It is frequently necessary to estimate several different specifications of the demand for money function, including different coverage of the variables in the relationship, in order to find the one that is reasonably satisfactory, i.e., where the relationship is plausible and relatively stable and where the probable magnitude of prediction errors is relatively small. However, in practice, many estimates of the demand for money function contain prediction errors that are uncomfortably large. This leaves room for judgmental considerations to be used in the projection.

If the demand for money is a function of nominal income alone, estimates of the real income and the level of prices over the next 12 months are needed in order to obtain the estimate for money.

The rate of growth of real national income is a policy objective that must be realistic and also be consistent with the other policy objectives. Hence, there is no simple and easy way to estimate the rate of growth of real national income over the next 12 months. It depends on numerous and complex relationships that underlie aggregate supply and demand. On the supply side, perhaps one of the crudest but simplest ways is to investigate the growth of real output over the last few years and then to consider any new factors that are likely to affect real output over the 12-month period. These would include factors affecting agricultural output, particularly in primary producing countries; new plants and equipment coming on stream; measures to increase the rate of capacity utilization, such as changes in import restrictions, particularly on raw materials and semifinished products, and in credit allocation; and changes in the labor force.

On the demand side, it is necessary to consider fiscal, monetary, exchange rate, and incomes policies, as well as economic conditions in the rest of the world that affect the prices and volumes of exports and imports. A simultaneity problem occurs in the estimation of real income. The estimated real income, which is used to estimate the demand for money, is in part determined by the monetary and fiscal policy stances. However, the domestic credit derived from the estimated demand for money (see below), given the amount of net foreign assets, may not be consistent with the monetary and fiscal policy stances envisaged initially. This implies that real income, the demand for money, and the monetary and fiscal policies must be determined simultaneously. Operationally, this difficulty may be circumvented by making general assumptions about the effects of these policies and by checking later to see whether these are borne out by the calculations. Thus, the estimated level of the real national income has to take into account the exogenous factors, as well as the effects of the initially envisaged monetary, fiscal, exchange rate, and incomes policies.

The level of prices over the next 12 months is a target variable. However, as in the case of real national income, the value of this target cannot be set arbitrarily. The prices of imports and exports in foreign currency may be largely outside the sphere of influence of the authorities of the country. The prices of domestic products for the home market may change not only because of events that have already occurred (such as an increase in the wage rate, already granted) or because of likely events over which the authorities have no control, but also because of monetary, fiscal, exchange rate, and incomes policies. The complication of simultaneity again arises—namely, that the level of prices is used to estimate the demand for money, which in turn, together with the supply of money, influences the level of prices. This implies that the demand for money, the supply of money, and the level of prices must be determined simultaneously. A procedure similar to the one described in connection with the estimation of real national income may be used here.

If the demand for money is a function of other variables besides nominal income, such as the expected rate of inflation or the expected rates of return on competing financial assets, these have to be estimated before the amount of money demanded can be calculated. The expected rate of inflation may be inferred from the already estimated level of prices over the next 12 months. Established techniques for generating expectation, such as adaptive expectation or rational expectation, can be utilized. Similarly, the expected rate of interest may be estimated on the basis of the stance of monetary policy and certain behavioral assumptions concerning expectation.

The next step involves the estimation of "quasi-money." Generally, quasi-money is explained by the same variables as those operating in the demand for money function, or by closely related variables. However, the interest rates on savings and time deposits tend to influence the demand for money and the demand for quasi-money in opposite directions.

For "other items (net)" in the monetary survey, it is useful to check whether this component changes very much from year to year. If it does, the cause of its variations should be investigated so as to derive some basis for estimating the numerical value of this item 12 months hence.

Once money, quasi-money, and other items (net) have been estimated and the target value for net foreign assets has been fixed, the amount of domestic credit of the banking system 12 months hence can be calculated; that is:

$$DC_t = MO_t + QMO_t + NOI_t - NFA_t \tag{1}$$

where *DC* stands for domestic credit, *MO* for money, *QMO* for quasi-money, *NOI* for other items (net), *NFA* for net foreign assets, and the subscript *t* stands for the value of the variable at the end of the 12-month program period.

Thus, in order to reach the specified target for net foreign assets, the authorities would have to ensure that domestic credit created by the banking system during the next 12 months *(ΔDC_t)* does not exceed the amount

$$\Delta DC_t = DC_t - DC_{t-1} \qquad (2)$$

where DC_t is given by equation (1) and the subscript $t-1$ stands for the value of the variable at the beginning of the 12-month program period.

If it is believed that the credit expansion can be limited to the amount calculated in equation (2) without upsetting the estimates of the macroeconomic variables, such as real income and prices, used in estimating the items in equation (1), then the calculated overall credit expansion is considered to be consistent with the policies initially envisaged. However, it is only rarely that the amount of credit expansion calculated in equation (2) turns out to be consistent with the policies initially envisaged, as well as with the estimated values of other variables in the economy. Furthermore, the amount of credit expansion yielded by equation (2) does not indicate how the new credit is to be allocated, for example, between the government and private sectors. Therefore, it is useful to continue the work and to project (on the basis of the estimated exogenous variables and the policy actions) government sector revenue and expenditure, private sector income and expenditure, and the major components of the balance of payments, in order to ensure the internal consistency of the financial program.

On the basis of the forecasts of national income and its major components (e.g., consumption, imports, etc.), it may be possible to estimate the bulk of government revenue. Typically, in fact, the major part of government revenue depends on income, consumption, exports, and imports (as illustrated in Workshop 7: Revenue Forecasting), as well as on the tax structure and the envisaged changes in tax laws and in collection procedure. Implicit or explicit assumptions must already have been made about government expenditure in estimating the national income. Any change in the exchange rate would also affect estimates of government revenue as well as expenditure. The resulting budgetary deficit, if any, may or may not be such that it can be financed through government borrowing abroad, which is reflected in net foreign assets in equation (1) or by the expansion of domestic credit calculated on the basis of equation (2). If such financing of the government is feasible, then the exercise can proceed. Account should be taken of the fact that the private sector and the rest of the public sector (see Workshop 2: Government Finance Statistics) also need bank credit to finance their economic and financial activities. Therefore, the entire amount of the calculated credit expansion is not available to finance the government deficit. If the deficit cannot be financed by borrowing from the banking system or abroad, various possibilities are open—such as borrowing from domestic nonbank sources, increase in taxation, or reduction in government expenditure below the level initially envisaged. But if some of these policy actions change the values of the endogenous variables already used to calculate credit expansion (such as net foreign assets, real national income, and prices), the calculated expansion of credit would also change. If this is the case, the initially envisaged policies are obviously not compatible with the objectives and therefore the exercise must be repeated with different policies or objectives. It may require several iterations before a consistent set of values for the relevant variables is obtained.

On the basis of the forecasts of the state of the world economy and of domestic supply and demand, exports and imports may be estimated. For the values of exports and imports in domestic currency, assumptions about exchange rate policies have to be made. In estimating private capital movements in a country where the exchange system is free of restrictions on capital transactions, it is necessary to take into account domestic interest rates in relation to the interest rates in international money and capital markets. For other items of the balance of payments, it is necessary to use the information available and to investigate the relationships in each specific case (see Workshop 8: Balance of Payments Forecasting). If these estimates yield a value for the outturn of the balance of payments that is compatible with the target for net foreign assets fixed in calculating the credit expansion, the exercise can proceed further.

If the outturn in the balance of payments is not the desired one, different policies (including possibly a different exchange rate) will be required and these will inevitably affect the endogenous variables used elsewhere in the calculations. Thus, it would be necessary to start all over again with fresh assumptions about the policies to be undertaken and perhaps new values for the target variables. This process would continue until policy measures are found that are compatible with the values of the target variables, given the estimated exogenous variables.

The next step would be to calculate the expansion of central bank credit that is compatible with the expansion of banking system credit. This step would be necessary in order to give the authorities an instrument that is essential for both the execution and control of a financial program. Some countries, for a variety of reasons, have strong objections to imposing credit ceilings on individual commercial banks and prefer to impose a single ceiling on central bank domestic credit. If the relationships involved in the estimation of the credit multiplier (i.e., the ratio between total bank domestic credit and central bank monetary liabilities) are stable, the imposition of a ceiling on the central bank domestic credit would effectively constrain bank credit, given the assumptions about net foreign assets. This would avoid involvement in the sensitive and difficult task of allocating credit among banks. Besides, the ceiling on the central bank domestic credit can be readily controlled.

The task is therefore to estimate the relationships between the monetary liabilities of the central bank and the principal components of the consolidated balance sheet of the commercial banks, taking into account the interest rates on both bank deposits and loans (if such interest rates play a role in the case investigated). This exercise may also give an indication of how a government deficit or surplus can be financed, that is, whether it can be financed through direct advances from the central bank, or from commercial banks, or both. It may be found that, for institutional or other reasons, the domestic credit of the central bank has to be higher than that derived from the credit multiplier. If this is so, a policy to reduce the size of the multiplier, such as the imposition of higher reserve requirements on banks or other similar policy actions, may be necessary.

The technical task of preparing a financial program is accomplished when the set of policy measures required to produce the desired targets has been determined.

The technique of financial programming described above has been presented in rather general terms. It should be noted that several iterations may be necessary in order to ensure the overall consistency of the financial program. In actual application of the program to specific cases, suitable modifications may have to be made in the light of the relevant economic circumstances and the availability of data. Furthermore, the order of steps in the financial programming exercise is not sacrosanct; in fact, in the formulation of a hypothetical financial program for Kenya as presented under Exercise and Issues for Discussion, the order of steps differs from that outlined above.

This workshop, which contains an illustration and application of one possible technique of financial programming, provides the elements for preparing a hypothetical financial program for Kenya for the calendar year 1978. The first section discusses the medium-term policy objectives, the annual targets, and the performance criteria incorporated in the International Monetary Fund's extended facility arrangement for Kenya in fiscal years 1976–78. The second section reviews the actual performance of the Kenyan economy and discusses the implementation of government policies during 1975 and 1976. The third section describes and analyzes Kenya's economic situation in 1977. In conclusion, the section on Exercise and Issues for Discussion contains a possible methodology to be utilized for the formulation of a hypothetical financial program for Kenya in 1978. It is assumed that the program is being formulated in early January 1978. The forecasting techniques and other elements of information from previous workshops may be used as ingredients in the preparation of this financial program.

OBJECTIVES AND POLICY CRITERIA FOR KENYA'S EXTENDED FACILITY PROGRAM

Kenya has experienced payments imbalances in recent years because of an adverse trend in the external terms of trade and policies that have resulted in increases in both the capital intensiveness and import intensiveness of production. Gross official international reserves declined from SDR 220 million (equivalent to six months' imports) at the end of 1970 to SDR 162 million (equivalent to two months' imports) at the end of 1974. The authorities considered that a lower rate of growth than the 6.5 per cent achieved during the 1965–74 period was more realistic, in view of these developments. In addition, to prevent further deterioration in the balance of payments, prices needed to be stabilized.

Accordingly, in July 1975, the Government of Kenya undertook a three-year program, supported by the use of the International Monetary Fund's resources under an extended facility arrangement, seeking the attainment of (1) an annual rate of growth in real gross domestic product (GDP) of 5 per cent, (2) a rate of increase in domestic prices substantially lower than that of import prices, and (3) the elimination of the need for balance of payments assistance by 1980. To achieve these objectives, the program stressed both medium-term policies, designed to change Kenya's structure of production and pattern of factor use, and short-term demand management policies. The medium-term policies attempted to shift public and private investment toward agriculture, mainly through increased development outlays on agriculture, provision for remunerative producer prices, and more adequate credit facilities; to reform the tariff structure, which had favored imports of capital goods and raw materials; and to hold down the labor-capital cost ratio through wage guidelines.

Within the medium-term framework, Kenya's financial program for fiscal year 1976 was formulated to promote specific objectives. The growth target for real GDP was set at 5.4 per cent in 1975 and 5.1 per cent in 1976 (Table 1). In spite of the intended policy shifts, the overall balance of payments deficits were forecast at KSh 732 million (SDR 84 million) in 1975 and KSh 400 million (SDR 41 million) in 1976. These targets implied a limitation of the increase in total domestic credit to 19 per cent in fiscal year 1976, with the increase in credit to the private sector being contained to 17 per cent. To control the expansion in total credit, ceilings

TABLE 1. Kenya: Total Availability and Use of Resources, 1974–78
(In billions of Kenya shillings)

Item	Provisional 1974	1975	Projections[1] 1976	1977	1978
GDP at factor cost	16.7	17.6	18.5	19.4	20.4
Nonmonetary	*3.2*	*3.4*	*3.5*	*3.7*	*3.8*
Monetary	*13.5*	*14.2*	*15.0*	*15.7*	*16.6*
Indirect taxes	2.4	2.2	2.4	2.6	2.8
Subsidies	0.1	0.1	0.1	0.1	0.1
GDP at market prices	**19.0**	**19.7**	**20.8**	**21.9**	**23.1**
Imports of goods and services	8.3	7.7	7.9	7.9	8.1
Exports of goods and services	6.6	6.9	7.1	7.5	7.9
Import surplus	**1.7**	**0.8**	**0.8**	**0.4**	**0.2**
Total resources available for domestic investment and consumption	**20.7**	**20.5**	**21.6**	**22.3**	**23.3**
Public fixed capital formation	1.8	1.9	2.0	2.1	2.2
Public consumption	3.4	3.7	3.8	4.0	4.2
Total public expenditure	**5.2**	**5.6**	**5.8**	**6.1**	**6.4**
Private fixed capital formation	2.0 }	3.2	3.6	3.6	3.7
Increase in stocks	2.1 }				
Private consumption	11.4	11.7	12.2	12.6	13.2
Total private expenditure	**15.5**	**14.9**	**15.8**	**16.2**	**16.9**
Total use of resources	**20.7**	**20.5**	**21.6**	**22.3**	**23.3**
Annual percentage change in GDP at factor cost	3.6	5.4	5.1	4.9	5.2
Imports as percentage of GDP at factor cost	0.50	0.44	0.43	0.41	0.40
Gross investment as percentage of GDP at market prices	0.31	0.26	0.27	0.26	0.26
Total consumption as percentage of GDP at market prices	0.78	0.78	0.77	0.76	0.75

Source: Rattan J. Bhatia and Saul L. Rothman, "Introducing the Extended Fund Facility: The Kenyan Case," *Finance and Development,* Vol. 12, No. 4 (December 1975), pp. 39–41, table on p. 41.

[1] At constant 1974 prices.

were put on the level of net domestic assets of the Central Bank of Kenya.[2] Government capital expenditure and lending minus repayments were to rise by about 20 per cent over fiscal-year 1975 actuals and were to be reoriented toward agriculture. The overall budget deficit was estimated at KSh 1.4 billion. A limit, consistent with the overall limitation on increase in bank credit, was placed on borrowing by the Government from the banking system for this fiscal year.

In the financial program formulated in June 1976 for fiscal year 1977, the second year of the extended facility arrangement, the targets for growth of real GDP were 4.9 per cent in calendar year 1976 and 5.2 per cent in 1977. The balance of payments targets were overall deficits of KSh 400 million (SDR 41.4 million) in 1976 and KSh 460 million (SDR 47.6 million) in 1977. The program envisaged an increase in money plus quasi-money of 10 per cent during the program period. It implied an overall increase in domestic credit of 21 per cent. Credit to the nongovernment sector was expected to increase by 18 per cent. These rates of credit expansion were calculated to contain imports to levels consistent with the GDP and balance of payments targets. The financial program for fiscal year 1977 also included one performance clause limiting the increase in net domestic assets of the Central Bank of Kenya and another limiting government borrowing from the banking system. The budgetary targets were to reduce the magnitude of the overall deficit and to maintain the real level of capital expenditure, thus implying a significant reduction in the rate of increase in real current expenditure.

The observance of the limits on the net domestic assets of the Central Bank, as well as of those on net credit to the Government, would be a condition for Kenya's access to Fund resources under the proposed arrangement.[3] In addition, the conditionality included the

[2] Defined as the sum of currency issued plus nonbank private deposits minus net foreign assets.

[3] Conditionality of this nature is required for extended facility programs that involve drawings from the International Monetary Fund above the first credit tranche.

Government's intention not to introduce any multiple currency practices or any new restrictions, nor to intensify existing ones on payments and transfers for current international transactions, nor to introduce restrictions or intensify existing ones on imports.

POLICY IMPLEMENTATION AND ECONOMIC PERFORMANCE IN KENYA IN 1975–76

The Kenyan authorities implemented several measures that were envisaged in the program. Following the 30 per cent rise in producer prices for domestically consumed agricultural commodities in January 1975, producer prices for maize, wheat, and milk were raised by an average of 28 per cent in September 1976. In mid-1975, the Government announced new wage guidelines limiting the average rate of increase in wages and salaries to 75 per cent of the increase in the consumer price index. These guidelines were revised further in February 1976 to limit average wage and salary increases to two thirds of the increase in the consumer price index. In July 1975, the Central Bank of Kenya issued a directive requiring commercial banks to increase the share of their deposits lent to the agricultural sector by 7 percentage points, to 17 per cent by the end of June 1976. Government capital expenditure and lending minus repayments were also shifted in favor of the agricultural sector. In October 1975, Kenya depreciated the shilling by about 12 per cent and changed its peg from the U.S. dollar to the special drawing right (SDR). A wide-ranging import tariff reform was initiated to discourage excessive use of imports and to encourage the use of domestic raw materials and factors of production.

The economic picture that emerged for 1975 was mixed. For the second successive year, there was a decline in the rate of economic growth. Real GDP increased by only 1.2 per cent, mainly because of unusually bad weather conditions. Nevertheless, there was a substantial improvement in the balance of payments, as well as some moderation of inflation. The balance of payments in 1975 showed a deficit of KSh 338 million (SDR 47 million), which was considerably smaller than the extended facility program's target of a deficit of KSh 732 million (SDR 84 million). The annual rate of increase in the cost of living for the lower-income group in 1975 as a whole was 19.2 per cent, which was slightly higher than in 1974. However, the increase in the second half of 1975 was much lower than in the first half. The budget outturn indicated a shortfall in revenue as well as greater current expenditure than initially budgeted. Development projects were cut back, but cost overruns kept the nominal level of capital expenditure only slightly short of the budgeted level. Net credit to the Government from the banking system amounted to KSh 400 million for fiscal year 1976 and KSh 837 million for the calendar year 1975. The domestic counterpart of Kenya's SDR allocation (KSh 134 million) was transferred in September 1975 to treasury deposits with the Central Bank. Money and quasi-money increased by 17 per cent in 1975. Domestic credit went up by 29 per cent, while net foreign assets (net of Fund credit) actually declined.

In 1976 economic conditions were much more favorable. Real GDP increased by 6.1 per cent, wage employment rose by 4.7 per cent, the inflation rate (in terms of the cost of living for the lower-income group) was reduced to 11.4 per cent, and the balance of payments recorded a large surplus of KSh 776 million. The rise in world prices for coffee, Kenya's major export, and the improvement in weather conditions were the most important factors underlying this turnaround, but the economy also might have responded to the policy shifts introduced in 1975 and 1976. The budgetary situation did not register the expected improvement, mainly because of a substantial increase in defense expenditure for fiscal year 1977. Nevertheless, there was a small reduction in the overall budget deficit. Net credit to the Government from the banking system amounted to minus KSh 5 million for fiscal year 1977 and KSh 131 million for calendar year 1976. The rate of growth in money and quasi-money accelerated to 24 per cent in 1976. Domestic credit expanded by 17 per cent, while net foreign assets increased by two and a half times to KSh 1,459 million.

ECONOMIC DEVELOPMENTS IN KENYA IN 1977

In 1977, the rate of Kenya's economic growth accelerated and the balance of payments registered a record surplus, mainly because of favorable weather conditions and a continued upsurge in coffee prices. However, inflation worsened, and the budgetary situation remained under pressure, as the Kenyan authorities were obliged to incur a substantial increase in expenditures on defense and development.

Production, Expenditure, and Prices

The rate of increase in real GDP accelerated from 6.1 per cent in 1976 to an estimated 7.3 per cent in 1977 (Tables 2 and 3).

TABLE 2. Kenya: Selected National Accounts Data, 1975–77
(In millions of Kenya shillings)

Item	1975	1976	1977[1]
Resources			
GDP at factor cost (current prices)	20,560	25,257	32,404
Indirect taxes and subsidies	2,783	3,325	4,249
GDP at market prices	23,343	28,581	36,653
Imports of goods and services	8,358	9,436	11,688
Total	**31,701**	**38,017**	**48,341**
Use of resources			
Private fixed investment	2,824	3,390	4,633
Public fixed investment	2,026	2,450	3,141
Change in stocks	—275	133	—14
Gross investment	**4,576**	**5,973**	**7,760**
Private consumption	15,731	17,542	21,338
Public consumption	4,256	4,943	6,250
Total consumption	**19,987**	**22,485**	**27,588**
Gross domestic expenditure	24,563	28,457	35,347
Exports of goods and services	7,138	9,560	12,994
Total	**31,701**	**38,017**	**48,341**
National income			
GDP at factor cost	20,560	25,257	32,404
Factor incomes received from abroad	428	352	372
Factor incomes paid abroad	1,256	1,444	1,786
GNP at factor cost	19,732	24,165	30,990
Indirect taxes and subsidies	2,783	3,325	4,249
GNP at market prices	22,515	27,490	35,239

Source: Kenya, *Economic Survey,* 1978.
[1] Provisional figures.

TABLE 3. Kenya: Sectoral Origin of Gross Domestic Product, 1974–77
(In millions of Kenya shillings)

Sectoral Origin	Current prices				Constant 1972 Prices			
	1974	1975	1976	1977[1]	1974	1975	1976	1977[1]
Private sector and public sector enterprises	**15,206**	**17,426**	**21,679**	**28,220**	**11,898**	**11,887**	**12,627**	**13,600**
Semimonetary economy	3,519	4,651	5,202	6,106	2,987	3,019	2,979	3,080
Agriculture, forestry, and fishing	2,741	3,621	4,000	4,650	2,375	2,388	2,329	2,406
Other	778	1,030	1,202	1,456	612	631	650	674
Monetary economy	11,687	12,775	16,477	22,114	8,911	8,868	9,648	10,520
Agriculture, forestry, and fishing	2,599	2,859	4,567	7,768	2,034	2,036	2,115	2,370
Mining and quarrying	63	66	83	93	58	60	68	71
Manufacturing	2,381	2,543	3,348	4,108	1,890	1,886	2,236	2,572
Building and construction	868	888	924	1,040	640	617	589	624
Electricity and water	209	264	284	433	202	224	263	285
Transport, storage, and communications	1,075	1,205	1,383	1,386	839	813	898	847
Wholesale and retail trade, restaurants, and hotels	2,317	2,437	2,889	3,807	1,433	1,325	1,434	1,588
Finance, insurance, real estate, and business services	936	1,093	1,361	1,570	768	813	916	964
Other services	1,239	1,420	1,638	1,909	1,050	1,094	1,129	1,199
Government services	**2,700**	**3,134**	**3,578**	**4,184**	**2,452**	**2,636**	**2,778**	**2,936**
Total GDP at factor cost	**17,906**	**20,560**	**25,257**	**32,404**	**14,350**	**14,523**	**15,405**	**16,536**

Source: Kenya, *Economic Survey,* 1978.
[1] Provisional figures.

Agricultural production is estimated to have increased by about 12 per cent, attributable mainly to favorable weather conditions and the continued increase in export prices. Production of coffee, tea, and sugarcane increased by 21 per cent, 39 per cent, and 14 per cent, respectively, while other crops and livestock products showed little change. Manufacturing output is estimated to have risen by 15 per cent. The effects on this industry of the expansion of rural output and incomes more than compensated for the disruptive effects of the breakup of the East African Community (EAC) in 1977. The output of building and construction is estimated to have increased by 6 per cent, compared with a decline of 5 per cent in 1976, reflecting a turnaround in private residential building activity and the start of several major government projects (e.g., the Upper Tana Reservoir, Mombasa Water Supply Development Program, and Bura Irrigation Project). Tourism was adversely affected by the closing of the Tanzanian border. Nevertheless, the decline in the number of visitors was offset by an increase in the average length of stay, resulting in a 7 per cent increase in the number of bed-nights for tourists. Output of transport and communications is estimated to have declined by 6 per cent, reflecting mainly the strains experienced by the EAC corporations and the closure of the Tanzanian border. Wholesale and retail trade, distribution, and other sectors of the economy all recorded reasonable rates of increase.

Aggregate domestic demand (as measured by the sum of consumption and investment expenditures) rose by an estimated 24 per cent in nominal terms, compared with 19 per cent in 1976. Gross fixed capital formation as a proportion of GDP rose from 20 per cent in 1976 to 21 per cent in 1977. The ratio of consumption to GDP declined from 79 per cent in 1976 to 75 per cent in 1977. Private sector investment in real terms increased most significantly in agriculture (44 per cent); transport, storage, and communications (30 per cent); and manufacturing (15 per cent). By type of asset, investment in 1977 mainly took the form of machinery and equipment. The decrease in the consumption ratio reflected, in part, the reinvestment of the gross farm revenue and business profits and, in part, the impact of the wage guidelines.

Wage employment rose by 5.3 per cent in 1977, with the most significant expansion occurring in finance, insurance, real estate, and business services (16 per cent); transport and communications (9 per cent); and manufacturing (8 per cent). Wage employment in agriculture also expanded by 4 per cent, compared with a decline of 1 per cent in 1975 and an increase of 1 per cent in 1976. Employment in the public sector went up by 5.6 per cent in 1977, compared with an increase of 4.1 per cent in 1976. While in 1976 growth of public sector employment was largely concentrated in central government employees, in 1977 the rise in public sector employment occurred mainly in the parastatal bodies and other enterprises partly owned by the public sector.

Average wage earnings rose by 8 per cent in 1977, compared with 16 per cent in 1976. The rate of increase of average earnings in the public sector decelerated more than that in the private sector. The 9 per cent increase in average earnings in the private sector was in accordance with the wage guidelines, which allowed an average increase in wage earnings equivalent to two thirds of the increase in the cost of living. The highest increase in average earnings in 1977 occurred in manufacturing (13 per cent); transport and communications (11 per cent); and trade, restaurants, and hotels (9 per cent). Average earnings in agriculture declined by about 1 per cent, compared with an increase of 17 per cent in 1976.

In spite of the increase in domestic supply, inflation emerged as the foremost problem in 1977. The sharp increase in domestic liquidity, together with an upward adjustment of retail prices of foods to correspond with higher producer prices, exerted considerable pressure on consumer prices. Between December 1976 and December 1977 consumer prices for the lower-income group in Nairobi rose by 21.0 per cent. The food index went up by 17.2 per cent while the rent index rose by 31.9 per cent for the lower-income group. In terms of the implicit GDP deflator, inflation was estimated at about 20 per cent in 1977.

Balance of Payments

Kenya's balance of payments recorded an overall surplus of more than KSh 2 billion in 1977 (Table 4). The value of merchandise exports rose by 51 per cent (4 per cent in volume), and that of merchandise imports rose by 31 per cent (21 per cent in volume). The terms of trade improved by about 32 per cent following an improvement of 17 per cent in 1976. The trade deficit declined sharply, while the combined surplus in invisibles and capital accounts remained broadly unchanged. At the end of December 1977, Kenya's gross international reserves were SDR 438 million, or the equivalent of about five months' imports.

The principal factor underlying the overall improvement in 1977 was the continued rise in the prices of coffee and tea, Kenya's major exports. While these prices peaked in late spring 1977, their weighted averages for the year were higher than in 1976 by 80 per cent and 91 per cent, respectively. Export volumes of coffee and tea also rose by 22 per cent and 19 per cent, respectively. Kenya's "other" exports, which include some manufactured products, rose slightly (5 per cent) in value despite the virtual loss of the Tanzanian market.

The increase in imports was due, in part, to higher incomes and greater availability of domestic credit and, in part, to greater government imports, including those of new capital equipment required for replacing some EAC corporations by Kenyan corporations and defense-related imports. The average propensity to import was 32 per cent, which was about the same as in 1976 but lower than in 1974 and 1975 when high oil prices raised the import propensity to an average of 39 per cent.

As a result partly of the dissolution of the East African Community, and even more as a result of the closure of the Tanzanian border, Kenya's tourist and other service receipts grew more slowly in 1977, while payments of investment income rose faster, reflecting higher profits of foreign firms, particularly those engaged in production and marketing of Kenya's major exports. Larger inflows of pri-

TABLE 4. Kenya: Balance of Payments Summary, 1976–77
(In millions of Kenya shillings)

Item	1976 Source	1976 Use	1976 Balance	1977 Source	1977 Use	1977 Balance
Current account	**10,552**	**11,250**	**–698**	**14,186**	**13,704**	**482**
Trade balance	6,224	8,158	–1,934	9,418	10,702	–1,284
Imports, c.i.f.		*8,158*	*–8,158*		*10,702*	*–10,702*
Exports, f.o.b.	*6,224*		*6,224*	*9,418*		*9,418*
Services	3,688	2,722	966	3,948	2,772	1,176
Freight and insurance	*550*	*92*	*458*	*566*	*80*	*486*
Other transportation	*1,516*	*558*	*958*	*1,490*	*354*	*1,136*
Foreign travel	*858*	*260*	*598*	*994*	*150*	*844*
International investment income	*310*	*1,262*	*–952*	*352*	*1,542*	*–1,190*
Government transactions, n.e.s.	*170*	*232*	*–62*	*190*	*344*	*–154*
Other services	*284*	*318*	*–34*	*356*	*302*	*54*
Transfers	640	370	270	820	230	590
Private	*144*	*186*	*–42*	*230*	*160*	*70*
Government	*496*	*184*	*312*	*590*	*70*	*520*
Capital account	**1,677**	**237**	**1,440**	**1,754**	**–59**	**1,813**
Private long-term	512	50	462	628	12	616
Government long-term	702	–8	710	678	14	664
Government corporations long-term	188	86	102	444	–20	464
Short-term	275	109	166	4	–65	69
Government	—	*12*	*–12*	—	—	—
Government corporations	*6*	*8*	*–2*	*4*	*8*	*–4*
Commercial banks	*–35*	*67*	*–102*	—	*–73*	*73*
Private	*304*	*22*	*282*	—	—	—
Errors and omissions	—	—	**34**	—	—	**–48**
Overall balance	—	—	**776**	—	—	**2,247**
Financing (increase in assets)	**158**	**934**	**–776**	**87**	**2,334**	**–2,247**
Gross official reserves	—	870	–870	—	1,973	–1,973
Use of Fund credit	158	—	158	—	361	–361
Other liabilities[1]	—	64	–64	87	—	87

Sources: For current account and capital account (except commercial banks), the data are taken from Kenya, *Economic Survey,* 1978. The data for commercial banks and financing are taken from International Monetary Fund, *International Financial Statistics,* July 1978, in order to ensure consistency with the monetary accounts for purposes of financial programming. The adjustment for the resulting discrepancy is contained in the residual item, errors and omissions.

Note: n.e.s. = not elsewhere specified.

[1] Includes foreign banks' deposits with the Central Bank of Kenya and International Monetary Fund deposits.

vate capital, mostly direct investment, were partly offset by a decline in government capital inflows.

Public Finance

Kenya's budgetary position improved considerably in fiscal year 1977, as the overall deficit declined by 22 per cent to KSh 1.3 billion (Table 5). Current revenue increased by 20 per cent as a result of a general economic recovery, while total expenditure increased by 17

TABLE 5. Kenya: Summary of Central Government Budgetary Operations, Fiscal Years 1976–78
(In millions of Kenya shillings; year ending June 30)

	Item	1976	1977	1978[1]
1	Current revenue	5,123	6,149	7,375
1.1	Tax	4,571	5,297	6,401
1.2	Nontax	552	852	975[2]
2	Capital revenue	—	—	—
3	Total revenue (1 + 2)	5,123	6,149	7,375[2]
4	Grants	201	234	440
4.1	Current	61	24	. . .
4.2	Capital	140	210	. . .
5	Total revenue and grants (3 + 4)	5,325	6,383	7,815
6	Current expenditure	4,904	5,580	. . .
7	Capital expenditure	1,259	1,660	. . .
8	Total expenditure (6 + 7)	6,164	7,240	9,416[3]
9	Lending minus repayments	870	470	783
10	Expenditure and lending minus repayments (8 + 9)	7,034	7,710	10,199[3]
11	Current account surplus or saving (without grants) (1 — 6)	219	569	. . .
12	Gross fixed capital formation	1,059	1,388	. . .
13	Gross capital formation	1,059	1,388	. . .
14	Overall deficit/surplus (5 — 10)	—1,709	—1,327	—2,384
15	Financing (= 14)	1,709	1,327	2,384
15.1	Abroad	639	464	686
15.2	Domestic	1,070	863	1,698
15.2.1	Nonbank	670	868	498
15.2.2	Deposit money banks	350	684	1,200 (15.2.2 and 15.2.3)
15.2.3	Central Bank	50	—689	

Sources: International Monetary Fund, *Government Finance Statistics Yearbook*, Vol. 2 (1978) and *International Financial Statistics*, various issues; Central Bank of Kenya, *Annual Report for the Financial Year Ended 30th June, 1977;* Kenya, *Estimates of Revenue*, 1977/78, *Estimates of Recurrent Expenditure*, 1977/78, and *Development Estimates*, 1977/78.

[1] Budget estimates.
[2] Includes operating revenue of departmental enterprises.
[3] Includes operating expenditure of departmental enterprises.

per cent. External financing fell short of the budgeted level, but the Government succeeded in mobilizing funds from the domestic nonbank sector. Thus, the recourse to the banking system decreased.

The budget for fiscal year 1978 was formulated against the background of the forecast of a record high balance of payments surplus. Although realizing the danger of renewed acceleration of inflation, the Government felt that there was a need to step up development effort. Budget estimates aimed at increasing the current account surplus by restraining the growth of current expenditure to below that of current revenue. New tax measures, including an export tax on coffee and tea, were estimated to generate KSh 500 million of revenue. Capital expenditure and lending minus repayments were projected to rise sharply, and the overall budget deficit was estimated at KSh 2.4 billion. About half of the deficit was expected to be financed by borrowing from the banking system, including financing by the Cereals and Sugar Finance Corporation.

Since the inception of the budget for fiscal year 1978, two developments have assumed increasing importance. First, the dissolution of the East African Community has necessitated additional expenditure to set up Kenyan replacements for various EAC corporations. Second, defense expenditure increased more than anticipated. The budgetary outturn during the first half of fiscal year 1978 showed an overall budget deficit of KSh 1.3 billion. Current revenue was increasing significantly faster than current expenditure. Capital expenditure was running below the budgeted rate, primarily because deliveries of equipment were later than expected. During this period, the budget deficit was financed almost equally by nonbank domestic borrowing (KSh 565 million) and by bank borrowing (KSh 537 million). The latter included KSh 232 million of financing from the Cereals and Sugar Finance Corporation.

Money and Credit

The growth in money and quasi-money accelerated sharply in Kenya from 25 per cent in 1976 to 47 per cent in 1977 (Table 6). Both the increase in net foreign assets and the increase in domestic credit contributed to the monetary expansion. Domestic credit increased by 24 per cent in 1977, as the 34 per cent increase in credit to the private sector was only partially offset by a decline of KSh 98 million in net credit to the Government. The expansion in private sector credit occurred in response to rising economic activity and to higher prices, as well as to a relaxation of the limits on domestic borrowing by foreign companies. Beginning in April 1977, foreign-controlled companies engaged in direct agricultural production and manufacturing and tourism industries were allowed to borrow locally up to 100 per cent of their investment while previously such borrowing had been limited to between 20 and 60 per cent.

In terms of the sectoral distribution, credit to all sectors, except building and construction, expanded sharply. Credit to the priority sectors of agriculture, manufacturing, and African small-scale enterprises rose by 34 per cent, 33 per cent, and 39 per cent, respectively. Because of the large expansion of deposits, credit to the agricultural sector in 1977 averaged only about 12 per cent of commercial bank deposits, considerably below the 17 per cent requirement set by the Central Bank.

The decline in net credit to the Government reflected a considerable improvement in the budgetary position, particularly during the first half of 1977. With a view to reducing the creation of primary liquidity, the Government shifted its bank borrowing from the Central Bank to commercial banks. Thus, the Government's position with the Central Bank changed from a net debtor position of KSh 778 million at the end of 1976 to a net creditor position of KSh 35 million by the end of 1977. At the same time, net credit from commercial banks to the Government rose by KSh 715 million.

Commercial banks were highly liquid throughout the year. Their liquidity ratios averaged 32 per cent, compared with the legal requirement of 18 per cent. In mid-1977, the Central Bank announced that, effective January 1, 1978, the liquidity ratio requirement would be raised to 20 per cent. In September 1977 the Central Bank announced a redefinition of liquid assets to net out interbank borrowing, which became effective January 1, 1978.

TABLE 6. Kenya: Monetary Survey, 1973–77
(In millions of Kenya shillings)

Item	1973 December	1974 June	1974 December	1975 June	1975 December	1976 June	1976 December	1977 June	1977 December
Net foreign assets	**1,558**	**1,434**	**969**	**854**	**581**	**1,189**	**1,459**	**3,776**	**3,633**
Central Bank[1]	1,584	1,494	1,061	933	681	1,192	1,449	3,717	3,689
Government[2]	25	31	4	—	8	9	16	13	23
Commercial banks	—51	—91	—96	—79	—108	—12	—6	46	—79
Domestic credit	**3,859**	**4,389**	**4,966**	**5,297**	**6,414**	**6,563**	**7,475**	**7,798**	**9,255**
Government (net)	479	466	930	1,100	1,767	1,500	1,898	1,495	1,800
Claims	*1,019*	*1,008*	*1,036*	*1,183*	*1,789*	*2,279*	*2,043*	*2,787*	*3,206*
Deposits	*540*	*542*	*106*	*83*	*22*	*779*	*145*	*1,292*	*1,406*
Nongovernment	3,380	3,923	4,036	4,197	4,647	5,063	5,577	6,303	7,455
Official entities	*237*	*176*	*223*	*221*	*303*	*250*	*215*	*205*	*259*
Private sector[3]	*3,143*	*3,747*	*3,813*	*3,976*	*4,344*	*4,813*	*5,362*	*6,098*	*7,196*
Other items (net)	**—69**	**—19**	**—18**	**—59**	**180**	**321**	**479**	**622**	**475**
Money and quasi-money	**5,356**	**5,708**	**5,819**	**6,077**	**6,814**	**7,432**	**8,454**	**10,952**	**12,413**
Money	3,862	4,083	4,016	4,052	4,540	4,966	5,674	7,496	8,427
Currency outside banks	*982*	*1,015*	*1,086*	*1,022*	*1,234*	*1,194*	*1,625*	*1,765*	*2,181*
Demand deposits[4]	*2,880*	*3,068*	*2,930*	*3,030*	*3,306*	*3,772*	*4,049*	*5,731*	*6,246*
Quasi-money	1,494	1,625	1,803	2,025	2,274	2,466	2,780	3,456	3,986
SDR allocations	**130**	**134**	**134**	**134**	—[5]	—	—	—	—

Sources: Central Bank of Kenya, *Annual Report for the Financial Year Ended 30th June, 1977;* International Monetary Fund, *International Financial Statistics*, July 1978.

[1] Foreign liabilities include use of Fund credit.
[2] Foreign exchange holdings.
[3] Includes Cereals and Sugar Finance Corporation and Agricultural Finance Corporation.
[4] Adjusted for "uncleared effects."
[5] The domestic counterpart of Kenya's SDR allocation was transferred in September 1975 to treasury deposits with the Central Bank of Kenya.

TABLE 7. Kenya: Summary Accounts of the Monetary Authorities, 1973–77

(In millions of Kenya shillings)

Item	1973	1974		1975		1976		1977	
	December	*June*	*December*	*June*	*December*	*June*	*December*	*June*	*December*
Net foreign assets	**1,609**	**1,525**	**1,065**	**933**	**689**	**1,201**	**1,465**	**3,730**	**3,712**
Foreign assets	1,615	1,559	1,354	1,380	1,439	1,867	2,309	4,477	4,282
Foreign exchange[1]	*1,371*	*1,305*	*1,338*	*1,340*	*1,403*	*1,862*	*2,282*	*4,432*	*4,143*
SDRs	*142*	*148*	*16*	*40*	*36*	*5*	*27*	*45*	*139*
Reserve position in the Fund	*102*	*106*	—	—	—	—	—	—	—
Foreign liabilities[2]	6	34	289	447	750	666	844	747	570
Domestic credit	**—88**	**—31**	**726**	**872**	**1,205**	**678**	**787**	**—53**	**—17**
Government (net)	—95	—33	490	586	1,171	636	778	—53	—35
Claims	369	399	526	575	1,112	1,295	851	1,100	1,243
Advances	*200*	*200*	*200*	*339*	*543*	*288*	*200*	*200*	*200*
Treasury bills	*60*	*22*	*148*	*87*	*284*	*164*	*20*	—	*133*
Government securities	*109*	*177*	*177*	*149*	*150*	*709*	*497*	*741*	*726*
SDR allocations used by Government	—	—	—	—	*134*	*134*	*134*	*134*	*134*
Trust Fund loans	—	—	—	—	—	—	—	*25*	*50*
Deposits	464	432	36	—11	—59	659	73	1,153	1,278
Official entities	7	—	—	—	—	—	—	—	—
Commercial banks	—	2	236	286	34	42	9	—	18
Other items (net)[3]	**—4**	**—40**	**—132**	**138**	**281**	**145**	**251**	**287**	**462**
Reserve money	**1,395**	**1,400**	**1,789**	**1,533**	**1,613**	**1,734**	**2,001**	**3,390**	**3,233**
Currency outside banks	982	1,015	1,086	1,022	1,234	1,194	1,625	1,765	2,182
Currency in commercial banks	137	117	253	161	174	189	205	217	241
Banks' deposits	221	261	381	313	131	311	133	1,268	730
Official entities' deposits	55	6	69	37	74	40	38	139	80
SDR allocations	**130**	**134**	**134**	**134**	—[4]	—	—	—	—

Sources: Central Bank of Kenya, *Annual Report for the Financial Year Ended 30th June, 1977;* International Monetary Fund, *International Financial Statistics*, July 1978.

[1] Includes balances with banks abroad and foreign securities.
[2] Includes use of Fund credit.
[3] Includes revaluation account, uncleared effects, and other unclassified assets and liabilities.
[4] The domestic counterpart of Kenya's SDR allocation was transferred in September 1975 to treasury deposits with the Central Bank of Kenya.

The composition of money and quasi-money stayed about the same as in 1976. Reflecting the increase in domestic liquidity, the average tender rate for treasury bills declined from over 4 per cent at the beginning of 1977 to about 1 per cent at the end of the year.

EXERCISE AND ISSUES FOR DISCUSSION

A Hypothetical Financial Program for Kenya in 1978

A discussion of the following issues may help in formulation of a financial program for Kenya for calendar year 1978.

Issues for Discussion

1. *Given the Kenyan authorities' objectives, what do you consider to be the principal problem areas in recent economic developments of the Kenyan economy? Would you suggest any change in the medium-term strategy? Are there corrective actions needed in 1978, particularly in the areas of bank liquidity, import restrictions, tax efforts, wage guidelines, and price controls?*
2. *Comment on the appropriateness and the effects of the 1975 and 1976 wage guidelines and the exchange rate depreciation of 1975.*
3. *What scenario would you anticipate in 1978 for government expenditure and coffee prices? How does this scenario affect the desire of the Kenyan authorities to curb inflation?*
4. *In general, how does the choice of the targets for growth, inflation, and international reserves influence the formulation of a financial program? Are these objectives conflicting?*
5. *Discuss the rationale for setting a ceiling on the expansion of domestic credit of either the Central Bank or the banking system, and the appropriateness of allocating total domestic credit among different sectors of the economy by administrative decision. What is the impact on the economy of a ceiling on government borrowing?*

Exercise: A Suggested Procedure

It is assumed that the financial program for Kenya for the calendar year 1978 is being formulated in early January 1978. A suggested, though by no means exclusive, procedure for drawing up the financial program is outlined below.

1. *Indicate the principal objectives that are to be attained for the calendar year 1978. Among the objectives that should be considered are the growth rate in real GDP,* the rate of price increase, and the desirable balance of payments outturn (a minimum surplus or a maximum deficit). In fixing the GDP target for 1978, it should be determined whether the medium-term growth objective is realistic.*

2. *Given the preliminary selected objectives, forecast the components of the balance of payments and the overall balance of payments deficit or surplus for 1978. Is the forecast balance of payments outturn compatible with the assumed objectives? If not, there are several choices available. First, you can change the assumed objectives to make them more consistent with your forecast. Alternatively, you can change policies if you insist on the attainment of the objectives. In this case, you may consider varying capital flows either through renegotiation of foreign debts or through drawing on official loans, or you may consider putting more restrictive controls on the foreign borrowing of the commercial banks. You may also consider a change in the exchange rate or a change in monetary and fiscal policy. Note that these changes will also affect domestic prices and production.*

3. *Having determined the target for the level of net foreign assets of the banking system and the policies involved, you can now proceed to construct the "desired" balance sheet for either the banking system or the monetary authorities of Kenya. For the*

* *Projections for sectoral growth and the demand components in the economy (Tables 2 and 3) are often useful in order to arrive at a reasonable target for the rate of growth in GDP.*

balance sheet of the banking system as a whole, this procedure may be followed:

(a) *Estimate the demand for money and quasi-money on the basis of the target rate of growth of output and prices established in (2) above. The observed ratio of money to quasi-money over several periods may be useful for this projection.*

(b) *Calculate the desired domestic credit for the banking system according to the monetary survey identity. Table 6 may be used for the calculations.*

For the balance sheet of the monetary authorities of Kenya, a possible procedure is the following:

(a) *Fix the desired net international reserves of the monetary authorities.*

(b) *Estimate the demand for money.*

(c) *Project the monetary liabilities of the monetary authorities. The observed ratios of these liabilities to total money stock over several periods may be useful for this projection.*

(d) *Project the net domestic assets of the monetary authorities that are equal to reserve money less the desired net international reserves of the monetary authorities, compatible with the estimated demand for money and the level of international reserves. Table 7 may be used for this purpose.*

4. *The credit projections so derived are in accordance with the target rate of growth in GDP and the target level of net international reserves. However, the projection for either domestic credit of the banking system or net domestic assets of the monetary authorities of Kenya may not be compatible with both the Kenyan Government's budgetary position and the private sector investment plan.*** *Make a forecast for the principal items in the Gov-*

** *Sometimes the credit expansion so calculated must be adjusted several times. The reason is that the change in the rate of credit expansion would have an impact on the macroeconomic aggregates, including both GDP and net international reserves, which have been taken as given (targets) in the initial calculations of the credit projection.*

ernment's budget (revenue as well as expenditure). The forecast of tax revenue has to be consistent with the target rate of growth in nominal income, flows of international trade that affect government receipts, and the proposed changes in tax laws, administration, or structure. Calculate the required borrowing (net) of the Government from the banking system for the program period. Seek to reconcile the projections for the balance of payments and the monetary aggregates with the projections for government revenue and expenditure and for investment of the private sector.

5. *Re-examine the entire program to see whether it is internally consistent and whether it is realistic and feasible. For this purpose, it may be useful to construct a summary of flow-of-funds accounts for the program period similar to that which appears in Workshop 4: Flow of Funds. Does the program imply substantial deviation from the past performance of the economy? If so, are the required changes in the available policy instruments feasible? If new instruments are proposed, to what extent can they be effectively used during the program period? Insofar as possible, state how your program can be implemented.*

6. *Determine the performance criteria for the program. Among possible criteria, the following are often utilized: (a) a limit on the domestic credit of the banking system, (b) a limit on the net domestic assets of the monetary authorities, (c) a limit on the net credit to the Government from the banking system, (d) a limit on new short-term and medium-term foreign borrowing by the public sector and the banking system, and (e) a limit for the decline in net foreign assets of the banking system. Are there other performance criteria that might produce the desired effect in the context of Kenya?*

APPENDIX

Kenya: Selected Statistical Data, 1966–77

Year	*CP*	*CG*	*IF*	*M*	*X*
1966	5,500	1,142	1,224	...	...
1967	5,864	1,244	1,644	2,326	1,580
1968	6,248	1,470	1,790	2,412	1,676
1969	6,538	1,712	1,874	2,434	1,804
1970	6,894	1,862	2,254	3,052	2,040
1971	8,212	2,284	2,884	3,930	2,098
1972	9,003	2,573	3,302	3,746	2,410
1973	10,848	2,796	3,645	4,384	3,290
1974	12,554	3,530	4,075	7,696	4,522
1975	15,731	4,256	4,851	7,324	4,758
1976	17,542	4,943	5,840	8,158	6,224
1977	21,338	6,250	7,774	10,702	9,418

Year	*PM*	*PX*	*VYW*	*YW*	*R1*	*R2*
1966	76	88	1,764	1,507	7.1429	7.1429
1967	78	83	1,829	1,610	7.1429	7.1429
1968	79	85	1,928	1,739	7.1429	7.1429
1969	80	86	2,018	1,904	7.1429	7.1429
1970	81	94	2,079	2,079	7.1429	7.1429
1971	89	90	2,158	2,311	7.7551	7.1429
1972	100	100	2,277	2,680	7.7551	7.1429
1973	119	115	2,415	3,243	8.3238	7.0012
1974	178	152	2,422	3,594	8.7454	7.1429
1975	225	175	2,409	4,019	9.6600	7.3432
1976	261	238	2,535	4,361	9.6600	8.3672
1977	281	337	2,630	4,903	9.6600	8.2766

Sources: *CP* = Private consumption at current prices, in millions of Kenya shillings (Kenya, *Economic Survey* and *Statistical Abstract*, various issues).

CG = Government consumption at current prices, in millions of Kenya shillings (Kenya, *Economic Survey* and *Statistical Abstract*, various issues).

IF = Gross fixed capital formation at current prices, in millions of Kenya shillings (Kenya, *Economic Survey* and *Statistical Abstract*, various issues).

M = Imports, c.i.f. (balance of payments basis), in millions of Kenya shillings (Kenya, *Economic Survey* and *Statistical Abstract*, various issues).

X = Exports, f.o.b., in millions of Kenya shillings (Kenya, *Economic Survey* and *Statistical Abstract*, various issues).

PM = Import prices, 1972 = 100 (Kenya, *Economic Survey*, 1978 and *Statistical Abstract*, various issues).

PX = Export prices, 1972 = 100 (Kenya, *Economic Survey*, 1978 and *Statistical Abstract*, various issues).

VYW = Total OECD income at constant 1970 prices and 1970 exchange rate, in billions of U.S. dollars (Organization for Economic Cooperation and Development, *National Accounts*, 1976 and *Main Economic Indicators*, May 1978).

YW = Total OECD income at current prices and current exchange rate, in billions of U.S. dollars (OECD, *National Accounts*, 1976 and *Main Economic Indicators*, May 1978).

R1 = Exchange rate, Kenya shillings per SDR, end of year (*International Financial Statistics (IFS)*).

R2 = Exchange rate, Kenya shillings per U.S. dollar, average during the year (*IFS*).

Kenya: Selected Statistical Data, 1966–77 (concluded)

Year	*MGDP*	*GDP*	*P1*	*P2*	*MO*
1966	7,622	9,125	83.5	57.0	1,333
1967	8,116	9,546	85.0	58.0	1,410
1968	8,858	10,282	86.2	58.2	1,627
1969	9,526	10,941	87.1	58.1	1,927
1970	10,378	11,673	88.9	59.3	2,410
1971	11,402	12,330	92.5	61.6	2,589
1972	13,172	13,172	100.0	65.0	3,029
1973	14,984	14,066	106.5	71.2	3,862
1974	17,906	14,350	124.8	83.9	4,016
1975	20,560	14,523	141.6	100.0	4,540
1976	25,257	15,405	164.0	111.4	5,674
1977	32,404	16,536	196.0	128.0	8,427

Year	*MQ*	*DC*	*DCP*	*RM*	*TAX*[1]	*T*[1]
1966	1,885	1,000	1,079	490	. . .	. . .
1967	2,086	1,293	1,339	625	. . .	. . .
1968	2,317	1,341	1,308	784	1,187	. . .
1969	2,748	1,429	1,370	1,133	1,293	. . .
1970	3,505	1,871	1,840	1,263	1,512	. . .
1971	3,770	2,527	2,394	1,152	1,840	. . .
1972	4,294	3,018	2,672	1,264	2,137	2,630
1973	5,356	3,859	3,380	1,395	2,318	2,817
1974	5,819	4,966	4,036	1,789	3,187	3,625
1975	6,814	6,413	4,647	1,613	3,943	4,347
1976	8,454	7,475	5,577	2,001	4,571	5,123
1977	12,413	9,255	7,455	3,233	5,297	6,149

Sources: *MGDP* = GDP at factor cost at current prices, in millions of Kenya shillings (Kenya, *Economic Survey* and *Statistical Abstract,* various issues).

GDP = GDP at factor cost at constant 1972 prices, in millions of Kenya shillings (Kenya, *Economic Survey* and *Statistical Abstract,* various issues).

P1 = GDP deflator, 1972 = 100, derived from *MGDP* and *GDP.*

P2 = Consumer prices, 1975 = 100 (Kenya, *Statistical Digest,* various issues).

MO = Money, i.e., currency outside banks plus demand deposits, in millions of Kenya shillings *(International Financial Statistics (IFS)).*

MQ = Money plus quasi-money, in millions of Kenya shillings *(IFS).*

DC = Total domestic credit of the banking system, in millions of Kenya shillings *(IFS).*

DCP = Total domestic credit less net credit to the Government, in millions of Kenya shillings *(IFS).*

RM = Reserve money, in millions of Kenya shillings *(IFS).*

TAX = Tax revenue of the Government, in millions of Kenya shillings (Kenya, *Statistical Abstract,* 1973; International Monetary Fund, *Government Finance Statistics Yearbook,* Vol. 1 (1977) and Vol. 2 (1978); and Kenya, *Appropriation Accounts, Other Public Accounts and the Accounts of the Funds for the Year 1967/68* to *1970/71).*

T = Total revenue of the Government, in millions of Kenya shillings (IMF, *Government Finance Statistics Yearbook,* Vol. 1 (1977) and Vol. 2 (1978); and Kenya, *Appropriation Accounts, Other Public Accounts and the Accounts of the Funds for the Year 1967/68* to *1970/71).*

[1] Fiscal year figures. For example, the figure for 1966 is for fiscal year July 1, 1965 to June 30, 1966.

ANSWERS TO EXERCISES

Chapter 3
WORKSHOP 1—Monetary and Financial Survey

page 49, Exercise A

Kenya: Monetary Survey, 1977
(In millions of Kenya shillings)

Net foreign assets	**3,633**
Foreign assets	4,616
Use of Fund credit	460
Other foreign liabilities	523
Domestic credit	**9,255**
Government (net)	1,800
Other public sector	259
Private sector [1]	7,196
Other items (net)	**475**
Money plus quasi-money	**12,413**
Money	8,427
Currency	*2,182*
Demand deposits	*6,269*
Uncleared effects	*—24*
Quasi-money	3,986

Source: Tables 7 and 8.
[1] Includes 683.5 million Kenya shillings corresponding to CSFC and AFC.

page 49, Exercise B

Kenya: Changes in Monetary Survey Items

Item	1977 Millions of Kenya shillings	1977 Per cent
1. Net foreign assets	2,174	149.0
2. Domestic credit	1,780	23.8
3. Credit to Government (net)	—98	—5.2
4. Credit to other general government	44	20.5
5. Credit to private sector	1,834	34.2
6. Assets = liabilities	3,954	44.3
7. Money	2,753	48.5
8. Quasi-money	1,206	43.4
9. Other items	—5	—1.0

Source: Tables 9 and 10.

Chapter 3
WORKSHOP 1—Monetary and Financial Survey

page 49, Exercise C

2. **Kenya: Net Foreign Assets of the Monetary Authorities**
(In millions of Kenya shillings)

Item	1976	1977
Assets	2,301	4,282
Liabilities	—844	—570
Net foreign assets	**1,457**	**3,712**
Percentage change		154.8
Reserve money	**2,001**	**3,233**
Percentage change		61.6

Source: Table 7.

3. **Accounts for the Kenyan Government in the Monetary Authorities and Commercial Banks in 1977**
Net Credit to Government
(In millions of Kenya shillings)

	Monetary Authorities		Commercial Banks	
Item	1976	1977	1976	1977
Claims	851	1,243	1,192	1,963
Deposits	—73	—1,278	—72	—128
Net credit	**778**	**—35**	**1,120**	**1,835**
Percentage change		—104.5		63.8

Source: Tables 7 and 8.

4. **Kenya: Monetary Survey**
(In millions of Kenya shillings)

Item	1976	1977
Money plus quasi-money	8,454	12,413
Percentage change		46.8
Percentage change in real GDP (1972 prices)		**7.5**
Percentage change in aggregate demand (current prices)		**21.5**

Sources: Table 9 and Kenya, *Economic Survey.*

Chapter 4
WORKSHOP 2—Government Finance Statistics

page 84, Exercise A

Kenya: Principal Aggregates, Fiscal Year 1977
(In millions of Kenya shillings; year ending June 30)

Revenue	6,149.2
Grants	234.1
Expenditure	7,240.0
Lending minus repayments	470.3
Overall deficit/surplus	—1,327.0
Financing	1,327.0
Abroad	*463.6*
Domestic	*863.4*

page 85, Exercise C

Kenya: Domestic Financing by Type of Debt Instrument, Fiscal Year 1977
(In millions of Kenya shillings; year ending June 30)

Domestic financing	863.4
Long-term bonds	*385.5*
Short-term bonds and bills	*552.0*
Long-term loans n.e.c.	*—0.5*
Short-term loans and advances n.e.c.	*42.2*
Changes in cash, deposits, etc.	*—115.8*

Note: n.e.c. = not elsewhere classified.

Chapter 5
WORKSHOP 3—Balance of Payments Statistics

page 121, Exercise 1

Kenya: Standard Presentation of the Balance of Payments, 1976
(In millions of SDRs)

Item	1976
A. Goods, Services, and Unrequited Transfers	**—72.3**
Goods and services	**—100.2**
Total credit	*1,007.0*
Total debit	*—1,107.2*
1. Merchandise: exports f.o.b.	644.3
2. Merchandise: imports f.o.b.	—734.7
3. Nonmonetary gold	—
4. Freight and insurance on merchandise credit	37.9
5. Freight and insurance on merchandise debit	—100.3
6. Other transportation: credit	156.9
7. Other transportation: debit	—57.8
8. Travel: credit	88.8
9. Travel: debit	—26.9
10. Undistributed income from direct investment abroad	0.6
11. Undistributed income from direct investment in Kenya	—24.0
12. Other direct investment income: credit	11.8
13. Other direct investment income: debit	—56.9
14. Other investment income: credit	19.7
15. Other investment income: debit	—49.7
16. Other government: credit	17.6
17. Other government: debit	—24.0
18. Other private: credit	29.4
19. Other private: debit	—32.9
Unrequited transfers	**27.9**
Total credit	*66.2*
Total debit	*—38.3*
20. Private: credit	27.1
21. Private: debit	—33.3
22. Government: credit	39.1
23. Government: debit	—5.0
B. Capital (excluding reserves and related items)	**150.0**
Nonmonetary sectors	**159.7**
24. Direct investment in Kenya	38.7
25. Direct investment abroad	—2.7
26. Other private long-term liabilities	24.9
27. Other private long-term assets	—2.5
28. Other private short-term liabilities	32.1
29. Other private short-term assets	—3.1

Kenya: Standard Presentation of the Balance of Payments, 1976
(concluded)
(In millions of SDRs)

Item	1976
B. Capital (excluding reserves and related items) *(concluded)*	
30. General government long-term liabilities	72.7
31. General government long-term assets	0.8
32. General government short-term liabilities	—
33. General government short-term assets	—1.2
Monetary sectors	**—9.7**
34. Deposit money banks: long-term	—
35. Deposit money banks: short-term	—10.5
36. Central institutions: long-term	—
37. Central institutions: short-term	0.8
C. Allocation of SDRs (item 38)	—
D. Reserves and Related Items	**—74.0**
Liabilities	**16.5**
39. Use of Fund credit	16.5
40. Other liabilities	—
Assets	**—90.5**
41. Monetary gold	—
42. SDRs	1.0
43. Reserve position in the Fund	—
44. Foreign exchange and other claims	—91.5
E. Net Errors and Omissions (item 45)	**—3.7**

Source: International Monetary Fund, *Balance of Payments Yearbook,* Vol. 28 (Washington, December 1977), p. 336.

Chapter 5
WORKSHOP 3—Balance of Payments Statistics

page 121, Exercise 1 (concluded)

Kenya: Analytic Presentation of the Balance of Payments, 1976
(In millions of SDRs)

	Code	1976
A. Goods, Services, and Unrequited Transfers	1 . . C Z	**—73.9**
Merchandise: exports f.o.b.	1 A . A Z	644.3
To Tanzania and Uganda	1 A 1 A Y	*137.9*
To other countries		
Coffee	1 A 1 A Q	*193.2*
Tea	1 A 1 A P	*65.8*
Other (Including adjustments)	1 A . A Y	*247.4*
Merchandise: imports f.o.b.	1 A . B Z	—734.7
Trade balance	1 A . C Z	**—90.4**
Services: credit	1 S . A Z	362.7
Transportation and merchandise insurance	1 C . A Y	*194.8*
Travel	1 D . A Z	*88.8*
Government services	1 I . A Z	*17.6*
Other services	1 M . A Y	*61.5*
Services: debit	1 S . B Z	—372.5
Transportation and merchandise insurance	1 C . B Y	*—158.1*
Investment income	1 N . B Z	*—130.6*
Government services	1 I . B Z	*—24.0*
Other services	1 M . B Y	*—59.8*
Total (goods and services)	1 . 1 C Z	**—100.2**
Private unrequited transfers	1 K . C Z	—6.2
Total (excluding government unrequited transfers)	1 . 2 C Z	**—106.4**
Government unrequited transfers: credit	1 H 8 AW	37.5
Grants and technical assistance from		
U.K. Government	1 H 8 A Y	*13.1*
Others	1 H 8 A X	*24.4*
Government unrequited transfers: debit	1 H . B Z	—5.0
B. Long-Term Capital, excluding Groups D and F	1 W 1 X Z	**131.9**
Direct investment	3 Z . X Z	36.0
Other private	8 Z 1 X Z	22.4
General government	7 Z 1 X Z	73.5
Long-term loans received	7 P . X Q	*62.1*
Other	7 Z 1 X Y	*11.4*
Total, A plus B	1 . BX Z	**58.0**

Kenya: Analytic Presentation of the Balance of Payments, 1976
(concluded)
(In millions of SDRs)

	Code	1976
C. Short-Term Capital, excluding Groups D and F	1W2X Z	**14.4**
Deposit money banks	5Z2X Z	—10.5
Liabilities	5Y2X Z	*—3.6*
Assets	5L2X Z	*—6.9*
Other private	8Z2X Z	29.0
General government	7Z2X Z	—1.2
Central monetary institutions	4Z2X Z	0.8
Net errors and omissions	9A . X Z	—3.7
Total, A through C	1 . CX Z	**72.4**
D. Exceptional Financing	1WZX Z	**1.6**
Grants to finance general imports	1H8AQ	0.9
Grants from Subsidy Account	1H8AV	0.7
Total, A through D	1 . DX Z	**74.0**
E. Counterpart Items	9B . X Z	—
Monetization/demonetization of gold	9B3X Z	—
Allocation of SDRs	9B1X Z	—
Total, A through E	1 . EX Z	**74.0**
F. Reserves and Related Items	2Z . X Z	**—74.0**
Use of Fund credit	2M . X Z	16.5
Other liabilities	2Q . X Z	—
Monetary gold	2A . X Z	—
SDRs	2B . X Z	1.0
Reserve position in the Fund	2C . X Z	—
Foreign exchange and other claims	2F . X Z	—91.5

Source: International Monetary Fund, *Balance of Payments Yearbook,* Vol. 28 (Washington, 1977), p. 335.

page 121, Exercise 2

As indicated in the text, there are alternative definitions of the current balance and the overall balance.

Balance	*Lines in Analytic Presentation*	*1976 (In millions of SDRs)*
Trade	Trade balance	—90.4
Current	A. Goods, Services, and Unrequited Transfers	—73.9
	Total (goods and services)	—100.2
	Total (excluding government unrequited transfers)	—106.4
Basic	Total, A plus B	58.0
Overall	Total, A through C	72.4
	Total, A through D	74.0
	Total, A through E	74.0

Chapter 6
WORKSHOP 4—Flow of Funds

page 142, Exercises 1 and 2

A Hypothetical Economic System

Item	Sector PS_H		Sector PS_C		Sector GS		Sector *B*		Sector *FS*		Total	
	Source	*Use*	*Source*	*Use*	*Source*	*Use*	*Source*	*Use*	*Source*	*Use*	*Source*	*Use*
I. Incomes and Expenditures												
1. Receipts												
Income	12,100		1,800						4,700		18,600	
Transfers and taxes					3,500						3,500	
2. Current expenditure												
Consumption		9,700				1,900						11,600
Imports										4,000		4,000
Transfers and taxes		2,000		1,500								3,500
Wages and salaries						1,000						1,000
Current account balance		400		300		600				700		2,000
3. Saving (current account balance)	400		300		600				700		2,000	
4. Investment expenditure		100		450		1,200				250		2,000
5. Overall position		300	150		600					450	750	750
II. Changes in Financial Balance Sheet												
1. Liabilities or claims												
to or on *B*	100	280	530	410	510					450	1,140	1,140
to or on *FS*							450				450	
to or on PS_H			70		50		280	100			400	100
to or on PS_C		70			40		410	530			450	600
to or on *GS*		50		40				510				600
2. Net financing	300			150		600			450		750	750

page 152, Exercises 1–4

Kenya: Summary of Income and Flow-of-Funds Accounts, 1976

(In millions of Kenya shillings)

Item	Sector *PS*		Sector *GS*		Sector *B*		Sector *FS*		Total	
	Source	*Use*	*Source*	*Use*	*Source*	*Use*	*Source*	*Use*	*Source*	*Use*
I. Incomes and Expenditures										
1. Receipts										
Exports	9,560						9,436		18,996	
Transfers	2,609		218				370		3,197	
Taxes			4,934						4,934	
Other income	9,358		702				1,444		11,504	
2. Current expenditure										
Consumption				1,241						1,241
Imports		9,436						9,560		18,996
Transfers		347		2,210				640		3,197
Taxes		4,934								4,934
Other		2,146		1,792				352		4,290
Current account balance		4,664		611				698		5,973
3. Saving (current account balance)	4,664		611				698		5,973	
4. Investment expenditure		4,749		1,224						5,973
5. Overall position	85		613					698	698	698
II. Changes in Financial Balance Sheet										
1. Liabilities or claims										
to or on *B*	930	1,939	254	123			905	27		
to or on *FS*	1,024		552		27	905				
to or on *PS*			600	670	1,939	930		1,024		
to or on *GS*	670	600			123	254		552		
2. Net financing		85		613			698			

Chapter 7
WORKSHOP 5—The Polak Model: An Application

page 163, Exercise 1

(a) $\hat{m} = \dfrac{2.946}{9} = 0.327$

$\hat{k} = \dfrac{2.598}{9} = 0.289$

Hence,

$$\alpha = \frac{m}{m+k} = \frac{0.328}{0.328 + 0.289} = 0.53$$

$$\beta = \frac{k}{m} = \frac{0.289}{0.328} = 0.88$$

Note that

$$\alpha\beta = 0.53\ .\ 0.88 = 0.47 < 1, \text{ hence}$$

$$M = 0.53A + 0.47\ M_{t-1}$$

is a stable dynamic equation.

(b) $M_t = \alpha A_t + \alpha^2\beta A_{t-1} + \alpha^3\beta^2 A_{t-2} + \ldots$

$A_t = X_t + CM_t + \Delta NDC_t$

(i) First period multiplier

$$\frac{\Delta M_t}{\Delta(\Delta NDC_t)} = \frac{\Delta M_t}{\Delta A_t} = \alpha = 0.53$$

(ii) Truncated multiplier at the end of second period

$$\frac{\Delta M_t}{\Delta A_t} + \frac{\Delta M_t}{\Delta A_{t-1}} = \alpha + \alpha^2\beta = 0.53\ (1 + 0.47) = 0.78$$

(iii) At the end of third period

$$\frac{\Delta M_t}{\Delta A_t} + \frac{\Delta M_t}{\Delta A_{t-1}} + \frac{\Delta M_t}{\Delta A_{t-2}} = \alpha + \alpha^2\beta + \alpha^3\beta^2 = 0.90$$

(iv) Long-run multiplier (total effect) is the sum of the declining geometric progression:

$$\alpha + \alpha^2\beta + \alpha^3\beta^2 \ldots = \frac{\alpha}{1 - \alpha\beta} = \frac{0.53}{1 - 0.47} = 1$$

Thus, a unit increase in one of the exogenous variables will cause an increase in imports of 0.53 unit in the first period, a total increase of

0.78 unit in the first two periods, 0.90 unit in the first three periods, etc. Over infinitely many periods the total effect will be 1 unit. Convergence is rapid, as 90 per cent of the total effect is manifested in the first three periods. Multiplier is the same for any component of A_t.

(c) $e_{M,CM} = \dfrac{\Delta M_t/M_t}{\Delta CM_t/CM_t} = \dfrac{\Delta M_t \,.\, CM_t}{\Delta CM_t \,.\, M_t} = \alpha \dfrac{CM_t}{M_t}$

(i) $\alpha = 0.53$ — *1969–76 ($n = 8$)*

$\overline{CM}_t = 1{,}233$

$\overline{M}_t = 5{,}842$

$\alpha \dfrac{\overline{CM}_t}{\overline{M}_t} = 0.53\ (0.21) = 0.11$

(ii) Long run

$\overline{M} = \dfrac{\alpha}{1 - \alpha\beta}(\overline{X} + \overline{CM} + \Delta\overline{NDC})$

$\dfrac{\Delta\overline{M}}{\Delta\overline{CM}} \,.\, \dfrac{\overline{CM}}{\overline{M}} = \dfrac{\alpha}{1 - \alpha\beta} \dfrac{\overline{CM}}{\overline{M}} = 1.(0.21) = 0.21$

(iii) $e_{M,X} = \dfrac{\Delta M_t/M_t}{\Delta X_t/X_t} = \alpha \dfrac{\overline{X}}{\overline{M}} = \alpha \cdot \dfrac{4{,}436}{5{,}507} = 0.43$ (mean elasticity)

Long run

$e_{M,X} = \dfrac{\alpha}{1 - \alpha\beta} \dfrac{\overline{X}}{\overline{M}} = 1 \cdot \dfrac{4{,}436}{5{,}507} = 0.81$

Elasticity compares percentage changes. As X is larger than CM, a given percentage change in X has a relatively larger effect on imports than a given percentage change in CM.

page 164, Exercise 2

(a) $M_t = \alpha A_t + \alpha\beta M_{t-1}$

$\hat{M}_{1977} = \alpha(X_{1977} + CM_{1977} + \Delta NDC_{1977}) + \alpha\beta M_{1976}$

$= 0.53\ (11{,}580 + 2{,}282 + 1{,}785) + 0.47\ (9{,}436) = 12{,}728$

$\Delta N\hat{F}A_{1977}$

$= X_{1977} + CM_{1977} - \hat{M}_{1977} = 11{,}580 + 2{,}282 - 12{,}728 = 1{,}134$

(b)

	Predicted	*Actual*	*Differences*
M	12,728	11,688	+1,040
ΔNFA	1,134	2,174	−1,040

M forecast was too high, and thus NFA forecast was too low.

Chapter 7
WORKSHOP 5—The Polak Model: An Application

page 164, Exercise 2 (concluded)

Given

$$MO_{1977} = 12{,}413 \qquad \hat{Y}_{1977} = \frac{1}{\hat{k}} MO_{1977} = \frac{12{,}413}{0.29} = 42{,}803$$

$$\hat{k} = 0.29$$

$$Actual\ k = \frac{MO_{1977}}{Y_{1977}} = \frac{12{,}413}{36{,}653} = 0.34$$

i.e., people held larger money balances than expected.

Given

$$M_{1977} = 11{,}688 \qquad \hat{M}_{1977} = 12{,}728$$

$$\hat{m} = 0.33$$

even with actual income (Y_t), there was over-prediction of M:

$$\hat{M}_{1977} = \hat{m}Y_{1977} = 0.33\,(36{,}653) = 12{,}095$$

$$M_{1977} = mY_{1977}, \text{ hence } m = \frac{M_{1977}}{Y_{1977}} = 0.32$$

i.e., actual $m <$ predicted $\hat{m}$.

page 164, Exercise 3

(a) Insertion of equation

$$M_t = \alpha\,(X_t + CM_t + \Delta NDC_t) + \alpha\beta M_{t-1}$$

into the identity

$$\Delta NFA_t = X_t + CM_t - M_t$$

yields

$$\begin{aligned}\Delta NFA_{1977} &= X_{1977} + CM_{1977} - \alpha\,(X_{1977} + CM_{1977} \\ &\quad + \Delta NDC_{1977}) - \alpha\beta M_{1976} \\ &= (1-\alpha)\,(X_{1977} + CM_{1977}) - \alpha\,\Delta NDC_{1977} \\ &\quad - \alpha\beta M_{1976} \\ &= 0\end{aligned}$$

$$\Delta NDC_{1977} = \frac{1-\alpha}{\alpha}(X_{1977} + CM_{1977}) - \beta M_{1976}$$

$$= \frac{0.47}{0.53}\,(11{,}580 + 2{,}282) - 0.88\,(9{,}436)$$

$$= 12{,}292.7 - 8{,}303.7$$

$$= 3{,}989$$

(b) $NFA_{1977} = \frac{1}{12} M_{1976} = \frac{9{,}436}{12} = 786$

$$\Delta NFA_{1977} = NFA_{1977} - NFA_{1976} = 786 - 1{,}459 = -673$$

$$(1 - \alpha)(X_{1977} + CM_{1977}) - \alpha \Delta NDC_{1977} - \alpha\beta M_{1976} = -673$$

$$\Delta NDC_{1977} = \frac{1 - \alpha}{\alpha}(X_{1977} + CM_{1977}) - \beta M_{1976} + \frac{673}{\alpha}$$

$$\Delta NDC_{1977} = \frac{0.47}{0.53}(11{,}580 + 2{,}282) - 0.88\,(9{,}436) + \frac{673}{\alpha}$$

$$= 3{,}989 + 1{,}432 = 5{,}421$$

(c) $\Delta MO_t = \Delta NDC_t + \Delta NFA_t$

$= 0$ if $\Delta NDC_t = \Delta NFA_t$

$\Delta M_t = m\Delta Y_t$

$\Delta MO_t = 0$, hence $\Delta Y_t = 0$ and hence, $\Delta M_t = 0$

$$\Delta Y_t = \frac{1}{k}\,\Delta MO_t$$

Chapter 8
WORKSHOP 6—Projection of Monetary Aggregates

page 181, Exercise A

Kenya: Monetary Survey, December 1977
(In millions of Kenya shillings)

Item	Projection December 1977
Net foreign assets	**3,650**
Central Bank[1]	3,665 (Central Bank and Government combined)
Government[2]	
Commercial banks	—15
Domestic credit	**11,012**
Government (net)	2,496
Claims	. . .
Deposits	. . .
Nongovernment	8,516
Official entities	. . .
Private sector[3]	. . .
Other items (net)	**479**
Money and quasi-money	**14,183**
Money	9,588
Currency outside banks	. . .
Demand deposits	. . .
Quasi-money	4,595
SDR allocations	—

[1] Foreign liabilities include use of Fund credit.
[2] Foreign exchange holdings.
[3] Includes Cereals and Sugar Finance Corporation and Agricultural Finance Corporation.

page 182, Exercise B

$$GDP_{1977} = 15{,}405\ (1.07) = KSh\ 16{,}483\ million$$
$$\dot{P}_{1977} = 17\ per\ cent$$
$$P_{1977} = 164\ (1.17) = 191.9$$
$$MO^*_{1977} = -1{,}883.91 + 0.3706\ (16{,}483) - 28.9752\ (17) = 3{,}732$$
$$MQ^*_{1977} = -\ 2{,}630.84 + 0.5243\ (16{,}483) - 34.9792\ (17) = 5{,}416$$
$$MO_{1977} = 3{,}732\ (2)\ (1.919) - 5{,}674 = KSh\ 8{,}649\ million$$
$$MQ_{1977} = 5{,}416\ (2)\ (1.919) - 8{,}454 = KSh\ 12{,}333\ million$$

Chapter 9
WORKSHOP 7—Revenue Forecasting

page 207, Exercise 1

Kenya: Tax Revenues Adjusted for the Effects of Discretionary Tax Measures, Fiscal Years 1968–77[1]
(In millions of Kenya shillings; year ending June 30)

	Tax Revenue Source	1968	1969	1970	1971	1972	1973	1974	1975	1976	1977
1.	Taxes on income, profits, and capital gains[2]	493.1	506.9	626.9	811.1	966.8	1,084.2	1,240.5	1,595.1	1,797.6	2,149.3
5.1	Sales tax	—	—	—	—	—	. . .[3]	853.8	1,027.0	1,215.9	1,308.4
5.2	Excises	269.7	290.7	320.4	372.8	392.2	404.8	515.9	546.7	521.4	574.1
6.1	Import duties	618.0	666.0	741.1	861.6	933.0	741.3	1,087.8	1,154.5	1,068.7	1,057.2

[1] Adjusted to the fiscal-year 1977 tax structure, using the proportional data adjustment method.
[2] Excluding the graduated personal tax, which was abolished December 31, 1973.
[3] The sales tax, which was introduced in April-May 1973, generated KSh 54.1 million of revenue in fiscal year 1973. No attempt was made here to adjust this amount to a full-year, fiscal-year 1977 tax structure.

page 207, Exercise 2

(a) In equation (2), the elasticity of taxes on income, profits, and capital gains with respect to GDP at factor cost at current prices is equal to:

$$El(ATI/Y) = \frac{d\,Ln\,ATI}{d\,Ln\,Y} = b$$

where

ATI = adjusted revenue from taxes on income, profits, and capital gains
Y = GDP at factor cost at current prices.

Thus, the null hypothesis is:

$$H_0\colon b = 1,$$

which will be tested against the alternative hypothesis:

$$H_1\colon b > 1,$$

as income taxes on individuals are progressive (see Chapter 9, Appendix II).

The following variable has a t distribution with $n - k$ degrees of freedom:

$$t = \frac{\hat{b} - b}{s_{\hat{b}}}$$

where

$\hat{b}$ is the least squares estimator of b

$s_{\hat{b}}$ is the estimated standard error of $\hat{b}$

n is the number of observations, here equal to 10

k is the number of parameters, here equal to 3.

Using equation (2a), one can calculate the value of t under the null hypothesis:

$$t_0 = \frac{1.09750 - 1}{0.05792} = 1.683.$$

Choosing a 5 per cent significance level for a one-tail test, one can find from a table of the t distribution that, with 7 degrees of freedom, the critical region is:

$$t > t^* = 1.895$$

where t^* is the critical value of t.

Since $t_0 < t^*$, the "unit elasticity" hypothesis cannot be rejected at the 5 per cent level of significance.

(b) In equation (6a) the elasticities of import duties with respect to import volume and import price are, respectively:

$$E1\ (ATM/L\bar{M}) = \frac{\delta\ Ln\ ATM}{\delta\ Ln\ L\bar{M}} = 0.40020 + 0.37235 = 0.77255$$

$$E1\ (ATM/LPM) = \frac{\delta\ Ln\ ATM}{\delta\ Ln\ LPM} = 0.40020$$

where

ATM = adjusted revenue from import duties

$L\bar{M}$ = lagged, calendar-year imports at constant prices

LPM = lagged, calendar-year import price index.

Note that $Ln\ LM = Ln\ L\bar{M} + Ln\ LPM$

where

LM = lagged, calendar-year imports at current prices.

page 207, Exercise 3

Kenya: Tax Revenue Forecasts for Fiscal Year 1978
(In millions of Kenya shillings; year ending June 30)

	Tax	Regression Equation	Base Values	AT_{78}[1]	BD_{78}[2]	T_{78}[3]
1.	Taxes on income, profits, and capital gains	(1a)	LY_{78} = 32,404; DA_{78} = 1	2,840.8	—90.0	2,750.8
4.3	Estate duty			10.4[4]	—	10.4[4]
5.1	Sales tax	(4a)	LCP_{78} = 21,338	1,574.3	205.0	1,779.3
5.2	Excises	(8a)	$L\bar{C}P_{78}$ = 16,670	596.2	—32.0	564.2
5.4	Taxes on specific services	(11a)	LCP_{78} = 21,338	60.7	10.0	70.7
5.5	Taxes on use of, or permission to use, goods or to perform activities	(9a)	$L\bar{Y}_{78}$ = 16,536	104.7	—	104.7
6.1	Import duties	(6a)	LM_{78} = 10,630; $L\bar{M}_{78}$ = 3,783	1,292.0	100.0	1,392.0
6.2	Export duties			—	300.0[5]	300.0[5]
7.2	Stamp duties	(10a)	$L\bar{Y}_{78}$ = 16,536	58.4	—	58.4
IV.	**Tax revenue**			**6,537.5**	**493.0**	**7,030.5**

[1] AT_{78} = Tax revenue forecast for fiscal year 1978 based on fiscal-year 1977 tax structure.
[2] BD_{78} = Budget estimate of the revenue effect of discretionary tax measures in fiscal year 1978.
[3] $T_{78} = AT_{78} + BD_{78}$.
[4] Average of the three preceding fiscal years.
[5] Export duties were introduced in the budget for fiscal year 1978.

page 208, Exercise 4

(a) The expected built-in elasticity of tax revenue for fiscal year 1978 with respect to lagged, calendar-year GDP at factor cost at current prices is equal to:

$$E1\ (AT_{78}/LY_{78}) = \frac{\dfrac{\Delta AT_{78}}{AT_{77}}}{\dfrac{\Delta LY_{78}}{LY_{77}}} = \frac{\dfrac{1{,}240.7}{5{,}296.8}}{\dfrac{7{,}147.0}{25{,}257.0}} = 0.828$$

where

AT_{78} = tax revenue forecast for fiscal year 1978 based on fiscal-year 1977 tax structure

LY_{78} = lagged, calendar-year 1977 GDP at factor cost at current prices.

(b) The expected overall elasticity (buoyancy) of tax revenue for fiscal year 1978 with respect to lagged, calendar-year GDP at factor cost at current prices is equal to:

$$E1\ (T_{78}/LY_{78}) = \frac{\dfrac{\Delta T_{78}}{T_{77}}}{\dfrac{\Delta LY_{78}}{LY_{77}}} = \frac{\dfrac{1{,}733.7}{5{,}296.8}}{\dfrac{7{,}147.0}{25{,}257.0}} = 1.157$$

where

T_{78} = tax revenue forecast for fiscal year 1978 based on fiscal-year 1978 tax structure

LY_{78} = lagged, calendar-year 1977 GDP at factor cost at current prices.

page 209, Exercise 6

The forecast of nontax revenue (in millions of Kenya shillings) for fiscal year 1978 is equal to:

$$NT_{78} = \frac{NT_{77}}{LY_{77}} \times LY_{78} = \frac{852.3}{25{,}257} \times 32{,}404 = 1{,}093.5$$

where

NT_{78} = nontax revenue forecast for fiscal year 1978

LY_{78} = lagged, calendar-year 1977 GDP at factor cost at current prices.

Chapter 10
WORKSHOP 8—Balance of Payments Forecasting

page 255, Exercise 3

Variable	Percentage Change	Index or Value 1976	Index or Value 1977
Import prices	7.7	261	281
GDP deflator	19.5	164	196
GDP (real)	7.34	15,405[1]	16,536[1]

[1] In millions of Kenya shillings.

(a) From equation (9):

$$MR = 2{,}471.379 + 0.2495\ (16{,}536) - 1{,}886.755\left(\frac{281}{196}\right)$$

Imports at constant prices are forecast to rise to 3,892—a rise of *24.8 per cent* over 1976. The value of imports rises by the product of the price and volume increase, i.e., *34.4 per cent.*

(b) Assume a 5 per cent devaluation increases the index of import prices for 1977 to 295. Substituting the revised import price data in equation (9):

$$MR = 2{,}471.379 + 0.2495\ (16{,}536) - 1{,}886.755\left(\frac{295}{196}\right)$$

Imports at constant prices are now forecast to rise to 3,757—an increase of 20.5 per cent over 1976. This calculation suggests that a 5 per cent devaluation would lead to a 4 per cent decline in import volume. Note, however, the important and almost certainly unrealistic assumption that domestic prices and output are not affected by the devaluation.

(c) Let *Ep* represent the price elasticity and *Ey* the income elasticity.

$$Ep_{1977} = \frac{\Delta MR}{MR_{1976}} \Big/ \frac{\Delta(PM/PGDP)}{(PM/PGDP)_{1976}} = \frac{\Delta MR}{\Delta(PM/PGDP)} \times \frac{(PM/PGDP)_{1976}}{MR_{1976}}$$

$$Ey_{1977} = \frac{\Delta MR}{MR_{1976}} \Big/ \frac{\Delta GDP}{GDP_{1976}} = \frac{\Delta MR}{\Delta GDP} \times \frac{GDP_{1976}}{MR_{1976}}$$

The marginal response of import volume to changes in relative prices or incomes for the forecast year can be taken from the coefficients in equation (9). Data for the base year 1976 can be found in the Appendix to Chapter 10.

$$Ep_{1977} = -1{,}886.755 \times \left(\frac{261/164}{3{,}119}\right) = -0.96$$

$$Ey_{1977} = 0.2495 \times \left(\frac{15{,}405}{3{,}119}\right) = 1.2$$

Equation (9′) uses a logarithmic specification, and the price and income elasticities can be taken directly from the estimated equation.